ISBN-8373-5822-1

122 ADMISSION TEST SERIES

 **RUDMAN'S QUESTIONS AND ANSWERS ON THE...**

PSAT/NMSQT

Preliminary SAT/
National Merit Scholarship Qualifying Test

Intensive preparation for the examination including...

Verbal Abilities

- Sentence Completion
- Verbal Analogies
- Reading Comprehension

Quantitative Abilities

- Mathematical Ability
- Quantitative Comparison

NLC
NATIONAL LEARNING CORPORATION

PASSBOOK®

NOTICE

PASSBOOK SERIES®

THE *PASSBOOK SERIES®* has been created to prepare applicants and candidates for the ultimate academic battlefield—the examination room.

At some time in our lives, each and every one of us may be required to take an examination—for validation, matriculation, admission, qualification, registration, certification, or licensure.

Based on the assumption that every applicant or candidate has met the basic formal educational standards, has taken the required number of courses, and read the necessary texts, the *PASSBOOK SERIES®* furnishes the one special preparation which may assure passing with confidence, instead of failing with insecurity. Examination questions—together with answers—are furnished as the basic vehicle for study so that the mysteries of the examination and its compounding difficulties may be eliminated or diminished by a sure method.

This book is meant to help you pass your examination provided that you qualify and are serious in your objective.

The entire field is reviewed through the huge store of content information which is succinctly presented through a provocative and challenging approach—the question-and-answer method.

A climate of success is established by furnishing the correct answers at the end of each test.

You soon learn to recognize types of questions, forms of questions, and patterns of questioning. You may even begin to anticipate expected outcomes.

You perceive that many questions are repeated or adapted so that you gain acute insights, which may enable you to score many sure points.

You learn how to confront new questions, or types of questions, and to attack them confidently and work out the correct answers.

You note objectives and emphases, and recognize pitfalls and dangers, so that you may make positive educational adjustments.

Moreover, you are kept fully informed in relation to new concepts, methods, practices, and directions in the field.

You discover that you are actually taking the examination all the time: you are preparing for the examination by "taking" an examination, not by reading extraneous and/or supererogatory textbooks.

In short, this PASSBOOK®, used directedly, should be an important factor in helping you to pass your test.

THE PSAT/NMSQT

THE PSAT/NMSQT

The Preliminary SAT/National Merit Scholarship Qualifying Test is cosponsored by the College Board and National Merit Scholarship Corporation. It is developed and administered for the College Board and National Merit Scholarship Corporation by Educational Testing Service (ETS).

THE COLLEGE BOARD

The College Board is a national nonprofit association that champions educational excellence for all students through the ongoing collaboration of more than 2,900 member schools, colleges, universities, educational systems, and associations. By means of responsive forums, research, programs, and policy development, the College Board promotes universal access to high standards of learning, equity of opportunity, and sufficient financial support so that every student is prepared for success in college and work. The Board produces college-planning materials and conducts workshops for educators.

NATIONAL MERIT SCHOLARSHIP CORPORATION (NMSC)

NMSC is an independent, not-for-profit organization that conducts two annual competitions for recognition and scholarships, the National Merit Scholarship Program and the National Achievement Scholarship Program for Outstanding African-American Students. The PSAT/NMSQT serves as the screening test for students who wish to participate in NMSC programs.

Please direct inquiries about any aspect of the Merit Program or the Achievement Program - including student eligibility, the selection process, and awards offered - to National Merit Scholarship Corporation, 1560 Sherman Avenue, Suite 200, Evanston, IL 60201-4897; (847) 866-5100.

If you have questions, comments, or suggestions about PSAT/NMSQT registration, administration, or score reports, write: PSAT/NMSQT, P.O. Box 6720, Princeton, NJ 08541-6720; call: (866) 433-7728; fax: (610) 290-8979.

The PSAT/NMSQT measures verbal and mathematical reasoning abilities you have developed over many years, both in and out of school. It does not measure other factors and abilities - such as creativity, special talents, and motivation - that may also help you do well in college.

You won't have to recall facts from literature, or history, or science. You won't have to answer grammar questions. You won't need to furnish math formulas, in fact, some will be given on the test for reference.

PSAT/NMSQT scores give you helpful feedback about your verbal reasoning and math problem-solving skills. In December your school will give you your PSAT/NMSQT score report and your test book. Your score report will include your verbal score, mathematics score, score ranges, percentiles, and Selection Index (twice your verbal score plus your math score, 2V+M), which is used by NMSC as an initial screen of the large number of participants in its competitions. So you can review your test performance and better understand the test, your score report will show the correct answers and your answers to the questions. (If you haven't received your score report by mid-January, see your counselor.)

The PSAT/NMSQT does not provide duplicate copies of score reports, but your school will have a copy of your score report. If you change schools within two years after you take the test, you may ask the PSAT/NMSQT office to report your scores to your new school.

Your scores and answer sheet information are stored indefinitely at Educational Testing Service for the College Board and NMSC. Information may be used in research studies, but none that can identify you will be released without your consent.

PSAT/NMSQT scores are not reported directly to colleges. You can ask your school to send your scores to colleges if you wish.

Colleges and universities that use the Student Search Service do not know your scores (although institutions may send information to students whose scores are within a specified range). They receive only your name, address, sex, birth date, school, grade level, social security number, and intended college major.

Your scores will be reported to your school and, in some cases, to your school district or state; to NMSC for consideration at the entry level of the National Merit Scholarship Program; and to other scholarship programs that you mark on your answer sheet. These include the National Achievement Scholarship Program for Outstanding African-American Students, conducted by NMSC, and the National Hispanic Scholar Recognition Program conducted by the College Board.

SPECIAL ACCOMMODATIONS MAY BE AVAILABLE:

IF you know in advance that you can't take the test on the date your school offers it. Your school may be able to arrange for you to take the test at a neighboring school that has selected the other test date. Tell your counselor as soon as possible that you have a conflict, such as not being able to test on Saturday for religious reasons.

If you will be tested at another school, take your school's code number and some form of identification, preferably with a photo.

DATES

IF you will be studying abroad when the test is given: You must make advance arrangements if you will studying abroad when the test is given. Send to the PSAT/NMSQT office the name of the city, country, and, if known, the name and address of the school you will be attending when the test is given. The PSAT/NMSQT office will send you instructions.

PROGRAMS

IF you miss the test but want to enter scholarship programs: If you do not take the PSAT/NMSQT because of illness or an emergency, see the note on NMSC 1 about possible alternate testing arrangements for entering the competitions conducted by National Merit Scholarship Corporation.

Contact the College Board by e-mail at nhrp@collegeboard.org, or call (800) 626-9795 for more information.

ARRANGEMENTS

IF you have a disability and need special arrangements: A student at any grade level with a documented disability whose school regularly provides accommodation for classwork, assignments, and tests may be eligible for special arrangements. If you need the test and practice materials in Braille or large type, your school can order them for administration on Tuesday, October 24; extended time is permitted.

If you have a disability that requires other accommodations (such as use of a reader, writer, or magnifying glass), your school can order the PSAT/NMSQT in regular type and administer it to you on the same day other students in your school are tested (Saturday, October 21 or Tuesday, October 24). Extended time is permitted.

In December you'll receive your test book and your PSAT/NMSQT score report. Your score report will give your verbal score, your math score, your Selection Index, correct answers, and your answers. To show that special arrangements were made, your score report will be marked *Nonstandard Administration.*

You and your parent or guardian will be asked to sign a form before the test date to verify that you are eligible for special arrangements and to acknowledge that you understand your score report will be marked *Nonstandard Administration.*

A student who is deaf or hard of hearing may have a sign language or oral interpreter to translate test instructions from spoken English. Score reports will not be marked *Nonstandard Administration,* as long as no other special testing accommodations are provided.

If you have a documented hearing, learning, physical, or visual disability, talk to your counselor or teacher.

THE NATIONAL MERIT SCHOLARSHIP PROGRAM

The National Merit Scholarship Program, an annual competition initiated in 1955, is conducted by National Merit Scholarship Corporation (NMSC). NMSC is a not-for-profit organization that operates without government funding.

More than one million high school students who take the PSAT/NMSQT and meet other participation requirements will enter the Merit Program that will end some 18 months later. Some 50,000 scholastically talented Merit Program entrants will be honored; more than 15,000 of them will continue in the competition, and about 6,900 will win Merit Scholarship® awards for college undergraduate study. The Merit Scholarship awards will be supported by some 600 independent sponsors - corporations and businesses, company foundations, professional associations, and colleges and universities - and by NMSC's own funds. In addition, approximately 1,300 other awards (called Special Scholarships) that are financed by corporate and business sponsors will be offered through the Merit Program. For eligibility requirements and scholarship information, contact your counselor or NMSC directly at: Department of Educational Services and Selection, National Merit Scholarship Program, 1560 Sherman Avenue, Suite 200, Evanston, IL 60201-4897; telephone (847) 866-5100.

THE TEST

The PSAT measures verbal and quantitative abilities.

VERBAL ABILITY

The verbal section consists of three parts: Sentence Completions, Verbal Analogies, and Critical Reading.

Sentence Completions

Sentence completion questions measure your knowledge of the meanings of words, and your ability to understand how the different parts of a sentence fit together logically. Sentences are given with one or two words omitted. The correct answer is the word or set of words that, when placed in the blanks, BEST fits the meaning of the sentence as a whole. The sentences, usually taken from published material, cover a wide variety of topics of the sort you are likely to have encountered in school or in your general reading. Your understanding of the sentences will not depend on specialized knowledge of science, literature, social studies, or any other field.

Below are the directions you will see on the test.

Each sentence below has one or two blanks, each blank indicating that something has been omitted. Beneath the sentence are five words or sets of words labeled A through E. Choose the word or set of words that, when inserted in the sentence, BEST fits the meaning of the sentence as a whole.

Example: Medieval kingdoms did not become constitutional republics overnight; on the contrary, the change was _____.

A. unpopular   B. unexpected
C. advantageous   D. sufficient
E. gradual

To answer a sentence completion question, you have to understand how the parts of the sentence relate to one another. In the example above, the first part of the sentence says that the kingdoms did not change overnight. The blank must describe the true nature of the change. So, the correct answer will be a word that describes a change that did not happen rapidly. Note that all five choices could describe changes but only choice E (gradual) best fits the logic and meaning of the sentence as a whole by describing a slow change.

1. The huge budget deficit places the city government in a _____ situation; financial _____ is an ever-present danger.

A. vulnerable; expansion   B. perilous; collapse
C. gainful; audit   D. hazardous; restoration
E. prosperous; bankruptcy

Look for important words and phrases that tell you what is going on: *danger* tells you that there is a threat to the city government, the *huge budget deficit* tells you the exact nature of the *danger* -not enough money to meet daily costs.

Now look at the choices and try to find the one that fits best. While both *vulnerable* and *hazardous* could describe threats, the second words in these choices do not describe financial dangers -choices A and D cannot be correct. You can further rule out two of the three remaining choices: *gainful* describes a profitable situation, not a budgetary crisis; *bankruptcy* does refer to a major problem for a city, but *prosperous* does not describe the result of a budget deficit. Choice B best fits the logic and meaning of the sentence: *The huge budget deficit places the city government in a perilous situation: financial collapse is an ever-present danger.*

2. The pursuit of scientific study can be _____ in that it often requires long hours of hard work.

A. arduous   B. amenable
C. collaborative   D. intermittent
E. insightful

This sentence indicates that the missing word must fit the definition *often requires long hours of hard work.* Consider the meanings of the words in each choice. Words such as *amenable, collaborative, intermittent,* and *insightful* could apply to *scientific study.* However, only *arduous* is a word that means *involving hard work.* Therefore, choice A is correct because it most logically completes the sentence: *The pursuit of scientific study can be* <u>arduous</u> *in that it often requires long hours of hard work.*

3. She is a skeptic, _____ to believe that the accepted opinion of the majority is generally

    _____.

       A.   prone; infallible   B.   afraid; misleading
       C.   inclined; justifiable   D.   quick; significant
       E.   disposed; erroneous

To answer this question correctly, you must know the meaning of the word *skeptic:* a person who doubts or disagrees with generally accepted conclusions or ideas. Which choice best fits this definition?

A *skeptic* would hardly consider the *accepted opinion of the majority* to be *infallible, justifiable,* or *significant,* so choices A, C, and D cannot be correct. A *skeptic* might believe that the *accepted opinion of the majority* is *misleading.* But would a *skeptic* be *afraid* that it was? No, a *skeptic* would feel certain that it was. Therefore, choice B is not correct. Only choice E makes a logical sentence where both words correctly define a *skeptic: She is a skeptic,* <u>disposed</u> *to believe that the accepted opinion of the majority is generally* <u>erroneous</u>.

Hints

1. Begin by reading the entire sentence to yourself to get a feel for the meaning of the whole thing, and to identify, if you can, the words or phrases that are at the heart of the meaning of the sentence.
2. Watch for introductory or connecting words and phrases like *but, not, because, however, moreover, if, even though,* and others that tell you how the parts of the sentence relate to each other.
3. In sentences with two blanks, make sure the words for both blanks make sense in the sentence. Wrong choices often include one correct and one incorrect word.
4. Start by working with one blank at a time. Narrow down the choices using one blank, then use the choices for the other blank to help you make your final decision.
5. Stay within the meaning of the sentence. You should be able to point to words or phrases in the sentence that support your answer choice.
6. Before you mark your answer, read the complete sentence with your choice filled in to be sure it makes sense.

Verbal Analogies

Analogy questions measure your knowledge of the meanings of words, your ability to see a relationship between a pair of words, and your ability to recognize a similar or parallel relationship in another pair of words. Each question consists of a pair of words in CAPITAL letters followed by five pairs of words; the correct answer is the pair whose relationship BEST matches that of the pair in capital letters.

Below are the directions you will see on the test.

Each question below consists of a related pair of words or phrases, followed by five pairs of words or phrases labeled A through E. Select the pair that BEST expresses a relationship similar to that expressed in the original pair.

Example:　　　CRUMB : BREAD ::
   A.　ounce : unit　　　　　　　　　B.　splinter : wood
   C.　water : bucket　　　　　　　　D.　twine : rope
   E.　cream : butter

The first step in answering an analogy question is to figure out the exact relationship between the words in capital letters. The best way is to make up a short sentence or phrase that states the relationship. In the example above, the relationship between CRUMB and BREAD can be stated as *a CRUMB is a very small piece of BREAD.* The second step is to decide which of the five pairs of words in the answer choices best fits the short sentence that you made up. In the example above, the correct answer is B: *a _splinter_ is a very small piece of _Wood_.*

None of the other choices shares a similar or parallel relationship with the capitalized pair of words: choice A, an *ounce* is a type of *unit,* not a *small piece* of a *unit;* choice C, *water* can be carried in a *bucket,* but is not a small piece of a *bucket;* choice D, *twine* is thinner and less strong than *rope,* but *twine* is not a small piece of *rope;* choice E, *cream* is made into *butter,* but it is not a small piece of *butter.*

Keep in mind that a pair of words can have more than one relationship. In choice E, the relationship can be expressed as *cream* is processed from the same material as *butter* or as *cream* can be made into *butter.* But neither of these matches the relationship in *CRUMB :: BREAD.* Choice B best expresses a relationship similar to that between CRUMB and BREAD.

For each of the following analogies, state the relationship between the words in capital letters and figure out the correct answer before you read the explanation.

4.　COUNTERFEITER : CURRENCY ::

   A.　Imposter : disguises　　　　　B.　collector : stamps
   C.　thief : plunder　　　　　　　　D.　forger : signatures
   E.　spy : secrecy

Be alert to multiple meanings of words; use only the meaning that establishes a reasonable relationship with the other word in the pair. CURRENCY can refer to the condition of being up to date. However, only the meaning referred to money, coins, and bills establishes a reasonable relationship with COUNTERFEITER. The relationship is *a COUNTERFEITER illegally produces CURRENCY.*

Try each of the choices to find the one that best matches this relationship. While an *imposter* may or may not make *disguises,* the relationship is that the COUNTERFEITER by definition is one who does produce illegal CURRENCY. A *collector* finds and preserves rare or unusual *stamps,* a *thief* illegally obtains but does not produce *plunder.* Now try D. Does a *forger* illegally produce *signatures?* Yes, a *forger* produces *signatures* and tries to pass them off as having been written by others. Choice E can be ruled out because *secrecy* is not an object illegally produced by a *spy.* The correct answer is choice D.

5.　IGNITE : COMBUSTIBLE ::

A. refrigerate : defrosted
B. bend : pliable
C. preserve : endangered
D. drain : clogged
E. magnify : observable

Sometimes the sentence you use to state the relationship of the capitalized word pairs rules out a few, but not all, of the choices. When that happens, your next step should be to describe the relationship between IGNITE and COMBUSTIBLE as *If something is COMBUSTI-BLE, one can IGNITE it.* When you try this relationship, you find that choice A fits the sentence: *If something is defrosted, one can refrigerate it.* You also find that choice B fits: *If something is pliable, one can bend it.* You must then restate your relationship more precisely. The most distinctive trait of something COMBUSTIBLE is that it is easy to IGNITE. Check all five of the choices to see which fits this new relationship best. Only choice B matches: *something pliable is easy to bend.*

6. REQUEST : ENTREAT ::

A. control : explode
B. admire : idolize
C. borrow : steal
D. repeat : plead
E. cancel : invalidate

When you answer analogy questions, you need to pay careful attention to the precise meanings of words. Recognizing shades of meaning will sometimes help you find the correct answer.

While the capitalized words have similar general meanings, they have precise definitions expressing different degrees of feeling. *To ENTREAT is to REQUEST, urgently, with strong feeling.* Only choice B fits this relationship: *To idolize is to admire in an extreme manner, with strong feeling.*

If you had limited your search to a word in the choices that was similar in meaning to the words in capital letters, you might have mistakenly selected choice D because of *plead.* But to *plead* is not to *repeat* with strong feeling - it is to ask with strong feeling. Therefore, choice D is incorrect. The correct answer is choice B.

Hints
1. First make up a sentence that shows how the two words in capital letters work together. Then see what pair of words among the choices works best in your sentence.
2. Remember that you are not looking for individual words that are similar to the words in capital letters or that have the same meaning. Don't look for a relationship between the first word in capital letters and the first word in each of the choices. Do look for a pair of words with the same relationship between them as the pair in capital letters.
3. Many pairs of words have more than one relationship between them. You may have to try a few relationships before you find the one that helps you choose the best answer.
4. If you find more than one answer that fits the first relationship you find in the pair of words in capital letters, you may have to define that relationship more precisely.

Critical Reading
Many verbal questions measure your critical reading skills. Critical reading selections are from social sciences, natural sciences, and the humanities. Some questions are based on a pair of passages on a shared theme or issue.

Some passages have an introduction or footnote. The information you need to answer the questions is in the passages, introductions, and footnotes.

Questions may ask you to:

- figure out the meaning of a word from its context
- understand significant information
- compare a pair of passages
- relate parts of a passage to each other, to the whole passage, or to a paired passage
- analyze and evaluate ideas, opinions, and arguments
- identify cause and effect
- make inferences and recognize implications
- follow the logic of an argument
- recognize consistency or inconsistency in an argument
- compare or contrast arguments

The passages on the next page are followed by questions based on their content; questions following a pair of related passages may also be based on the relationship between the paired passages. Answer the questions on the basis of what is <u>stated</u> or <u>implied</u> in the passages and in any introductory material that may be provided.

In Passage 1, the author presents his view of the early years of the silent film industry. In Passage 2, the author draws on her experiences as a mime to generalize about her art. (A mime is a performer who, without speaking, entertains through gesture, facial expression, and movement.)

Passage 1

Talk to those people who first saw films when they were silent, and they will tell you the experience was magic. The silent film had extraordinary powers to draw members of an audience into the story, and an equally potent capacity to make their imaginations work. It required the audience to become engaged - to supply voices and sound effects. The audience was the
5 final, creative contributor to the process of making a film.

The finest films of the silent era depended on two elements that we can seldom provide today - a large and receptive audience and a well-orchestrated score. For the audience, the fusion of picture and live music added up to more than the sum of the respective parts.

The one word that sums up the attitude of the silent filmmakers is *enthusiasm*, conveyed
10 most strongly before formulas took shape and when there was more room for experimentation. This enthusiastic uncertainty often resulted in such accidental discoveries as new camera or editing techniques. Some films experimented with players; the 1915 film REGENERATION, for example, by using real gangsters and streetwalkers, provided startling local color. Other films, particularly those of Thomas Ince, provided tragic endings as often as films by other compa-
15 nies supplied happy ones.

Unfortunately, the vast majority of silent films survive today in inferior prints that no longer reflect the care that the original technicians put into them. The modern versions of silent films may appear jerky and flickery, but the vast picture palaces did not attract four to six thousand people a night by giving them eyestrain. A silent film depended on its visuals; as soon as you
20 degrade those, you lose elements that go far beyond the image on the surface. The acting in silents was often very subtle, very restrained, despite legends to the contrary.

Passage 2

Mime opens up a new world to the beholder, but it does so insidiously, not by purposely injecting points of interest in the manner of a tour guide. Audiences are not unlike visitors to a foreign land who discover that the modes, manners, and thoughts of its inhabitants are not meaningless odd-
25   ities, but are sensible in context.

I remember once when an audience seemed perplexed at what I was doing. At first, I tried to gain a more immediate response by using slight exaggerations. I soon realized that these actions had nothing to do with the audience's understanding of the character. What I had believed to be a failure of the audience to respond in the manner I expected was, in fact, only
30   their concentration on what I was doing: they were enjoying a gradual awakening - a slow transference of their understanding from their own time and place to one that appeared so unexpectedly before their eyes. This was evidenced by their growing response to succeeding numbers.

Mime is an elusive art, as its expression is entirely dependent on the ability of the per-former to imagine a character and to recreate that character for each performance. As a mime,
35   I am a physical medium, the instrument upon which the figures of my imagination play their dance of life. The individuals in my audience also have responsibilities - they must be alert col-laborators. They cannot sit back, mindlessly complacent, and wait to have their emotions titil-lated by mesmeric musical sounds or visual rhythms or acrobatic feats, or by words that tell them what to think. Mime is an art that, paradoxically, appeals both to those who respond
40   instinctively to entertainment and to those whose appreciation is more analytical and complex. Between these extremes lie those audiences conditioned to resist any collaboration with what is played before them; and these the mime must seduce despite themselves. There is only one way to attack those reluctant minds - take them unaware! They will be delighted at an unex-pected pleasure.

Questions 7 through 9 relate to the pair of reading passages shown above.

7.   Both passages are primarily concerned with the subject of

   A.   shocking special effects
   B.   varied dramatic styles
   C.   visual elements in dramatic performances
   D.   audience resistance to theatrical performances
   E.   nostalgia for earlier forms of entertainment

This question asks you to think about both passages. You need to figure out the main subject or focus of the pair of passages, not simply to recognize that one passage is about silent film and the other is about mime.

In Passage 1, the discussion of silent films emphasizes the effectiveness of these films for audiences of that era. In Passage 2, the discussion of a mime's techniques focuses on fac-tors that make a performance effective for the audience. Thus, the main subject for both pas-sages is the way that a visual form of entertainment affects an audience. Recognizing this similarity, you are ready to search for the correct answer.

Choice A is wrong because *shocking special effects* is not a main subject. Choice E is incorrect because a tone of mild *nostalgia* appears only in Passage 1: since this question asks about the pair, the correct choice must be true for both passages. Although *varied dramatic styles* (used by film performers and by a mime) is an idea briefly touched upon in both pas-sages, it is not their subject. And even though both authors are making points about the overall role of audiences in the performances, D is incorrect because *audience resistance to theatrical performances* is addressed only in Passage 2. Choice C is the correct answer because it refers to performances in a visual art form.

8. In Passage 1, the statement *but the...eyestrain* (lines 18-19) conveys a sense of

    A. irony regarding the incompetence of silent film technicians
    B. resentment at the way old silent films are now perceived
    C. regret that the popularity of picture palaces has waned
    D. pleasure in remembering a grandeur that has passed
    E. amazement at the superior quality of modern film technology

   This question asks you to think carefully about the attitude expressed in part of Passage 1. Consider the lines: *but the vast picture palaces did not attract four to six thousand people a night by giving them eyestrain.* By mentioning large numbers of customers and the absence of *eyestrain,* the author emphasizes that watching silent films was not a physically uncomfortable experience (as it is for modern viewers). Previous sentences in Passage 1 also emphasize this point by referring to *inferior prints* and *the care that the original technicians* took, as well as the *jerky and flickery* impression of modern versions of silent films. The correct choice must accurately reflect the author's attitude while specifically answering the question being asked.
   In this question, *irony, resentment, regret,* and *pleasure* are all attitudes conveyed in Passage 1. However, the question directs you specifically to what is suggested in lines 18-19. Further, each choice mentions both an attitude and a specific situation. Choice A is wrong because the irony in lines 18-19 is not about the *incompetence of silent film technicians* - the author praises silent film technicians for their competence. Choice B reflects the author's point that modern audiences are mistaken in assuming that silent films have always been hard to watch. But, consider all choices before selecting your answer. Choice C is wrong because while the author does convey a sense of *regret* (that the old pleasure of watching silent films is lost), the regret, in lines 18-19, is not for the lost *popularity of picture palaces.* Choices D and E are wrong because lines 18-19 do not express either *pleasure* or *amazement.* Choice B is the correct answer; it is the only choice that accurately represents the attitude and the situation specified by the question.

9. Both passages mention which of the following as being important to the artistic success of the dramatic forms they describe?

    A. Effective fusion of disparate dramatic elements
    B. Slightly exaggerated characterization
    C. Incorporation of realistic details
    D. Large audiences
    E. Audience involvement

   This question asks you to compare the two passages and identify an idea shared by both authors. One good way to begin is by ruling out any choices that do not apply to both passages. For example, because only Passage 1 discusses *Effective fusion of disparate dramatic elements* and *Large audiences,* you can rule out choices A and D. Now examine the three remaining choices, B, C, and E. Although both passages touch on the ideas of *Incorporation of realistic details* and *Slightly exaggerated characterization,* neither of these is presented in both passages as being *important to the artistic success* of silent films and mime. Choice E is correct because *Audience involvement* is presented in both passages as an element *important to the artistic success* of silent films and mime.

The passage below is followed by questions based on its content. Answer the questions following the passage on the basis of what is <u>stated</u> or <u>implied</u> in that passage and in any introductory material that may be provided.

The following passage was written by a twentieth century commentator.

Nineteenth-century scientists made enormous strides in most fields, but they had obsessions that have dramatically changed Western attitudes toward nature. I think the most harmful of the changes has been the development of the idea that our relation with the physical world must always have a goal, that we must always be industriously seeking knowledge as we walk
5   among the trees. This dreadfully serious approach has made the study of nature too much like a school lesson and has turned people away from nature. The far saner eighteenth-century attitude, that nature is a mirror for philosophers, an evoker of emotion, a pleasure, a poem, has been forgotten. This attitude was replaced by an obsession with machines and with classification. Charles Darwin's theory and method of scientific inquiry made it seem possible to analyze
10   the natural world with as much certainty as if it were made up of parts like a steam engine. Only the other day I found a letter in the museum of which I am curator. It was from a well-known fern expert of the period and concerned some twenty or so specimens that had been sent to him. A modern botanist would class these ferns in three categories, but this worthy gentleman felt obliged to grant each plant its own lengthy appellation. By giving each fern a specific
15   name, he seemed to feel that he could increase his understanding of the world.
I do not mean to devalue the accomplishments of the nineteenth century. By contrast, seventeenth- and eighteenth-century science is absolute nonsense in modern scientific terms. Its diffuse reasoning, misinterpreted evidence, and frequent blend of the humanities with science proper are of little use to modern scientists. But one general, if unconscious, assumption
20   guiding almost all pre-nineteenth-century science - that it is comprehensible to most human beings in spite of its complexities - has been much too soon dismissed, and we should learn from it. It is not the fault of modern scientists that most of their work is now so complex that only their fellow specialists can understand it and that their writing is mechanical, with words reduced to cogs and treated as poor substitutes for purely scientific formulas. Nor is it directly
25   their fault that their vision of empirical knowledge, their absolute reliance on demonstrable fact, has seeped down to dominate the popular view of nature. Our mistake lies in accepting that modern scientific attitudes should govern our everyday relationship with nature.

10.   As it is used in the passage, *vision* (line 24) MOST NEARLY means

    A.   representation   B.   foresight
    C.   revelation   D.   conception
    E.   illusion

This type of question asks you to recognize the meaning of a word in a specific context. Words often have more than one meaning and writers sometimes use familiar words in inventive ways to make a point. Think carefully about how this word is used in this sentence. While several choices fit the dictionary definition of *vision,* you must consider the meaning of the word in the context in which it is used: *Nor is it directly their fault that their vision of empirical knowledge, their absolute reliance on demonstrable fact, has seeped down to dominate the popular view of nature.* The sentence states that society as a whole accepts the modern scientists' view of empirical knowledge. That is, society accepts their *conception* of empirical knowledge.

Choice D is the correct answer. None of the other words makes a meaningful sentence if substituted for the word *vision.*

11. In the passage as a whole, the author's attitude toward nineteenth-century science is BEST described as

    A. partisan disdain   B. tempered criticism
    C. ambivalence   D. toleration
    E. praise

To answer this question, you must recognize and analyze an important part of the author's argument. That is, you need to compare the choices to the author's overall attitude toward nineteenth-century science. The first paragraph says that nineteenth-century scientists brought about *harmful...changes.* Choices D and E are incorrect because they are attitudes more positive than the author's attitude. The second paragraph says *I do not mean to devalue the accomplishments of the nineteenth century,* allowing you to rule out choice A - it is too negative. Choices B and C apply to people who express apparently inconsistent opinions. Is the author *ambivalent,* indicating that he is uncertain and that he believes two directly opposite things? No, the author confidently expresses his opinion about two different aspects of nineteenth-century science. Choice B, *tempered criticism,* is the BEST answer to this question: it shows the author as criticizing nineteenth-century science while also tempering (modifying) his criticism with praise.

12. The author relates an anecdote about a well-known fern expert primarily to

    A. contradict the notion that nineteenth-century botanical classification is inferior to current classification
    B. illustrate the preoccupation of nineteenth-century scientists with classification
    C. provide an example of the nineteenth-century scientist's personal closeness to nature
    D. mention a scientist whose work reflects eighteenth-century attitudes
    E. contrast nineteenth-century methods of botanical classification with eighteenth-century methods

This question asks you to think carefully about the way the author presents the argument. How does the anecdote about the fern expert in lines 10-15 fit into that part of the passage? In the sentences before the anecdote, you will see that the author makes two general statements: that nineteenth-century scientists had *an obsession with machines and with classification*, and that they thought it was *possible to analyze the natural world with as much certainty as if it were made up of parts like a steam engine.* The point of the story is that a nineteenth-ceintury scientist *felt obliged* to create a *classification* for every fern - that he was obsessed with *classification.*
Now try to find the choice that best expresses this idea. You need to make thoughtful distinctions in selecting the correct answer to this question because every choice reflects some topic discussed in the passage. Don't select a choice simply because it contains an idea you read in the passage. Compare the fern expert story with each choice. Choices C and D reflect ideas from the overall passage; but, they do not reflect the point of the story - *classification.* While choices A, B, and E do discuss *classification,* choice A is wrong because the value of one system of *classification* is not the point of the story, and E is wrong because the story does not contrast nineteenth-century *classification* with eighteenth-century *classification.* Only

choice B accurately states how the author uses the anecdote in presenting the argument. The author *relates* (or tells) the story to provide an example of - to *illustrate* - the *preoccupation* with *classification* among *nineteenth-century scientists.*

13. In line 23, *reduced* MOST NEARLY means

A. divided
C. transposed
E. deleted

B. abridged
D. demoted

This question, like question 10, asks you to recognize the meaning of a word in a specific context. Begin by considering how the word is actually used: *It is not the fault of modern scientists that most of their work is now so complex that only their fellow specialists can understand it and that their writing is mechanical, with words reduced to cogs and treated as poor substitutes for purely scientific formulas.* In the sentence, *treated as poor substitutes* indicates that the value of *words* has decreased for modern scientists.

Consider the five choices and select the one that best captures that meaning of *reduced* in line 23. Choice D represents the way *reduced* is used in the sentence: it conveys the idea of lowering the value of words. Words have, in effect, been *demoted* to cogs. The other choices are incorrect because, while they do involve making changes to words, they do not necessarily involve changing the value of the words. Only choice D can be substituted for *reduced* without changing the meaning of the sentence in the passage. Choice D is the correct answer.

Hints

1. Don't skip introductions to passages. Information provided in the introduction is sometimes useful in analyzing and evaluating the passage.

2. Read each passage and any accompanying information carefully. Follow the author's reasoning and be aware of features such as assumptions, attitudes, and tone.

3. You may find it helpful to mark the passages as you are reading, but don't spend too much time making notes.

4. Read each question and all the answer choices carefully. Don't be misled by choices that are only partially correct.

5. When a question asks you to compare an aspect of a pair of passages, don't be misled by choices that are correct for only one of the two passages. The correct choice will be accurate for both passages.

6. Select the choice that best answers the question asked. Don't select a choice just because it is a true statement about the passage.

7. Some students find it helpful to read the questions first to get an idea of what to look for in the passage. Others prefer to read the passage and then try to answer the questions. Try both methods when you take your practice test to see which works better for you.

MATHEMATICS

Mathematical ability section consists of three parts: Standard Multiple-Choice, Quantitative Comparison, and Student-Produced Response that require you to produce and grid your own answer.

The mathematics questions call upon the skills you have learned in arithmetic, algebra, and geometry and test how well you can use these skills. Some of the questions are like those in your textbooks. Others require you to use your mathematical skills in original ways to solve problems.

The PSAT/NMSQT does not require you to know proofs of geometric theorems or concepts from intermediate algebra such as the quadratic formula or negative and fractional exponents.

Standard Multiple-Choice

Directions for Standard Multiple-Choice Questions:

Solve each problem using any available space on the page for scratchwork. Then decide which is the best of the choices given and fill in the corresponding oval on the answer sheet.

Notes:
1.   The use of a calculator is permitted. All numbers used are real numbers.
2.   Figures that accompany problems in this test are intended to provide information useful in solving the problems. They are drawn as accurately as possible EXCEPT when it is stated in a specific problem that the figure is not drawn to scale. All figures lie in a plane unless otherwise indicated.

Reference Information: The following reference information is given at the beginning of both mathematics sections.

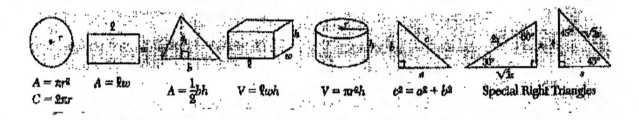

$A = \pi r^2$ $A = \ell w$ $A = \frac{1}{2}bh$ $V = \ell wh$ $V = \pi r^2 h$ $c^2 = a^2 + b^2$ Special Right Triangles

$C = 2\pi r$

The number of degrees of arc in a circle is 360.
The measure in degrees of a straight angle is 180.
The sum of the measures in degrees of the angles of a triangle is 180.

1.   In the figure shown at the right, x =

   A.   25
   B.   30
   C.   40
   D.   45
   E.   60

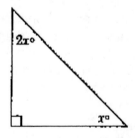

[When a question includes a figure not drawn to scale, you should not make any assumptions about the degree measures of angles or about the length of segments based only on the way the figure looks.]

Since it is noted that the figure is not drawn to scale, you can be certain only that the triangle is a right triangle and that the angle with measure 2x° is twice as large as the angle with measure x°. You can not accurately estimate the size of these angles from the way they look in the figure.

To answer the question, you can use the fact that the sum of the measures of the angles of a triangle is 180°. In this case, that means 2x + x + 90 = 180. This equation simplifies to 3x = 90 or x = 30. So, the correct answer is B.

2. A boat rental costs x dollars total for the first 4 hours of use. After the first 4 hours, the rate is y dollars per hour or part thereof.
   If the rental for a boat for 10 hours one day was $50, which of the following represents how x is related to y? 50 =

   A. x + 4y
   C. x + 10y
   E. 4x + 10y

   B. x + 6y
   D. 4x + 6y

The rental cost for 4 hours is x dollars. The rental cost for the remaining 6 hours is 6y dollars. Therefore, the 50 dollar rental cost for 10 hours is equal to x dollars plus 6y dollars or 50 + x + 6y. The correct answer is B.

3. In the figure shown at the right, line *l* passes through the origin and point A. Which of the following points is not on *l*?

   A. (2.5,1)
   B. (4,1.6) C (7,3)
   C. (10,4)
   D. (15,6)

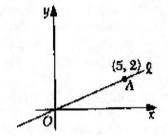

To solve this problem, you may want to use the concept of slope. To find the slope of *l*, use the coordinates of the two given points (5,2) and (0,0). The slope is defined as:

$$\frac{\text{the difference of the y coordinates}}{\text{the difference of the x coordinates}} \quad \text{or} \quad \frac{2-0}{5-0} = \frac{2}{5}$$

Therefore, the slope between any two points on *l* must be $\frac{2}{5}$. It may be easier to use the origin with each of the points given to see which of the points will not yield a slope of $\frac{2}{5}$. Using the origin as one of the points and subtracting 0 from both of the x and y coordinates means that for a point to be on l, the ratio of its y coordinate to its x coordinate must be $\frac{2}{5}$. In option A, $\frac{1}{2.5}=\frac{2}{5}$;

in option B, $\frac{1.6}{4}=.4=\frac{2}{5}$; in option D $\frac{4}{10}=\frac{2}{5}$ and in option E $\frac{6}{15}=\frac{2}{5}$.. Only in option C

$\frac{3}{7}\neq\frac{2}{5}$.

Therefore, the point (7,3) is not on l and C is the correct answer. A calculator may be helpful in computing the slopes, especially on options A and B. However, quick inspection may

tell you that the ratio of the y coordinate to the x coordinate in option C cannot equal $\frac{2}{5}$, so you can determine that C is the correct answer without even computing the ratios of the other answer choices.

4. Which of the following can be the average (arithmetic mean) of four consecutive positive even integers?

A. 212   B. 216   C. 220
D. 225   E. 228

In this case, you are asked to determine which of the answer choices can be the average of four consecutive positive even integers.

Remember that in order to find the average (arithmetic mean) of a list of numbers, add the numbers together and divide by the number of numbers you are averaging.

If you use algebra, the integers could be x, x+2, x+4, and x+6 since consecutive even

integers differ by 2. The sum of these integers is 4x + 12, and the average is $\frac{4x+12}{4}=x+3$.

Since x is a positive even integer, x + 3 must be odd (Even + Odd = Odd). The eliminates choices A, B, C, and E, so D is the correct answer.

This problem can also be solved intuitively by realizing that the average of four consecutive positive even integers will always be between the two middle integers and therefore will be an odd integer. The number 225 is the only odd integer among the answer choices. It is the average of the four consecutive even integers 222, 224, 226, and 228.

5. Let S be the set of all integers that can be written as $n^2 + 1$ where n is a nonzero integer. If x and y are two different integers in S, which of the following must be the square of an integer?

$(x-1)(y-1)$
$4(x-1)$

I.   (x-l)(y-l)
II.   4(x-l)
III. $x^2 + y^2$

A. I *only*   B. II*only*   C. III *only*
D. I, II   E. I, III

[This question format is used occasionally in both mathematics and verbal sections. Consider statements I, II, and III one at a time. Sometimes you can determine the correct answer by eliminating answer choices as you go.]

In this question, you must check each of the expressions I, II, and III and decide which must be the square of an integer. Since x and y are two different integers in S, let $x = n^2 + 1$ and $y = m^2 + 1$ where n and m are unequal integers. The expression (x-1)(y-l) in I equals $(n^2+1-1)(m^2+1-1) = n^2m^2 = (nm)^2$. Since n and m are integers, $(nm)^2$ is the square of an integer. Looking at the answer choices, you see that B and C can be eliminated as the correct answer since neither contains I. If you do not know how to evaluate II or III, it would be to your advantage to guess between choices A, D, and E. This type of guessing is called *educated guessing*. The more choices you can eliminate before making educated guesses, the better your chances of improving your score. In fact, if you can eliminate just one choice, it is to your advantage to guess.

Continuing to work the problem, you see that in II the expression $4(x-1) = 4(n^2+1-1) = 4n^2$ $= (2n)^2$, which is also the square of an integer. Therefore, A and E can be eliminated since neither contains II. The correct answer is D. For this problem, you can determine the correct answer without considering III.

However, if you want to be certain that III is not true, you can think of an example that shows the expression $x^2 + y^2$ is not always equal to the square of an integer. An example would be if x = 1 and y = 2. Since $0^2 + 1 = 1$ and $1^2 + 1 = 2$, 1 and 2 are both in set S. The expression $x^2 + y^2$ would equal 5, and 5 is not the square of an integer.

Hints

1.   Look at the answer choices before you begin to work on each question. The answer choices often will help you focus on what it is you are supposed to look for in the problem.

2.   Read each question carefully, even if it looks like a question you don't think you can answer. Good arithmetic skills can help you solve some simple algebra problems. Many geometry questions also test your algebra skills. Don't let the form of the question keep you from trying to answer it.

3.   You may find that your answer is a different mathematical expression that equals one of the choices. If you don't find your answer among the answer choices, write your answer in a different form. For example: 3x + 6 is the same as 3(x+2) and is the same as $2 + \dfrac{b}{a}$.

Quantitative Comparison

A second type of mathematics question that you will find on the PSAT/NMSQT is the Quantitative Comparison. The answer choices are always the same for these questions. This type of question usually involves less reading, takes less time to answer, and requires less computation than standard multiple-choice questions.

For this type of question, two quantities are compared and the correct answer choice is:
A if the quantity in Column A is greater,
B if the quantity in Column B is greater,
C if the two quantities are equal, or
D if the relationship cannot be determined from the information given.
You should memorize these choices so you do not have to refer to them for each question.

Directions for Quantitative Comparison Questions:

Quantitative Comparison questions consist of two quantities in boxes, one in Column A and one in Column B. You are to compare the two quantities and on the answer sheet fill in oval

A if the quantity in Column A is greater;
B if the quantity in Column B is greater;
C if the two quantities are equal;
D if the relationship cannot be determined from the information given

Notes:

1. In some questions, information is given about one or both of the quantities to be compared. In such cases, the given information is centered above the two columns and is not boxed.
2. In a given question, a symbol that appears in both columns represents the same thing in Column A as it does in Column B.
3. Letters such as x, n, and k stand for real numbers.

Examples:

	Column A	Column B	Answers
E1	5^2	20	● ⑧ © ⑩

$150°$ $x°$

	Column A	Column B	Answers
E2	x	30	ⓐ ⑧ ● ⑩

r and s are integers.

	Column A	Column B	Answers
E3	$r + 1$	$s - 1$	ⓐ ⑧ © ●

Column A   Column B

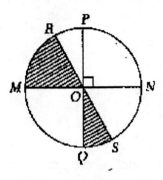

0 is the center of the circle and
MN, PQ, and RS are diameters.

6. | The fraction of the cir-
cle that is shaded. | 30%

You need to determine the percent of the circle that is shaded in order to determine the relationship between the two quantities. There are two shaded regions to consider, the region formed by angle MOR and the region formed by angle QOS. Angle QOS and angle ROP have the same degree measures since they are vertical angles. Therefore, the regions formed by these angles have the same area. Now combine the regions formed by angles MOR and ROP. This new region is one of the 4 equal regions formed by the perpendicular diameters MN and PQ. (The figure shows the right angle symbol for angle PON). The shaded region is or *25%* of the circle. The correct answer is B.

$$2 < x < 4$$
$$3 < y < 4$$

7. | X | | Y |

The problem states that x is a number between (but not including) 2 and 4, and y is a number between (but not including) 3 and 4. You are asked to compare x and y.

Since you are not told specific values for x and y, choose values that satisfy the given conditions. For example, if x = 3, the value of y would be greater than 3. If x = 3.5, y could also be 3.5 since 3.5 satisfies both conditions. If x = 3.5, y could be 3.25. This time x is greater than y.

There is not enough information given to tell you which quantity is greater. The correct answer is D. When the relationship between the quantity in Column A and the quantity in Column B changes like this, depending on the value of the variables, the answer is D.

Column A

Column B

One marble is selected at
random from a bowl that
contains exactly 9 marbles -
4 green, 3 red, and 2 yellow.

8.
The probability that the marble selected is red

$$\frac{1}{3}$$

To solve this problem, you must find the probability of selecting a red marble. Use the information stated in the problem, and write the probability as a fraction.

The probability of selecting a red marble is equal to

$$\frac{\text{Number of red marbles}}{\text{Total number of marbles}} = \frac{3}{9} = \frac{1}{3}$$

Since the quantity in Column B is also the correct answer is C.

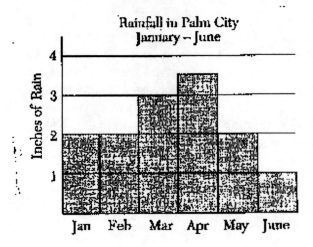

9.
The total number of inches or rainfall in January, February, and March

The total number of inches in rainfall in April, May, and June

Since in Quantitative Comparison questions you are comparing the quantity in Column A with the quantity in Column B, it may not always be necessary to arrive at the correct answer to a Quantitative Comparison question by calculating exact values. The answer to this problem, for example, can be found by visually comparing the bars for the various months. Since the number of inches in February and May are the same, it is only necessary to compare January and March with April and June. The rainfall in January is a full inch more than the rainfall in June, whereas the rainfall in April is less than an inch more than the rainfall in March. Therefore, the total number of inches of rainfall is greater for Column A than for Column B. The correct answer is A.

<u>Column A</u>   <u>Column B</u>

10.
| The perimeter of a rectangle with diagnonal of length 5 and one side of length 2 |

| The perimeter of a square with diagonal of length |

Remember the perimeter of a figure is the sum of the lengths of the sides of the figure. To compute the quantities in the two columns, it may be helpful to draw diagrams.

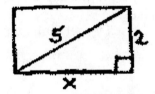   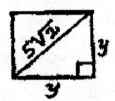

Since you are given the length of one side of the rectangle, you will need to find the length of the other side as well as the length of a side of the square.

Using the Pythagorean Theorem, $x^2 + 2^2 = 5^2$ which yields $x^2 = 21$, so $x = \sqrt{21}$. The perimeter of the rectangle is . You could use a calculator to get the exact perimeter or you could estimate the perimeter by realizing that is between 4 and 5, so the perimeter in Column A is between 12 and 14.

For Column B, use the fact that the diagonal of the square is the hypotenuse of a 45-45-90 triangle. Since the hypotenuse $\sqrt{2}$ is times the length of the side of this triangle (this formula is given with the reference information at the beginning of each mathematics section), the length of the side of the square is 5. The perimeter of the square will then be 20 and since 14 < 20, the correct answer is B.

<u>Hints</u>

1. Learn Quantitative Comparison answer choices:
    A if the quantity in Column A is greater;
    B if the quantity in Column B is greater;
    C if the two quantities are equal;
    D if the relationship cannot be determined from the information given

2. Make sure you are familiar with the layout of Quantitative Comparison questions:

Labels for *Column A* and *Column B* appear at the top of each page, not with each question

Lines separate each question

Information relating to both columns is centered

Quantities to be compared are boxed

Lines separate this question from the next

Column A   Column B
_____

$x > 0$

x^2 $\frac{1}{x}$

3. Many Quantitative Comparisons can be answered without working out the complete expressions in each column. For instance, simplifying fractions and factoring algebraic expressions is sometimes all you have to do to compare the two quantities.
4. When working with algebraic expressions, don't forget that a variable could stand for a fraction, a negative number, 0, etc.

Student-Produced Response

Mathematics questions in the student-produced response format do not include any answer choices. You are required to solve 10 problems and enter your answers in the special grids provided on the answer sheet. Read these directions carefully so you will know them thoroughly before the test.

Directions for Student-Produced Response Questions:
Student-Produced Response questions require you to solve the problem and enter your answer by marking the ovals in the special grid, as shown in the examples on the next page.

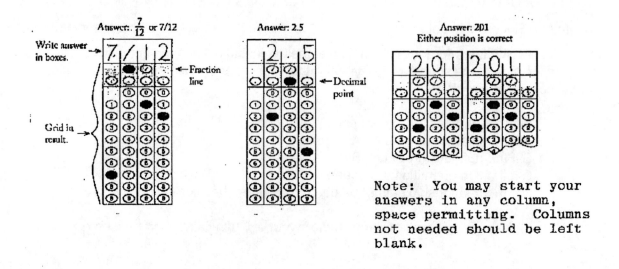

Note: You may start your answers in any column, space permitting. Columns not needed should be left blank.

- Mark no more than one oval in any column.
- Because the answer sheet will be machine-scored, you will receive credit only if the ovals are filled in correctly.
- Although not required, it is suggested that you write your answer in the boxes at the top of the columns to help you fill in the ovals accurately.
- Some problems may have more than one correct answer. In such cases, grid only one answer.
- Mixed numbers such as 2 1/2 must be gridded as 2.5 or 5/2.
- If is gridded, it will be interpreted as , not 2 1/2
- Decimal accuracy: If you obtain a decimal answer, enter the most accurate value that the grid will accommodate. For example, if you obtain an answer such as 0.6666..., you should record the result as .666 or .667. Less accurate values such as .66 or .67 are not acceptable.

Acceptable ways to grid $\dfrac{2}{3}$ = .6666...

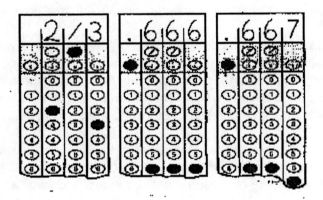

11.   If operation # is defined by the equation a # b = 3a + b, what is the value of x in the equation 2 # x = x # 3?

This question requires you to use a newly defined symbol. You are not expected to be familiar with the # operation, but rather to use the definition given. You need to solve an equation for x, but first you must determine the equation using the definition. The definition 2 # x = x # 3 becomes 3(2) + x = 3(x) +3. This simplifies to 6 + x = 3x + 3, which yields x = 3/2 or 1.5. You would then grid in your answer as either 3/2 or 1.5.

Note: The grid will not accommodate mixed numbers such as 1 1/2. If you grid 11/2, the result will be interpreted as , not 1 1/2.

So if you obtain a mixed number as an answer, you will need to change the mixed number to an improper fraction and enter the improper fraction on the grid or enter its decimal equivalent. The mixed number 1 1/2 can be entered as 3/2 or the decimal 1.5. It is not necessary, however, to reduce fractions to lowest terms.

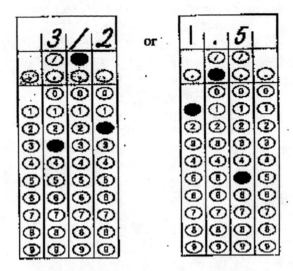

12. Each of 24 students selected exactly 3 colleges from a given list of colleges. If each college on the list was selected exactly 4 times, how many colleges were on the list?

You are trying to find how many colleges were on the list. There were 24 students, and each student selected exactly 3 colleges. So the total number of colleges selected by students was 24 x 3 = 72. Now consider the fact that more than one student selected the same college. The problem states that each college was selected exactly 4 times. To find the number of different colleges, divide 72 by 4, which gives 18. You would then grid in 18 as your answer.

Note: On Question 12, the number 18 can be gridded, as shown on the next page, in the center of the grid or it can be gridded to the far left or to the far right. All possibilities will be counted as correct. This gridding procedure holds for integers as well as for fractions and decimals.

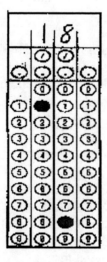

13. How many integers from -5,000 to 5,000, inclusive, are divisible by 5?

Divisible by 5 means that the remainder is zero when the integer is divided by 5. Therefore, you need to find how many integers from -5,000 to 5,000 will yield a remainder of 0 when divided by 5. Since 5 = 1.5, 10 = 2.5, 15 = 3.5,...5,000 = 1,000.5, there are 1,000 numbers between 1 and 5,000, inclusive, that are divisible by 5. Likewise, there are 1,000 numbers between -1 and -5,000, inclusive, that are divisible by 5. Remember that zero is also divisible by 5 since 0/5 = 0 with a remainder of 0 (zero is divisible by every nonzero integer). Therefore, there are 2,001 integers from -5,000 to 5,000, inclusive, that are divisible by 5.

Note: Since there is no provision for including a comma on the grid, you would grid 2001 as the correct answer.

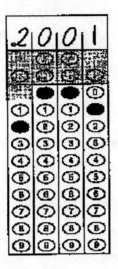

14.   If x = 12k where 6 < k < 10, and k is an integer, what is one possible value of x/2?

Since k is an integer and 6 < k < 10, then k could equal 7, 8, or 9. The possible values of x would then be 12.7 = 84, 12.8 = 96, or 12.9 = 108.

Evaluating yields 42, 48, or 54 as possible answers.

Any of these three answers would be counted as correct for this question. Note: You can only grid one of the possible correct answers.

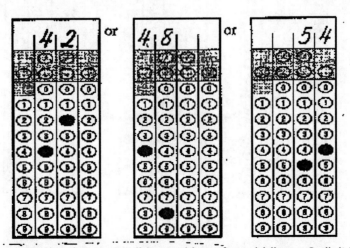

Also note the three possible positions for gridding a 2-digit integer - in the center of the grid or to the far left or to the far right.

15.   K, L, M, and N are points on a line in that order. If the length of segment LM is twice the length of segment KL, MN = 14 and KN = 40, what is the length of segment KL?

[For a geometry problem, if a figure is not drawn, it may be helpful to draw the figure so you can visualize the problem.]

You may want to draw and label a line to help you solve this problem. Since the length of segment LM is twice the length of segment KL, you can label LM with length 2x and KL with length x.

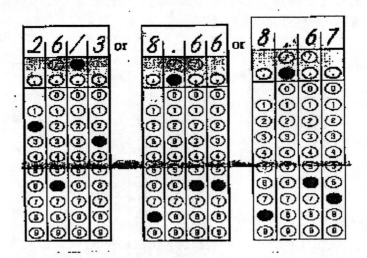

Since KN = 40, the information in the figure above tells you that the following equation can be written.

$$
\begin{aligned}
x + 2x + 14 &= 40 \\
3x &= 26 \\
x &= \frac{26}{3}
\end{aligned}
$$

You could grid either or its decimal equivalent. Since 8.666... is a repeating decimal, the decimal 8.66 or 8.67 can be gridded.

Note: Since 8.6 and 8.7 do not completely fill the grid, they are not correct answers for this question. Remember the directions say that if you obtain a decimal answer, enter the most accurate value that the grid will accommodate.

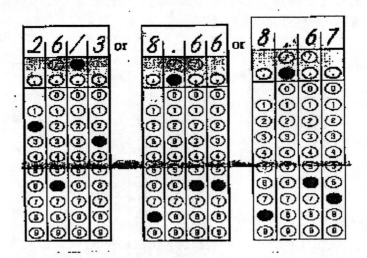

Hints

1.   Since answer choices are not given, a calculator may be more helpful in avoiding careless mistakes on these questions than on the other types of questions on the test.

2.   Although it is not necessary to write your answer in the boxes above the grid, it is suggested that you do so to avoid making errors in gridding. Remember that only the gridded answers will be scored.

3.   The grid can hold only four places and can accommodate only positive numbers and zero.

4.   Do not worry about which column to begin writing the answer in. As long as the answer is gridded completely, you will receive credit. Remember that for repeating decimal answers, you must enter the most accurate value that the grid will accommodate. Therefore, you must begin gridding at the far left-hand side of the grid and fill the answer grid completely.

5.   Unless a problem indicates otherwise, an answer can be entered on the grid either as a decimal or as a fraction. Do not grid zeros before decimal points.

6.   If you obtain an answer such as 3/24, it is not necessary to reduce it to lowest terms.

7.   It is not possible to grid mixed numbers. If you obtain an answer of a mixed number, convert it to an improper fraction or to a decimal. If the answer is a repeating decimal, you must grid the most accurate value the grid will accommodate.

8.   Some of the Student-Produced Response questions may have more than one correct answer. Under these circumstances, simply choose one of the possible answers to grid on your answer sheet.

9.   You do not lose points for a wrong answer to a Student-Produced Response question.

10.   Know the gridding rules for the Student-Produced Response questions before taking the test. Familiarity with them will save you time during the testing period.

————

HOW TO TAKE A TEST

You have studied hard, long, and conscientiously.

With your official admission card in hand, and your heart pounding, you have been admitted to the examination room.

You note that there are several hundred other applicants in the examination room waiting to take the same test.

They all appear to be equally well prepared.

You know that nothing but your best effort will suffice. The "moment of truth" is at hand: you now have to demonstrate objectively, in writing, your knowledge of content and your understanding of subject matter.

You are fighting the most important battle of your life — to pass and/or score high on an examination which will determine your career and provide the economic basis for your livelihood.

What extra, special things should you know and should you do in taking the examination?

BEFORE THE TEST

YOUR PHYSICAL CONDITION IS IMPORTANT

If you are not well, you can't do your best work on tests. If you are half asleep, you can't do your best either. Here are some tips:

1. Get about the same amount of sleep you usually get. Don't stay up all night before the test, either partying or worrying — DON'T DO IT.

2. If you wear glasses, be sure to wear them when you go to take the test. This goes for hearing aids, too.

3. If you have any physical problems that may keep you from doing your best, be sure to tell the person giving the test. If you are sick or in poor health, you really cannot do your best on any test. You can always come back and take the test some other time.

AT THE TEST

EXAMINATION TECHNIQUES

1. Read the *general* instructions carefully. These are usually printed on the first page of the examination booklet. As a rule, these instructions refer to the timing of the examination; the fact that you should not start work until the signal and must stop work at a signal, etc. If there are any *special* instructions, such as a choice of questions to be answered, make sure that you note this instruction carefully.

2. **When you are ready to start work on the examination,** that is as soon as the signal has been given, read the instructions to each question booklet, underline any key words or phrases, such as *least, best, outline, describe,* and the like. In this way you will tend to answer as requested rather than discover on reviewing your paper that you *listed without describing,* that you selected the *worst* choice rather than the *best* choice, etc.

3. If the examination is of the objective or so-called multiple-choice type, that is, each question will also give a series of possible answers: A, B, C, or D, and you are called upon to select the best answer and write the letter next to that answer on your answer paper, it is advisable to start answering each question in turn. There may be anywhere from 50 to 100 such questions in the three or four hours allotted and you can see how much time would be taken if you read through all the questions before beginning to answer any. Furthermore, if you come across a question or a group of questions which you know would be difficult to answer, it would undoubtedly affect your handling of all the other questions.

4. If the examination is of the essay-type and contains but a few questions, it is a moot point as to whether you should read all the questions before starting to answer any one. Of course if you are given a choice, say five out of seven and the like, then it is essential to read all the questions so you can eliminate the two which are most difficult. If, however, you are asked to answer all the questions, there may be danger in trying to answer the easiest one first because you may find that you will spend too much time on it. The best technique is to answer the first question, then proceed to the second, etc.

5. Time your answers. Before the examination begins, write down the time it started, then add the time allowed for the examination and write down the time it must be completed, then divide the time available somewhat as follows:

   a. If 3½ hours are allowed, that would be 210 minutes. If you have 80 objective-type questions, that would be an average of about 2½ minutes per question. Allow yourself no more than 2 minutes per question, or a total of 160 minutes, which will permit about 50 minutes to review.

   b. If for the time allotment of 210 minutes, there are 7 essay questions to answer, that would average about 30 minutes a question. Give yourself only 25 minutes per question so that you have about 35 minutes to review.

6. **The most important instruction is *to read each question*** and make sure you know what is wanted. The second most important instruction is to *time yourself properly* so that you answer every question. The third most important instruction is to *answer every question*. Guess if you have to but include something for each question, Remember that you will receive no credit for a blank and will probably receive some credit if you write something in answer to an essay question. If you guess a letter, say "B" for a multiple-choice question, you may have guessed right. If you leave a blank as the answer to a multiple-choice question, the examiners may respect your feelings but it will not add a point to your score. Some exams may penalize you for wrong answers, so in such cases *only*, you may not want to guess unless you have some basis for your answer.

7. Suggestions

    a. Objective-Type Questions

        (1) Examine the question booklet for proper sequence of pages and questions.

        (2) Read all instructions carefully.

        (3) Skip any question which seems too difficult; return to it after all other questions have been answered.

        (4) Apportion your time properly; do not spend too much time on any single question or group of questions.

        (5) Note and underline key words — *all, most, fewest, least, best, worst, same, opposite*.

        (6) Pay particular attention to negatives.

        (7) Note unusual option, e.g., unduly long, short, complex, different or similar in content to the body of the question.

        (8) Observe the use of "hedging" words — *probably, may, most likely, etc.*

        (9) Make sure that your answer is put next to the same number as the question.

      (10) Do not second guess unless you have good reason to believe the second answer is definitely more correct.

      (11) Cross out original answer if you decide another answer is more accurate; do not erase, *until* you are ready to hand your paper in.

      (12) Answer all questions; guess unless instructed otherwise.

      (13) Leave time for review.

b. Essay-Type Questions
  (1) Read each question carefully.
  (2) Determine exactly what is wanted. Underline key words or phrases.
  (3) Decide on outline or paragraph answer.
  (4) Include many different points and elements unless asked to develop any one or two points or elements.
  (5) Show impartiality by giving pros and cons unless directed to select one side only.
  (6) Make and write down any assumptions you find necessary to answer the question.
  (7) Watch your English, grammar, punctuation, choice of words.
  (8) Time your answers; don't crowd material.

8. Answering the Essay Question

Most essay questions can be answered by framing the specific response around several key words or ideas. Here are a few such key words or ideas:

M's: manpower, materials, methods, money, management

P's: purpose, program, policy, plan, procedure, practice, problems, pitfalls, personnel, public relations

a. Six basic steps in handling problems:
  (1) preliminary plan and background development
  (2) collect information, data and facts
  (3) analyze and interpret information, data and facts
  (4) analyze and develop solutions as well as make recommendations
  (5) prepare report and sell recommendations
  (6) install recommendations and follow up effectiveness

b. Pitfalls to Avoid
  (1) *Taking Things for Granted*
      A statement of the situation does not necessarily imply that each of the elements is necessarily true; for example, a complaint may be invalid and biased so that all that can be taken for granted is that a complaint has been registered
  (2) *Considering only one side of a situation*
      Wherever possible, indicate several alternatives and then point out the reasons you selected the best one.
  (3) *Failing to indicate follow up*
      Whenever your answer indicates action on your part, make certain that you will take proper follow-up action to see how successful your recommendations, procedures, or actions turn out to be.
  (4) *Taking too long in answering any single question*
      Remember to time your answers properly.

EXAMINATION SECTION

SENTENCE COMPLETION

1.   In this section, the test maker plants one or two clues in the sentence. The student is required to do a careful reading and come to the correct conclusion.

2.   TYPICAL TYPES

   A. Contrast - These contain words such as *but, although, however,* and *yet.* The general rule is that when you see these words the opposite is coming.

   The harshness of political struggle _____ Ralph but at the same time fascinated him, so that he could neither _____ the battle nor fully commit himself to it.
   A. frightened; dread   B. inspired; comprehend
   C. repelled; abandon   D. intrigued; forsake
   E. annoyed; influence

   With all its _____, the journey had, nonetheless, been an extremely eventful and successful one.
   A. discomfort   B. adventure
   C. glory   D. diligence
   E. accomplishment

   B. Words that connect ideas that are similar: *and, also, besides, for example, in other words, likewise, another, in addition, moreover, furthermore,* mean that more of the same is coming.

   Self-consciously and _____, but insistently, philosophers keep asking these traditional questions.
   A. confidently   B. diffidently
   C. frequently   D. pugnaciously
   E. progressively

   C. Definition Types - These commonly have one blank. The descriptive or relative clause defines the appropriate answer.

   His _____ disposition, by turns sunny and sullen, was a reflection not of inner but of external stimuli.
   A. somber   B. contentious   C. stoic
   D. volatile   E. callous
Sunny and sullen define volatile.

Much in keeping with its _____ start, the cooperative is doing a thriving business and is making plans to expand in the near future.
   A. problematic   B. premature   C. blemished
   D. auspicious   E. erratic
Thriving business defines auspicious.

D. Words that connect ideas in cause and effect relationships: *because, consequently, therefore, thus, hence, as a result, in order to.*

E. Some words mean that a certain condition must be considered: *if, when.*

If your garden plot is small, it will not pay to grow crops that require a large amount of _____ in order to develop.
   A. sun   B. rain   C. fertilizer
   D. space   E. care

In this sentence, the key words are *If* and *small*. If the garden is *small*, then the crops will not have a lot of room in which to grow. The answer must be a word that suggests area. Only the word space, choice D, does this, so D is the correct answer. Without the condition *If your garden plot is small*, you would not know which choice makes the most sense in this sentence. Make up some conditions under which the other answers would be the best choice. For example, *If your garden is in the desert, it will not pay to grow crops that require a large amount of rain in order to develop.* (This is an exercise to help you understand sentence logic; you would not want to waste actual testing time making up different conditions!)

PROBLEM-SOLVING TECHNIQUES

1. Read the sentence out loud saying *blank* for the space. This helps you understand how the parts of the sentence relate to each other.

2. Think about the definitions of the words in both the sentence and the answer choices.

3. Pay attention to the detail words of contrast, definition, and transition.

4. It is particularly difficult to understand a sentence completion with negatives. Look for the transitional word to give you clues to the correct choices.

5. Fill in the blanks with your own words before looking at the choices.

6. Answer the two blank questions, one blank at a time. Begin by working on the first blank alone. If it doesn't make sense, you can eliminate that choice. Then work on the second blank alone. You may eliminate any choices for which the second word doesn't make sense. If you have one choice left that's the correct answer. If you have more than one choice, work on both blanks together, only for the choices left. Read the complete sentence to be sure it makes sense.

SENTENCE COMPLETION

COMMENTARY

To test your ability to use and understand words when used in normal context (in the course of a paragraph or passage), the *Sentence Completion* question is used.

In this type of question you are required to complete a sentence, or sentences, from which one word (*One Blank*) or two words (*Two Blanks*) have been purposely omitted. You are then asked to choose from five given <u>words</u>, or five given <u>pairs of words</u>, the missing word or words, respectively.

This type of question is, perhaps, the best functional test of your knowledge of, and your ability to actually use, words. In the truest sense, this is the *fair* test of vocabulary: You are *not* being tested on words in isolation, but on your understanding of words in the form in which you generally meet them and deal with them -- in sentences, in paragraphs, in exposition.

It is, therefore, a much more difficult type of vocabulary question than the opposite, same-opposite, or verbal analogy types, for it probes depth and scope and functioning of vocabulary all at once. Moreover, because of the nature of the question and the fact that the words occur in context, the words or pairs of words presented as possible answers are likely to be representative of a cultured level of vocabulary.

The *sentence-completion* type of question is usually attended by the following directions:

Each of the following sentences has one or more blank spaces, each blank representing a word that has been omitted. Select the numbered word or pair of words that BEST completes each sentence.

The candidate may very well find that one or more of the possible answers can be used in an acceptable way and may, therefore, be regarded as a correct answer, based upon the criterion of grammatical correctness alone. But this standard, by itself, is not sufficient here. It is <u>not</u> enough that the word or pair of words selected should be possible of acceptance because of language correctness <u>per se</u>. It is mandatory that the word or pair of words selected be the very best choice from the points of view of the sense and intent of the passage, greater significance, and idiomatic felicity.

In this type of question, you will meet with sentences of the kind that you deal with regularly, in newspapers, books, and magazines. There will be no mystery about the sentence or sentences as a whole. But the test will be whether you have fully comprehended the intent of the passage in thought and in nuance.

SAMPLE QUESTIONS AND EXPLANATIONS

DIRECTIONS: Each question in this part consists of sentences which have one or more blank spaces, each blank representing a word that has been omitted. Select the lettered word or pair of words that BEST completes each sentence. *PRINT THE LETTER OF THE CORRECT WORD IN THE SPACE AT THE RIGHT.*

1. _____ the trials and tribulations of the Hungarian people, 1. ...
   they have not given up their hope of freedom.
   A. For   B. To the contrary of   C. According to
   D. Notwithstanding   E. In accordance with

2. As the queen walked through the hall, she was the _____ of   2. ...
   all who were present.
   A. toast   B. dream   C. cynosure   D. darling   E. interest

3. When the first automobiles appeared in our city, a host of · 3. ...
_____ regulations were _____ for controlling their use,
which were ridiculous in the extreme.
   A. fantastic-issued   B. promulgated-unusual
   C. unconventional-assumed   D. plausible-advanced
   E. incontrovertible-passed

EXPLANATION OF QUESTION 1
   Notwithstanding, Item D, is the only suitable answer.
   It is the proper conjunction balancing the clause "they have not
_____." All the other items are inconsistent with the sense of the
sentence.

EXPLANATION OF QUESTION 2
   Cynosure, Item C, is the correct answer.
   This question is (a rare) one of power of vocabulary. Unless the
candidate knows that cynosure means center of attraction, he will not
be able to answer this question correctly.
   All the other items are grammatical acceptabilities; however, none
of these idiomatically and ideologically carries out the intent of the
sentence.

EXPLANATION OF QUESTION 3
   Fantastic-issued, Item A, is correct. Fantastic means "queer," "freak-
ish," "fanciful," "bizarre." When used in conjunction with issued, it
makes the sentence most meaningful.
   Item B, promulgated-unusual, must be discarded because of the reverse
order of the words, since these must be fitted into the blanks in the
word sequence in which the item is presented.
   Item C, unconventional-assumed, must be deemed incorrect, principally
because of the unidiomatic word, assumed. The proper word which is indicated in its place is "issued," "passed," "published," "promulgated," or
"advanced."
   Item D, plausible-advanced, is incorrect because of the word plausible,
which entirely negates the phrase, "which were ridiculous in the extreme
   Item E, incontrovertible-passed, must be disregarded because the word
incontrovertible, while grammatically correct, adds nothing to the meaning of the sentence.

———

SUGGESTIONS FOR ANSWERING THE SENTENCE COMPLETION QUESTION

1. The first consideration must be whether the fill-in word or words
   that constitute the answer are in accord with the sense of the sentence and help to carry it out or reinforce it.
2. A second consideration is that the answer word(s) is(are) idiomatic
   and grammatical.
3. A third consideration is whether the answer word extends or disturbs
   the thought and sequence of the sentence.
4. A fourth consideration -- with special reference to the two-blank
   type question -- is that the paired words are presented in the question stem in the same order as the blank spaces occur in the senten-
   ce(s). Otherwise, this possibility is incorrect and must be discarded
5. Sometimes, the fill-in calls for a connective word, e.g., a conjunction. Be especially careful with this type of item. The conjunction
   must be in accord with the sense of the relationship of the elements
   of the sentence to be joined together.

6. The two-blank fill-in makes it necessary that the candidate attempt to answer this question by inserting both words of the possible pair at the same time. At times paired words are used that neutralize or cancel each other out in respect to content or meaning. In almost all cases, in a well-drawn question, one of the proposed words is correct. Therefore, there is little point in trying one word at a time.
7. The two-blank type is usually more difficult. It would be wise, when time is a factor, to answer the one-blank type first.
8. Particularly, with the paired fill-ins, one of the words may cancel out the other in meaning or content. Be alert for this, and discard such an item at once. Cf. 6. above.
9. Sometimes, there are more than two sentences -- often as many as three or four, sometimes even a paragraph -- encasing the sentence completion question. Some of these sentences may have no blanks. Even so, they have a most important purpose and must be read carefully. These sentences are presented to define more distinctly the *exact* meaning and *precise* purpose of the writer. The possible item-answers offered for the question will all, probably, be attractive, feasible, and seemingly acceptable.

   In effect, this question will be testing you on the highest basis of all -- the value judgment: the ability to make a verbal decision among items on the basis of fineness and firmness of understanding and shade and sensitivity of meaning.
10. The best way to answer this type of question -- one blank or two blanks--is to read the sentence carefully in order to capture the full import. Then, quickly scanning the possible answers, choose the most likely one and use it to complete the blanks. This should prove to be an effective as well as time-conserving device.

Exercises (*Tests*) in the Sentence-Completion-type question, organized for convenience into one-blank and two-blank categories, follow. These constitute a representative sampling of the nature, scope, and quality of this question-type.

———

EXAMINATION SECTION
TESTS IN SENTENCE COMPLETION/1-BLANK

DIRECTIONS FOR THIS SECTION:
    Each question in this section consists of a sentence in which one word is missing; a blank line indicates where the word has been removed from the sentence. Beneath each sentence are five words, *one* of which is the missing word. You are to select the letter of the missing word by deciding which one of the five words BEST fits in with the meaning of the sentence. *PRINT THE LETTER OF THE CORRECT ANSWER IN THE SPACE AT THE RIGHT.*

TEST 1

1. A man who cannot win honor in his own _____ will have a   1. ...
   very small chance of winning it from posterity.
       A. right   B. field   C. country D. way   E. age
2. The latent period for the contractile response to direct   2. ...
   stimulation of the muscle has quite another and shorter
   value, encompassing only a utilization period. Hence it
   is that the term *latent period* must be _____ carefully
   each time that it is used.
       A. checked   B. timed   C. introduced
       D. defined   E. selected
3. Many television watchers enjoy stories which contain vio-   3. ...
   lence. Consequently those television producers who are
   dominated by rating systems aim to _____ the popular taste.
       A. raise   B. control C. gratify D. ignore E. lower
4. No other man loses so much, so _____, so absolutely, as   4. ...
   the beaten candidate for high public office.
       A. bewilderingly   B. predictably   C. disgracefully
       D. publicly   E. cheerfully
5. Mathematics is the product of thought operating by means   5. ...
   of _____ for the purpose of expressing general laws.
       A. reasoning   B. symbols   C. words
       D. examples   E. science
6. Deductive reasoning is that form of reasoning in which the   6. ...
   conclusion must necessarily follow if we accept the premise
   as true. In deduction, it is _____ for the premise to be
   true and the conclusion false.
       A. impossible   B. inevitable   C. reasonable
       D. surprising   E. unlikely
7. Because in the administration it hath respect not to the   7. ...
   group but to the _____, our form of government is called
   a democracy.
       A. courts   B. people   C. majority
       D. individual   E. law
8. Before criticizing the work of an artist one needs to   8. ...
   _____ the artist's purpose.
       A. understand   B. reveal   C. defend
       D. correct   E. change
9. Their work was commemorative in character and consisted   9. ...
   largely of _____ erected upon the occasion of victories.
       A. towers   B. tombs   C. monuments
       D. castles   E. fortresses
10. Every good story is carefully contrived: the elements of   10. ...
    the story are _____ to fit with one another in order to
    make an effect on the reader.
        A. read B. learned C. emphasized D. reduced E. planned

4

TEST 2

1. One of the most prevalent erroneous contentions is that   1. ...
   Argentina is a country of _____ agricultural resources
   and needs only the arrival of ambitious settlers.
      A. modernized   B. flourishing   C. undeveloped
      D. waning   E. limited

2. The last official statistics for the town indicated the   2. ...
   presence of 24,212 Italians, 6,450 Magyars, and 2,315
   Germans, which ensures to the _____ a numerical preponderance.
      A. Germans B. figures C. town D. Magyars E. Italians

3. Precision of wording is necessary in good writing; by   3. ...
   choosing words that exactly convey the desired meaning,
   one can avoid _____.
      A. duplicity   B. incongruity   C. complexity
      D. ambiguity   E. implications

4. Various civilians of the liberal school in the British   4. ...
   Parliament remonstrated that there were no grounds for
   _____ of French aggression, since the Emperor showed less
   disposition to augment the navy than had Louis Philippe.
      A. suppression   B. retaliation   C. apprehension
      D. concealment   E. commencement

5. _____ is as clear and definite as any of our urges; we   5. ...
   wonder what is in a sealed letter or what is being said
   in a telephone booth.
      A. Envy   B. Curiosity   C. Knowledge
      D. Communication   E. Ambition

6. It is a rarely philosophic soul who can make a _____ the   6. ...
   other alternative forever into the limbo of forgotten things.
      A. mistake B. wish   C. change   D. choice E. plan

7. A creditor is worse than a master. A master owns only   7. ...
   your person, but a creditor owns your _____ as well.
      A. aspirations   B. potentialities C. ideas
      D. dignity   E. wealth

8. People _____ small faults, in order to insinuate that they   8. ...
   have no great ones.
      A. create   B. display C. confess D. seek E. reject

9. Andrew Jackson believed that wars were inevitable, and to   9. ...
   him the length and irregularity of our coast presented a
   _____ that called for a more than merely passive navy.
      A. defense   B. barrier   C. provocation
      D. vulnerability E. dispute

10. The progressive yearly _____ of the land, caused by the   10. ...
    depositing of mud from the river, makes it possible to
    estimate the age of excavated remains by noting the depth
    at which they are found below the present level of the
    valley.
       A. erosion   B. elevation   C. improvement
       D. irrigation   E. displacement

TEST 3

1. The judge exercised commendable _____ in dismissing the   1. ...
charge against the prisoner. In spite of the clamor that
surrounded the trial, and the heinousness of the offense,
the judge could not be swayed to overlook the lack of
facts in the case.
   A. avidity   B. meticulousness C. clemency
   D. balance   E. querulousness

2. The pianist played the concerto _____, displaying such   2. ...
facility and skill as has rarely been matched in this old
auditorium.
   A. strenuous   B. spiritedly   C. passionately
   D. casually   E. deftly

3. The Tanglewood Symphony Orchestra holds its outdoor con-   3. ...
certs far from city turmoil in a _____, bucolic setting.
   A. spectacular   B. atavistic   C. serene
   D. chaotic   E. catholic

4. Honest satire gives true joy to the thinking man. Thus,   4. ...
the satirist is most _____ when he points out the hypocrisy
in human actions.
   A. elated   B. humiliated   C. ungainly
   D. repressed   E. disdainful

5. She was a(n) _____ who preferred the company of her books   5. ...
to the pleasures of cafe society.
   A. philanthropist B. stoic   C. exhibitionist
   D. extrovert   E. introvert

6. So many people are so convinced that people are driven by   6. ...
_____ motives that they cannot believe that anybody is
unselfish!
   A. interior   B. ulterior   C. unworth
   D. selfish   E. destructive

7. These _____ results were brought about by a chain of for-   7. ...
tuitous events.
   A. unfortunate   B. odd   C. harmful
   D. haphazard   E. propitious

8. The bank teller's _____ of the funds was discovered the   8. ...
following month when the auditors examined the books.
   A. embezzlement B. burglary   C. borrowing
   D. assignment   E. theft

9. The monks gathered in the _____ for their evening meal.   9. ...
   A. lounge   B. auditorium   C. refectory
   D. rectory   E. solarium

10. Local officials usually have the responsibility in each area 10. ...
of determining when the need is sufficiently great to
_____ withdrawals from the community water supply.
   A. encourage   B. justify   C. discontinue
   D. advocate   E. forbid

TEST 4

1. The life of the mining camps as portrayed by Bret Harte -   1. ...
boisterous, material, brawling - was in direct _____ to the

6

contemporary Eastern world of conventional morals and
staid deportment depicted by other men of letters.
 A. model   B. parallel   C. antithesis
 D. relationship   E. response

2. The agreements were to remain in force for three years   2. ...
and were subject to automatic _____ unless terminated by
the parties concerned on one month's notice.
 A. renewal   B. abrogation   C. amendment
 D. confiscation   E. option

3. In a democracy, people are recognized for what they do   3. ...
rather than for their _____.
 A. alacrity   B. ability   C. reputation
 D. skill   E. pedigree

4. Although he had often loudly proclaimed his _____ concern-   4. ...
ing world affairs, he actually read widely and was usually
the best informed person in his circle.
 A. weariness   B. complacency   C. condolence
 D. indifference   E. worry

5. This student holds the _____ record of being the sole   5. ...
failure in his class.
 A. flagrant   B. unhappy   C. egregious
 D. dubious   E. unusual

6. She became enamored _____ the acrobat when she witnessed   6. ...
his act.
 A. of   B. with   C. for   D. by   E. about

7. This will _____ all previous wills.
 A. abrogates   B. denies   C. supersedes
 D. prevents   E. continues

8. In the recent terrible Chicago _____, over ninety children   8. ...
were found dead as a result of the fire.
 A. hurricane   B. destruction   C. panic
 D. holocaust   E. accident

9. I can ascribe no better reason why he shunned society than   9. ...
that he was a _____.
 A. mentor   B. Centaur   C. aristocrat
 D. misanthrope   E. failure

10. One who attempts to learn all the known facts before he   10. ...
comes to a conclusion may most aptly be described as a
_____.
 A. realist   B. philosopher   C. cynic
 D. pessimist   E. skeptic

TEST 5

1. The prime minister, fleeing from the rebels who had seized   1. ...
the government, sought _____ in the church.
 A. revenge B. mercy C. relief D. salvation E. sanctuary

2. It does not take us long to conclude that it is foolish to   2. ...
fight the _____, and that it is far wiser to accept it.
 A. inevitable   B. inconsequential C. impossible
 D. choice   E. invasion

3. _____ is usually defined as an excessively high rate of   3. ...
interest.
 A. Injustice   B. Perjury   C. Exorbitant
 D. Embezzlement   E. Usury

4. "I ask you, gentlemen of the jury, to find this man guilty   4. ...
   since I have _____ the charges brought about him."
   A. documented   B. questioned   C. revised
   D. selected   E. confused
5. Although the critic was a close friend of the producer,   5. ...
   he told him that he could not _____ his play.
   A. condemn   B. prefer   C. congratulate
   D. endorse   E. revile
6. Knowledge of human nature and motivation is an important   6. ...
   _____ in all areas of endeavor.
   A. object B. incentive C. opportunity D. asset E. goal
7. Numbered among the audience were kings, princes, dukes, and 7. ...
   even a maharajah, all attempting to _____ one another in the
   glitter of their habiliments and the number of their escorts.
   A. supersede B. outdo C. guide D. vanquish E. equal
8. There seems to be a widespread feeling that peoples who   8. ...
   are located below us in respect to latitude are _____ also
   in respect to intellect and ability.
   A. superior   B. melodramatic   C. inferior
   D. ulterior   E. contemptible
9. This should be considered a(n) _____ rather than the usual 9. ...
   occurrence.
   A. coincidence   B. specialty   C. development
   D. outgrowth   E. mirage
10. Those who were considered states' rights adherents in the 10. ...
    early part of our history, espoused the diminution of the
    powers of the national government because they had always
    been _____ of these powers.
    A. solicitous   B. advocates   C. apprehensive
    D. mindful   E. respectful

TEST 6

1. We can see in retrospect that the high hopes for lasting   1. ...
   peace conceived at Versailles in 1919 were _____.
   A. ingenuous   B. transient   C. nostalgic
   D. ingenious   E. specious
2. One of the constructive effects of Nazism was the passage   2. ...
   by the U.N. of a resolution to combat _____.
   A. armaments   B. nationalism   C. colonialism
   D. genocide   E. geriatrics
3. In our prisons, the role of _____ often gains for certain   3. ...
   inmates a powerful position among their fellow prisoners.
   A. informer B. clerk C. warden D. trusty E. turnkey
4. It is the _____ liar, experienced in the ways of the world, 4. ...
   who finally trips upon some incongruous detail.
   A. consummate   B. incorrigible   C. congenital
   D. flagrant   E. contemptible
5. Anyone who is called a misogynist can hardly be expected   5. ...
   to look upon women with _____ contemptuous eyes.
   A. more than   B. nothing less than   C. decidedly
   D. other than   E. always

6. Demagogues such as Hitler and Mussolini aroused the masses 6. ...
by appealing to their _____ rather than to their intellect.
    A. emotions   · B. reason   C. nationalism
    D. conquests   E. duty

7. He was in great demand as an entertainer for his _____ 7. ...
abilities: he could sing, dance, tell a joke, or relate
a story with equally great skill and facility.
    A. versatile   B. logical   C. culinary
    D. histrionic   E. creative

8. The wise politician is aware that, next to knowing when 8. ...
to seize an opportunity, it is also important to know when
to _____ an advantage.
    A. develop B. seek C. revise D. proclaim E. forego

9. Books on psychology inform us that the best way to break 9. ...
a bad habit is to _____ a new habit in its place.
    A. expel B. substitute C. conceal D. curtail E. supplant

10. The author who uses one word where another uses a whole 10. ...
paragraph, should be considered a _____ writer.
    A. successful   B. grandiloquent   C. experienced
    D. prolix   E. succinct

TESTS IN SENTENCE COMPLETION / 2-BLANKS

DIRECTIONS FOR THIS SECTION:
    Each question in this section consists of a sentence (or sentences) in which two words are missing; blank lines indicate where the words have been removed from the sentence. Beneath each sentence (or sentences) are five pairs of words, *one* of which is the missing words. You are to select the letter of the missing pair of words by deciding which one of the five pairs BEST fits in with the meaning of the sentence. *PRINT THE LETTER OF THE CORRECT ANSWER IN THE SPACE AT THE RIGHT.*

TEST 1

1. It appears that the _____ attacks of government committees 1. ...
investigating the personal and political leanings of government employees and officials are now a thing of the past
and that the attendant _____ are to be heard no more.
    A. patriotic - protestations B. iniquitous - eulogies
    C. malignant - vilifications D. noxious - impieties
    E. capricious - beatitudes

2. There has been a conspicuous attempt in children's courts 2. ...
in recent years to _____ some of the onus for juvenile de-
linquency from school and society to the home since studies
have revealed that failures in the home are the _____ factor
for this condition.
    A. exaggerate - principal   B. reconvert - basic
    C. shift - substitionary   D. minimize - prize
    E. transfer - prime

3. I have never seen so huge a "fat lady" at the circus. She 3. ...
was so _____ fat that even my neighbor who weighs over 300
pounds, appeared almost _____ in comparison.
    A. flagrantly - revolting   B. egregiously - Lilliputian
    C. startlingly - herculean   D. blandly - emaciated
    E. grotesquely - corpulent

4. The police department is usually accompanied by a _____.   4. ...
   type of supervision, which gives us a picture of its leaders
   as _____, not democratic administrators
      A. demoralizing - philosophers
      B. elevated - brigands   C. superior - trainers
      D. relaxed - disciplinarians E. rigid - martinets
5. The carnival show _____ with barkers, fakers, peddlers,   5. ...
   and medicine men selling their _____.
      A. grew - instruments   B. prospered - acts
      C. swarmed - panaceas   D. resounded - toys
      E. clamored - enigmas
6. It is often the conservative but _____ leader who advocates 6. ...
   circumspection; just as often it is the radical but _____
   leader who would tear down and re-do the past.
      A. practical - inflexible   B. conventional - visionary
      C. myopic - adamant   D. iconoclastic - socialist
      E. consistent - inconsistent
7. Considering the state of affairs _____ in the world today,   7. ...
   what is needed are statesmen of _____ wisdom and patience
   who can discuss matters without anger or threats and can
   plan constructively for the future.
      A. lambent - occluded   B. existing - callow
      C. rampant - infinite   D. raging - traditional
      E. subsiding - illimitable
8. The increase in obscene and sensational literature has   8. ...
   caused leaders from all walks of life to _____ the threat
   to public morals and to demand legislation providing for
   the _____ of these publications.
      A. palliate - confiscation   B. bemoan - improvement
      C. eulogize - censor   D. point up - expurgation
      E. condemn - ramification
9. The numerous "muggings" in the city parks and the destruc-   9. ...
   tion of public property in these places make it _____ to
   increase police protection against these criminals and _____.
      A. mandatory - trespassers   B. necessary - outlaws
      C. imperative - vandals   D. unnecessary - delinquents
      E. dubious - interlopers
10. Many of our conferences with the Soviets in recent years   10. ...
    have ended in _____, revealing a _____ conflict of inter-
    ests.
       A. stalemate - basic   B. compromise - fundamental
       C. conciliation - minor   D. cold war - discordant
       E. irreconciliability - growing

TEST 2

1. Paris, with its old worldliness, its cafes, its roof-tops   1. ...
   and its gay boulevards, has provided a(n) _____ stories
   and themes for the _____.
      A. copiosity - misanthrope   B. scarcity - novelist
      C. plethora - screen   D. ebullience - pedantic
      E. sheaf - untutored
2. Many of us, because we are lacking in verbal facility,   2. ...
   resort to _____ instead of using _____ expression.
      A. hyperbole - sardonic   B. innuendo - vernacular
      C. emotion - hackneyed   D. cliche - creative
      E. vituperation - acceptable

3. There is an interesting anecdote about one of our great   · 3. ...
   mathematicians. _____, he had failed in mathematics while
   a school boy. Today, this great man can assemble and re-
   assemble intricate numbers, formulae, symbols and equations,
   which are _____ only to the initiated.
      A. Coincidentally - lucid   B. Simultaneously - known
      C. Peculiarly - fathomable   D. Incredibly - credulous
      E. Ironically - unidentifiable

4. A(n) _____ of our own freedom is that we do not _____   4. ...
   others in their efforts to practice it.
      A. necessity - encourage   B. obligation - subvert
      C. concomitant - hinder   D. corollary - inspire
      E. goal - discourage

5. This is the place made famous in literature as bucolic   5. ...
   and serene, where the turbulence of the city is far away.
   Alas, it is no longer so. It is now _____ and _____.
      A. restricted - pedantic   B. grievous - bewildering
      C. historic and pandering   D. agrarian - bustling
      E. cosmopolitan - teeming

6. A national education association has revealed the _____   6. ...
   fact that many of our teachers are receiving _____ less
   than that of porters.
      A. startling - respect   B. interesting - not
      C. incongruous - remuneration   D. innocuous - a stipend
      E. heartening - far

7. We wondered why this dictator had deposited moneys in   7. ...
   foreign banks _____ suddenly the revolution broke out and
   his regime was _____ in a cataclysm which caused him to
   flee.
      A. when - engulfed   B. until - embroiled
      C. before - shaken   D. while - drowned
      E. whence - destroyed

8. While the study of Latin is now generally considered a(n)   8. ...
   _____ subject, as is true of any other subject or field,
   it is as meaningful as our _____.
      A. silent - impressions   B. recondite - comprehension
      C. impractical - interests   D. basic - predilections
      E. dead - prejudices

9. Winston Churchill has remarked that Russia is a puzzle   9. ...
   wrapped in an enigma. That is to say, Russia's purposes
   and plans are _____ and _____.
      A. irreligious - behavioristic   B. latent - patent
      C. contrary - translucent   D. inscrutable - ambiguous
      E. equivocal - ingenuous

10. It is the _____ man who says little and knows much and   10. ...
    moves about as though he had a _____.
       A. tactful - tumor   B. malevolent - philippic
       C. sage - masterpiece   D. grandiloquent - secret
       E. disciplined - plan

TEST 3

1. This city is rapidly becoming prosperous since its stores,   1. ...
   theatres and institutions can now be easily reached by the
   new _____ highway. As a result, _____ crowds are being at-
   tracted throughout the year.
      A. accessible - good   B. slow - huge
      C. dim - anxious   D. speedy - affluent
      E. tortuous - inordinate

2. When we characterize a student's conduct as _____, we mean   2. ...
   that he is _____.
   A. elephantine - impulsive   B. refractory - infectious
   C. recidivistic - relapsing   D. intransigent - conciliatory
   E. pusillanimous - resolute

3. The audience soon comes to recognize the _____, raging   3. ...
   speaker for a bombastic, pompous _____.
   A. pithy - ass   B. succinct - realist
   C. diffuse - buffoon   D. prolix - leader
   E. long-winded - authority

4. This tourist town is distinguished for its quaintness and   4. ...
   its quiet streets, where automobile traffic is forbidden.
   But there is the inevitable saloon from which, now and
   then, loud noises and screams emanate, to present a marked
   _____ to the general _____ of the town.
   A. antithesis - tenor   B. contrast - composition
   C. similarity - tone   D. revelation - reputation
   E. relief - population

5. Some of our operas start off in a _____ and turgid manner.   5. ...
   However, a refinement seems to set in and they usually con-
   clude on a restrained and _____ note.
   A. quiet - discordant   B. artificial - supercilious
   C. histrionic - subdued   D. clamorous - bombastic
   E. realistic - conventional

6. _____ is a science or a study (as one may regard it) which   6. ...
   is concerned with _____ life.
   A. Anthropology - lengthening B. Epistemology - enriching
   C. Pediatrics - extending   D. Entomology - shortening
   E. Geriatrics - prolonging

7. The son is like his father, _____ and grasping, giving   7. ...
   only so much as the occasion warrants but making sure to
   get more in turn; the daughter is like her mother, warm,
   and _____, ready to give herself completely to any principle that she believes in.
   A. sincere - generous   B. covetous - devoted
   C. belligerent - cordial   D. jealous - invidious
   E. martial - credulous

8. The _____ that the baseball player felt at his error was   8. ...
   evidenced in his _____.
   A. pleasure - grimace   B. anger - smile
   C. annoyance - chuckle   D. disgust - grim silence
   E. despair - shrug

9. The elevator operator was most _____ in his manner for the   9. ...
   Christmas gift _____ he could ill afford so useful but ex-
   pensive an object.
   A. sycophantic - since   B. abject - on account of
   C. profuse - inasmuch as   D. indignant - since
   E. subdued - because

10. In _____ the mayor to establish new housing projects, the   10. ...
    committee sincerely hoped to _____ the lot of the unfortu-
    nate slum dwellers.
    A. vexing - aggravate   B. pushing - buttress
    C. harassing - condign   D. cautioning - pacify
    E. urging - mitigate

TEST 4

1. Those living in the North who displayed a strong interest 1. ...
in, and sympathy toward, the Southern point of view, were
called "copperheads" and were subjected to an unceasing
_____ of vituperation and _____.
    A. flow - rejection   B. supply - castigation
    C. salutation - approbation   D. attack - integration
    E. barrage - excoriation

2. One of the _____ marks of the well-trained, well-cultivated 2. ...
gentleman is that he never displays a _____ manner to any
man.
    A. defective - grim   B. predominating - light
    C. outstanding - supercilious   D. prominent - penurious
    E. visible - sanguinary

3. In our law courts, the defendant is _____ innocent until he 3. ...
has been _____ guilty.
    A. tenuously - proved   B. deemed - resolved
    C. presumed - adjudged   D. considered - marked
    E. not - found

4. If you want to know the value of an old coin, you should 4. ...
go to a _____ who will give you a fairly accurate _____ of
its value.
    A. philatelist - estimate   B. curator - appraisal
    C. anthropologist - surmise   D. assayer - account
    E. numismatist - assessment

5. _____ are always a good sign as to whether businesses are 5. ...
operating _____.
    A. Estimates - at a profit   B. Shortages - at a loss
    C. Orders - efficiently   D. Deficits - uneconomically
    E. Forecasts - fairly well

6. Joan of Arc was _____ as a _____ because she was adjudged 6. ...
to have digressed from the accepted beliefs of the church.
    A. prescribed - witch   B. described - saint
    C. lampooned - barrister   D. proscribed - heretic
    E. inscribed - satyr

7. The _____ Richard the Lion Hearted was so called because 7. ...
of his _____ fortitude.
    A. dashing - glamorous   B. futile - puny
    C. infallible - leonine   D. indomitable - resolute
    E. invidious - persistent

8. This insurance company assures us that once this policy 8. ...
has been _____, it will be _____.
    A. revised - amended   B. modified - incorrigible
    C. signed - clear   D. refuted - disputable
    E. entered into - irrevocable

9. Taking note of the defendant's youth, poor home background, 9. ...
lack of opportunity, and other _____ matters, the court de-
cided to suspend sentence but administered a severe _____
to the defendant.
    A. mollifying - encomium   B. mitigating - rebuke
    C. pacific - reprimand   D. magnifying - lashing
    E. provocative - scolding

10. It was a _____ group of people who _____ the welfare sta- 10. ...
tions for food and clothing.
    A. mean - stared at   B. tremendous - attacked
    C. homogenous - berated   D. motley - queued up at
    E. beleaguered - railed at

TEST 5

1. It is not uncommon to hear the _____ man extol his own   1. ...
   virtues for all to hear; nor is it unusual to watch the
   modest man _____ his own.
   - A. self-made - proclaim   B. concupiscent - aggrandize
   - C. magnanimous - disparage D. credulous - bolster
   - E. timorous - depreciate

2. The proof-reader must be possessed of _____ skill for he   2. ...
   discovered all these errors in the text after what appeared
   to be only a _____ reading.
   - A. great - minute   B. real - regular
   - C. little - brief   D. consummate - cursory
   - E. artistic - single

3. It is disheartening to witness how often those who pose as   3. ...
   paragons of virtue, and, as though looking down from the
   paths of the godly, counsel others to a life of honest purpose, altruism, and serenity, are themselves _____, depredatory, and _____.
   - A. resolute - savage   B. puerile - violent
   - C. shiftless - seething   D. voracious - bristling
   - E. inchoate - pacific

4. General MacArthur, upon his return to the United States,   4. ...
   was given a(n) _____ by the people who turned out in _____
   array to greet the hero.
   - A. greeting - disheveled   B. plaudit - motley
   - C. ovation - vast   D. reward - sardonic
   - E. medal - unprecedented

5. A(n) _____ statement is _____ in manner.   5. ...
   - A. interrogatory - exclamatory B. sudorific - tortuous
   - C. dogmatic - peremptory   D. ambiguous - blatant
   - E. platitudinous - relevant

6. A very useful and popular device on the part of government   6. ...
   executives in situations of the utmost controversy is to
   appoint _____ committees and, thereby, to _____ criticisms
   of partiality or slanted viewpoint.
   - A. secular - avert   B. sub- - prevent
   - C. non-partisan - escape   D. bi-partisan - disseminate
   - E. expert - dispel

7. The detectives _____ from the _____ signs that a violent   7. ...
   struggle had taken place.
   - A. inferred - tantalizing   B. assumed - meretricious
   - C. estimated - raucous   D. deduced - enigmatic
   - E. surmised - patent

8. Such conduct as yours is impossible to _____. Your display   8. ...
   of _____ would have been worthy of a Hitler or an Attila.
   - A. overlook - thoughtfulness B. condone - frenzy
   - C. ignore - disputation   D. equal - implementation
   - E. forgive - magnanimity

9. What distinguishes the _____ person is his _____.
   - A. arrogant - fairness   B. profligate - wastefulness
   - C. superior - diffidence   D. introverted - garrulity
   - E. unconventional - conservatism

10. Have you noted how often prominent politicians, when asked 10. ...
    to _____ themselves, engage in what can only be called
    _____?
    - A. distend - recession   B. promote - modesty
    - C. declare - equivocation   D. disinter - morbidity
    - E. remove - alacrity

TEST 6

1. On the one hand scientific research introduces new methods   1. ...
   of _____ ; on the other it invents new devices to _____
   their effects.
   - A. production - implement
   - B. observation - reduce
   - C. destruction- counteract
   - D. warfare - increase
   - E. experimentation - enhance

2. It is a mistake to _____ the beliefs of an entire people   2. ...
   from the _____ of a few representatives.
   - A. deduce - actions
   - B. influence - appointment
   - C. question - success
   - D. glorify - failures
   - E. criticize - abilities

3. Poets are observing and thinking while others are robbing   3. ...
   and fighting, and they accomplish their ends by _____ rather
   than _____ .
   - A. scholarly - literary
   - B. obvious - subtle
   - C. intellectual - physical
   - D. active - passive
   - E. bodily-mental

4. The characteristic statesman of that day was a conscientious   4. ...
   _____ crushed under the weight of responsibilities to which
   he felt himself _____ .
   - A. intellectual - opposed
   - B. imbecile - adequate
   - C. figurehead - immune
   - D. plodder - unequal
   - E. worker - superior

5. He stamped his feet and blew on his hands, thinking that it   5. ...
   was _____ that the grass had been _____ only last week.
   - A. unbelievable - green
   - B. fortunate - seared
   - C. tragic - cut
   - D. impossible - planted
   - E. paradoxical - brown

6. The research worker does not desire an _____ of supervision   6. ...
   or of planning; he _____ the annoyance of not knowing what
   is expected of him.
   - A. excess - resents
   - B. elimination - minimizes
   - C. absence - dislikes
   - D. extension - exaggerates
   - E. understanding - shuns

7. Dogmas are the _____ of some _____ system of thought of a   7. ...
   particular opoch.
   - A. meaning - philosophical
   - B. by-product - new
   - C. crystallizations-dominant
   - D. axioms - fallacious
   - E. affirmations - historical

8. Science is always _____ , expecting that _____ of its pre-   8. ...
   sent theories will sooner or later be found necessary.
   - A. final - ramifications
   - B. original - reversals
   - C. tentative-modifications
   - D. practical - identifications
   - E. improving - deletions

9. One of the advantages that a large investor should enjoy is   9. ...
   the ability to take advantage of the _____ yields obtainable
   on certain speculative _____ .
   - A. uncertain - propositions
   - B. guaranteed - securities
   - C. higher - investments
   - D. flexible - properties
   - E. limited - occasions

10. If your planting field is _____ , it will not pay to grow   10. ...
    crops which require a large amount of _____ in order to
    develop.
    - A. irregular - moisture
    - B. enclosed - rain
    - C. small - space
    - D. large - fertilizer
    - E. unattractive - care

15

KEYS (CORRECT ANSWERS)

ONE-BLANK

TEST 1		TEST 2		TEST 3		TEST 4		TEST 5		TEST 6	
1.	E	1.	C	1.	D	1.	C	1.	E	1.	A
2.	D	2.	E	2.	E	2.	A	2.	A	2.	D
3.	C	3.	D	3.	C	3.	E	3.	E	3.	A
4.	D	4.	C	4.	A	4.	D	4.	A	4.	A
5.	B	5.	B	5.	E	5.	D	5.	D	5.	D
6.	A	6.	D	6.	B	6.	A	6.	D	6.	A
7.	D	7.	D	7.	D	7.	C	7.	B	7.	A
8.	A	8.	C	8.	A	8.	D	8.	C	8.	A
9.	C	9.	D	9.	C	9.	D	9.	A	9.	B
10.	E	10.	B	10.	B	10.	E	10.	C	10.	E

TWO-BLANKS

TEST 1		TEST 2		TEST 3		TEST 4		TEST 5		TEST 6	
1.	C	1.	C	1.	D	1.	E	1.	E	1.	C
2.	E	2.	D	2.	C	2.	C	2.	D	2.	A
3.	B	3.	C	3.	C	3.	C	3.	C	3.	C
4.	C	4.	C	4.	A	4.	E	4.	C	4.	D
5.	C	5.	E	5.	C	5.	D	5.	C	5.	A
6.	A	6.	C	6.	E	6.	D	6.	C	6.	C
7.	E	7.	A	7.	B	7.	D	7.	E	7.	C
8.	D	8.	C	8.	D	8.	E	8.	B	8.	C
9.	C	9.	D	9.	C	9.	B	9.	B	9.	C
10.	A	10.	E	10.	E	10.	D	10.	C	10.	C

16

SENTENCE COMPLETION

EXAMINATION SECTION

TEST 1

DIRECTIONS: Each question in this part consists of a sentence in which one word is missing; a blank line indicates where the word has been removed from the sentence. Beneath each sentence are five words, one of which is the missing word. You are to select the number of the missing word by deciding which one of the five words BEST fits in with the meaning of the sentence. *PRINT THE LETTER OF THE CORRECT ANSWER IN THE SPACE AT THE RIGHT.*

1. Although they had little interest in the game they were playing, rather than be _____, they played it through to the end.
   - A. inactive
   - B. inimical
   - C. busy
   - D. complacent
   - E. vapid

   1.____

2. That he was unworried and at peace with the world could be, perhaps, observed from his ____ brow.
   - A. unwrinkled
   - B. wrinkled
   - C. furrowed
   - D. twisted
   - E. askew

   2.____

3. Among the hundreds of workers in the assembly plant of the factory, one was ____ because of his skill and speed.
   - A. steadfast
   - B. condemned
   - C. consistent
   - D. outstanding
   - E. eager

   3.____

4. The story of the invention of many of our best known machines is a consistent one: they are the result of a long series of experiments by many people; thus, the Wright Brothers in 1903 ____ the airplane rather than invented it.
   - A. popularized
   - B. regulated
   - C. perfected
   - D. contrived
   - E. developed

   4.____

5. As soon as the former political exile returned to his native country, he looked up old supporters, particularly those whom he knew to be ____ and whose help he might need.
   - A. potent
   - B. pusillanimous
   - C. attentive
   - D. free
   - E. retired

   5.____

6. A recent study of the New Deal shows that no other man than the President could have brought together so many ____ interests and combined them into so effective a political organization.
   - A. secret
   - B. interior
   - C. predatory
   - D. harmonious
   - E. conflicting

   6.____

7. A study of tides presents an interesting ____ in that, while the forces that set them in motion are universal in application, presumably affecting all parts of our world without distinction, the action of tides in particular areas is completely local in nature.

    A. phenomenon   B. maneuver   C. paradox
    D. quality   E. spontaneity

7.__

8. Many of the facts that are found in the ancient archives constitute ____ that help shed light upon human activities in the past.

    A. facts   B. reminders   C. particles
    D. sources   E. indications

8.__

9. It is a regrettable fact that in a caste society which deems manual toil a mark of ____, rarely does the laborer improve his social position or gain political power.

    A. inferiority   B. consolation   C. fortitude
    D. hardship   E. brilliance

9.__

10. As a generalization, one can correctly say that crises in history are caused by the re-opening of questions which have been safely ____ for long periods of time.

    A. debated   B. joined   C. recondite
    D. settled   E. unanswered

10.__

TEST 2

1. We can see in retrospect that the high hopes for lasting peace conceived at Versailles in 1919 were ____.

    A. ingenuous   B. transient   C. nostalgic
    D. ingenious   E. species

1.__

2. One of the constructive effects of Nazism was the passage by the U.N. of a resolution to combat ____.

    A. armaments   B. nationalism   C. colonialism
    D. genocide   E. geriatrics

2.__

3. In our prisons, the role of ____ often gains for certain inmates a powerful position among their fellow prisoners.

    A. informer   B. clerk   C. warden
    D. trusty   E. turnkey

3.__

4. It is the ____ liar, experienced in the ways of the world, who finally trips upon some incongruous detail.

    A. consummate   B. incorrigible   C. congenital
    D. flagrant   E. contemptible

4.__

5. Anyone who is called a misogynist can hardly be expected to look upon women with ____ contemptuous eyes.

    A. more than   B. nothing less than   C. decidedly
    D. other than   E. always

5.__

6. Demagogues such as Hitler and Mussolini aroused the masses   6.___
   by appealing to their ____ rather than to their intellect.
        A. emotions   B. reason   C. nationalism
        D. conquests   E. duty

7. He was in great demand as an entertainer for his ____   7.___
   abilities: he could sing, dance, tell a joke, or relate
   a story with equally great skill and facility.
        A. versatile   B. logical   C. culinary
        D. histrionic   E. creative

8. The wise politician is aware that, next to knowing when   8.___
   to seize an opportunity, it is also important to know when
   to ____ an advantage.
        A. develop B. seek   C. revise   D. proclaim E. forego

9. Books on psychology inform us that the best way to break   9.___
   a bad habit is to ____ a new habit in its place.
        A. expel   B. substitute   C. conceal
        D. curtail   E. supplant

10. The author who uses one word where another uses a whole   10.___
    paragraph, should be considered a ____ writer.
        A. successful   B. grandiloquent   C. succinct
        D. prolix   E. experienced

TEST 3

1. The prime minister, fleeing from the rebels who had   1.___
   seized the government, sought ____ in the church.
        A. revenge   B. mercy   C. relief
        D. salvation   E. sanctuary

2. It does not take us long to conclude that it is foolish   2.___
   to fight the ____, and that it is far wiser to accept it.
        A. inevitable   B. inconsequential C. impossible
        D. choice   E. invasion

3. ____ is usually defined as an excessively high rate of   3.___
   interest.
        A. Injustice   B. Perjury   C. Exorbitant
        D. Embezzlement   E. Usury

4. "I ask you, gentlemen of the jury, to find this man guilty   4.___
   since I have ____ the charges brought against him."
        A. documented   B. questioned   C. revised
        D. selected   E. confused

5. Although the critic was a close friend of the producer,   5.___
   he told him that he could not ____ his play.
        A. condemn   B. prefer   C. congratulate
        D. endorse   E. revile

6. Knowledge of human nature and motivation is an important ____ in all areas of endeavor.
   A. object   B. incentive   C. opportunity
   D. asset   E. goal

6.___

7. Numbered among the audience were kings, princes, dukes, and even a maharajah, all attempting to ____ one another in the glitter of their habiliments and the number of their escorts.
   A. supersede   B. outdo   C. guide
   D. vanquish   E. equal

7.___

8. There seems to be a widespread feeling that peoples who are located below us in respect to latitude are ____ also in respect to intellect and ability.
   A. superior   B. melodramatic   C. inferior
   D. ulterior   E. contemptible

8.___

9. This should be considered a(n) ____ rather than the usual occurrence.
   A. coincidence   B. specialty   C. development
   D. outgrowth   E. mirage

9.___

10. Those who were considered states' rights aherents in the early part of our history espoused the diminution of the powers of the national government because they had always been ____ of these powers.
   A. solicitous   B. advocates   C. apprehensive
   D. mindful   E. respectful

10.___

TEST 4

1. The life of the mining camps as portrayed by Bret Harte - boisterous, material, brawling - was in direct ____ to the contemporary Eastern world of conventional morals and staid deportment depicted by other men of letters.
   A. model   B. parallel   C. antithesis
   D. relationship   E. response

1.___

2. The agreements were to remain in force for three years and were subject to automatic ____ unless terminated by the parties concerned on one month's notice.
   A. renewal   B. abrogation   C. amendment
   D. confiscation   E. option

2.___

3. In a democracy, people are recognized for what they do rather than for their ____.
   A. alacrity   B. ability   C. reputation
   D. skill   E. pedigree

3.___

4. Although he had often loudly proclaimed his ____ concerning world affairs, he actually read widely and was usually the best informed person in his circle.
   A. weariness   B. complacency   C. condolence
   D. indifference   E. worry

4.___

5. This student holds the ____ record of being the sole   5.____
   failure in his class.
     A. flagrant   B. unhappy   C. egregious
     D. dubious   E. unusual

6. She became enamored ____ the acrobat when she witnessed   6.____
   his act.
     A. of   B. with   C. for   D. by   E. about

7. This will ____ all previous wills.   7.____
     A. abrogates   B. denies   C. supersedes
     D. prevents   E. continues

8. In the recent terrible Chicago ____, over ninety children   8.____
   were found dead as a result of the fire.
     A. hurricane   B. destruction   C. panic
     D. holocaust   E. accident

9. I can ascribe no better reason why he shunned society than   9.____
   that he was a ____.
     A. mentor   B. Centaur   C. aristocrat
     D. misanthrope   E. failure

10. One who attempts to learn all the known facts before he   10.____
    comes to a conclusion may most aptly be described as a
    ____.
      A. realist   B. philosopher   C. cynic
      D. pessimist   E. skeptic

TEST 5

1. The judge exercised commendable ____ in dismissing the   1.____
   charge against the prisoner. In spite of the clamor that
   surrounded the trial, and the heinousness of the offense,
   the judge could not be swayed to overlook the lack of
   facts in the case.
     A. avidity   B. meticulousness   C. clemency
     D. balance   E. querulousness

2. The pianist played the concerto ____, displaying such   2.____
   facility and skill as has rarely been matched in this old
   auditorium.
     A. strenuously   B. deftly   C. passionately
     D. casually   E. spiritedly

3. The Tanglewood Symphony Orchestra holds its outdoor   3.____
   concerts far from city turmoil in a ____, bucolic setting.
     A. spectacular   B. atavistic   C. serene
     D. chaotic   E. catholic

4. Honest satire gives true joy to the thinking man. Thus,   4.____
   the satirist is most ____ when he points out the hypocrisy
   in human actions.
     A. elated   B. humiliated   C. ungainly
     D. repressed   E. disdainful

5. She was a(n) ____ who preferred the company of her books   5.___
   to the pleasures of cafe society.
       A. philanthropist   B. stoic   C. exhibitionist
       D. extrovert   E. introvert

6. So many people are so convinced that people are driven by   6.___
   ____ motives that they cannot believe that anybody is
   unselfish!
       A. interior   B. ulterior   C. unworthy
       D. selfish   E. destructive

7. These ____ results were brought about by a chain of   7.___
   fortuitous events.
       A. unfortunate   B. odd   C. harmful
       D. haphazard   E. propitious

8. The bank teller's ____ of the funds was discovered the   8.___
   following month when the auditors examined the books.
       A. embezzlement   B. burglary   C. borrowing
       D. assignment   E. theft

9. The monks gathered in the ____ for their evening meal.   9.___
       A. lounge   B. auditorium   C. refectory
       D. rectory   E. solarium

10. Local officials usually have the responsibility in each   10.___
    area of determining when the need is sufficiently great
    to ____ withdrawals from the community water supply.
        A. encourage   B. justify   C. discontinue
        D. advocate   E. forbid

____

KEYS (CORRECT ANSWERS)

TEST 1	TEST 2	TEST 3	TEST 4	TEST
1. A	1. A	1. E	1. C	1. D
2. A	2. D	2. A	2. A	2. B
3. D	3. A	3. E	3. E	3. C
4. C	4. A	4. A	4. D	4. A
5. A	5. D	5. D	5. D	5. E
6. E	6. A	6. D	6. A	6. B
7. C	7. A	7. B	7. C	7. D
8. D	8. E	8. C	8. D	8. A
9. A	9. B	9. A	9. D	9. C
10. A	10. C	10. C	10. E	10. B

____

VERBAL ANALOGIES

This type of question involves more than merely a knowledge of the meaning of words - it tests your ability to see relationships, your power to reason, and your knowledge of subject matter and everyday affairs. Often the words are simple but you must be careful to distinguish the fine shades of meaning.

Before you see the types of analogies, we shall work out one example:

       HAMMER : CARPENTER ::
          A. reins : horse   B. brush : painter
          C. shaves : barber   D. anchor : sailor
          E. blueprint : architect

FIRST STEP. Examine the relationship in the first pair from all possible angles. Express the relationship not *as this is to that* but in more specific terms. Example: A hammer is used by a carpenter as an essential tool.

SECOND STEP. Repeat the formula for each of the choices. Discard those that obviously do not fit, such as A and C.

THIRD STEP. Weigh the arguments for each of the choices that appear to fit: B, D, and E, then make the final decision. Where two or more seem to fit because of general agreement with the original pair, you must find additional specific agreement to narrow the choice to only one pair. In the above question, the sailor and the architect make use of an anchor or blueprint, respectively. However, a sailor does not handle the anchor or make anything with it, as a carpenter does with a hammer. The architect constructs but does not wield a blueprint. Therefore, the remaining choice, B, is correct, because the correspondence with the original choice is the closest.

Remember that in order for a relationship to remain the same in the answer words as in the question pair, the same sequence of ideas must remain.

The parts of speech used in an analogy must remain the same in the answer words as in the question pair for the relationship to be the same.

Keep in mind that many words have more than one meaning and that many pairs of words have more than one relationship between them. You may have to try a few relationships before you find the one that helps you choose the single best answer.

You may find the correct relationship but not refine it quite enough for the first time. If you can eliminate two or three answer choices with the first relationship you find, you may be able to get the correct answer by defining the relationship more precisely rather than by trying an entirely different one. You should practice stating precise, accurate relationships.

If you don't know the meaning of either of the words in CAPITAL letters, it probably won't help you to guess at the answer. On the other hand, if you know the words in CAPITAL letters but don't know some of the words in the answer choices, you may still be able to answer the question correctly. Remember, if you can eliminate even one of the answer choices, the odds of improving your score are in your favor if you guess.

Of course, you might have made the correct choice at first glance, but remember what Alexander Pope wrote about 230 years ago, *For fools rush in where angels fear to tread.* Be an angel. Test all possibilities; beware of traps.

TYPES OF ANALOGIES

Relationship	Example	Sentence
A type of	tulip:flower	A tulip is a type of flower.
A part of	wheel:car	A wheel is a part of a car.
A word that describes	carnivorous:lion	Carnivorous is a word that describes a lion.
A result of	transgression: punishment	Punishment is a result of a transgression.
A cause (or effect) of	puncture:blowout	Puncture is a cause of a blowout.
Is used to	mop:clean	A mop is used to clean.
Is used by	hammer:carpenter	A hammer is used by a carpenter.
Is created (or made) by	cabinet:carpenter	A cabinet is made by a carpenter
Is made from	shirt:fabric	A shirt is made from fabric.
Is larger (or smaller) than	lake:pond	A lake is larger than a pond.
To an extreme degree	careful:meticulous	A meticulous person is extremely careful.
Is a measure of	mile:distance	A mile is a measure of distance.
Has the purpose of	needle:sew	The purpose of a needle is to sew.
Is located in	sink:kitchen	A sink is located in a kitchen.
Is characterized by	miser:greed	A miser is characterized by greed.
Lacks	somber:light	A somber room lacks light.
Lacks	somber:cheer	A somber person lacks cheer.

ANALOGY QUESTIONS

1. The most important error on these questions is made because the student does not establish a specific relationship with the pair of words.

2. The second most common error is that the student does not apply this relationship in a consistent way with all the possible answers. The student allows the test maker to distract him.

PROBLEM-SOLVING TECHNIQUES

A. Go back to the original pair and establish a more specific relationship.

B. Eliminate unrelated parts.

C. Students should use the common types of analogies as a model; e.g., are these words synonyms, is one word the cause of another, etc.

D. When you don't know one of the words, work backward from the choices.

A single word can have several meanings. Choose the meaning of the word that works in a relationship with the other word in the pair. For example, in the last two relationships listed, somber can mean dark and gloomy, which is the meaning you would use if somber were used with light: *something that is somber lacks light*. Somber also can describe a quiet, perhaps depressed, person, the meaning you would use if somber were used with cheer: *a somber person does not express cheer*.

VERBAL ANALOGIES

The verbal-analogy type question is now a staple component of tests of general and mental ability, scholastic aptitude, professional qualification, and civil service examinations. This question-type is also being used for achievement testing.

The verbal analogy is considered an excellent measure for evaluating the ability of the student to reason with and in words. It is not, primarily, a test of vocabulary *per se*, for very rarely are the words that are used in this type of question difficult or abstruse in meaning (as they are, for example, in the same-opposite or sentence-completion type). Rather, they are everyday terms and phrases descriptive of materials and actions familiar to all of us.

The verbal analogy is a test of *word relationships* and *idea relationships*, involving a neat and algebraic-like arrangement in ratio (proportion) form not of numbers but of words. Some testers see in this type of question the development on the verbal (linguistic or qualitative) side of the same logical reasoning as occurs on the mathematical (numerical or quantitative) side in number problems. This type of question is ranked just after the reading-comprehension type in difficulty. However, it constitutes by far the most fascinating and challenging area in aptitude testing.

In general, three levels of ability are involved in answering the verbal analogy question.

First, and easiest in this connection, is the ability to understand the meanings of the words used in the question (understanding).

Second, and more difficult , is the ability to comprehend the relationship between the subject-, or question-, pair of words (the process of logical reasoning).

Third, and most difficult of all, is the ability to select from the five (pairs of) choices given, that choice which bears the same relationship to (within) itself as the subject words bear to one another. This involves analysis, comparison, and judgment (the process of evaluation).

In the verbal-analogy type of question, two important symbols are employed, which must be thoroughly understood beforehand. These are the colon(:), which is to be translated into words, when reading the question, in the same way as its mathematical equivalent, that is, "is to"; and the double colon (::), which is to be translated as "in the same way as." Thus, the analogy, BURGLAR: PRISON :: juvenile delinquent : reformatory, is to be read, A burglar is to a prison in the same way as a juvenile delinquent is to a reformatory. Or, reading for meaning, we could say instead, "A burglar is punished by being sent to a prison in the same way as a juvenile delinquent is punished by being sent to a reformatory."

SAMPLE QUESTIONS AND EXPLANATIONS

DIRECTIONS: Each question in this part consists of a pair of words in capital letters, which have a certain relationship to each other, followed *either* by a third word in capital letters and five lettered words in small letters (1 blank missing) OR by five lettered pairs of words in small letters (2 blanks missing). Choose *either* the letter of the word that is related to the third word in capital letters OR of the pair of words that are related to each other in the same way as the first two capitalized words are related to each other, and mark the appropriate space on your answer sheet.

1. EROSION : ROCKS :: DISSIPATION : _____
   A. character   B. temperance   C. penance   D. influence
   E. sincerity
2. MUNDANE : SPIRITUAL :: SECULAR : _____
   A. scientist   B. clerical   C. pecuniary   D. municipal
   E. teacher
3. ANARCHY : LAWLESSNESS :: _____ : _____
   A. autocracy : peace   B. disturbance : safety
   C. government : order   D. confusion : law
   E. democracy : dictatorship
4. UMBRELLA : RAIN :: _____ : _____
   A. roof : snow   B. screen : insects
   C. sewer : water   D. body : disease
   E. gong : dinner

                              ─

EXPLANATION OF QUESTION 1
   Item A, character, is correct.
   Erosion is a geological development that wears away Rocks. This
is an example of a cause-effect relationship -- a concrete relationship.
   Dissipation wears away character (Item A)in the same way --however,
this is an abstract relationship.
   But the comparison is apt and appropriate. This is a usual,general
type of analogy whose difficulty is compounded by the fact that a concrete relationship is compared with an abstract one.
   Item B,temperance(moderation),is merely one aspect of character.
   Item C,penance(repentance),bears no relationship to dissipation
in the sense of the subject words.
   Item D,influence, and Item E,sincerity, may or may not be affected
by dissipation.
   This question is an example of a one-blank analogy,that is,only one
word is to be supplied in the answer (a subject pair and a third subject
word being given in the question itself).

                              ─

EXPLANATION OF QUESTION 2
   Item B, clerical, is correct.
   Mundane means worldly,earthly. The opposite of this word is spiri-
tual -- unworldly,devout,eternal. This is a relationship of opposites.
   Secular means worldly, earthly,temporal. It is a synonym for mundane.
What is needed as the answer is an opposite equal in meaning to spiritual
   A. A scientist may or may not be worldly or spiritual. At any rate,
an adjective is needed as an answer, and scientist is a noun.
   B. Clerical("pertaining to the clergy") denotes, usually, apiritual
or religious qualities. It is an adjective. This is the correct answer.
   C. Pecuniary refers to money, and may, therefore,be regarded as a
synonym for secular.
   D. Municipal refers to municipalities or cities, and has no standing here as an answer.
   E. A teacher may or may not be worldly or spiritual. At any rate,
just as for A. scientist, it is a noun and not an adjective, which is
needed as an answer here.

                              ─

EXPLANATION OF QUESTION 3

Item C, government : order, is correct.

Anarchy, or no government, is characterized by lawlessness while a government is characterized by order. This is an example of an object (situation) : characteristic relationship.

Item A, autocracy : peace, is incorrect since very often autocracy (absolute monarchy or rule by an individual) is characterized by war.

Item B, disturbance : safety, is manifestly untrue.

Item D, confusion : law, is likewise untrue.

Item E, democracy : dictatorship, bears no relationship to the meaning conveyed by the subject pair.

This is an example of a two-blank analogy, that is, a pair of words is to be supplied. This is the more difficult type of analogy, and the one most frequently encountered on advanced-level examinations.

————

EXPLANATION OF QUESTION 4

Item B, screen : insects, is correct.

By means of an umbrella, one keeps the rain off his person just as a screen keeps insects out of the house. This is an example of an object: assists relationship.

Item A, roof : snow, is not correct since a roof keeps out many other things as well, e.g., light, heat, rain, insects, etc.

Item C, sewer : water, is incorrect since a sewer keeps water in or water flows through and in a sewer.

Item D, body : disease, is incorrect since often disease enters and destroys the body.

Item E, gong : dinner, is incorrect since the gong merely summons to dinner but does not keep anyone away.

————

As can be discerned from the examples above, there are many possible relationships on which word analogies may be formed. Some of these will be listed and illustrated below. However, the important point is not to ponder over labels and attempt to peg the relationships thereby. This is as unnecessary as it is time-consuming. The real object, or the real method, is to examine and to fully comprehend the relationship expressed in the subject pair and *then* to select as the correct answer that item which *most approximately* is in greatest consonance with all or most of the aspects of the given relationship.

————

TYPES AND FORMS OF ANALOGY QUESTIONS

Some or all of the following types of analogies or relationships are to be encountered on examinations.
1. PART : WHOLE
    Example: LEG : BODY :: wheel : car
2. CAUSE : EFFECT
    Example: RAIN : FLOOD :: disease : epidemic
3. CONCRETE: ABSTRACT
    Example: ROAD : VEHICLE :: life : person
4. WORD : SYNONYM
    Example: VACUOUS : EMPTY :: seemly : fit
5. WORD : ANTONYM
    Example: SLAVE : FREEMAN :: desolate : joyous

6. OBJECT : MATERIAL
     Example: COAT : WOOL :: dress : cotton
7. OBJECT : DEFINITION
     Example: ASSEVERATE : AFFIRM :: segregate : separate
8. OBJECT : SEX
     Example: COLT : MARE :: buck : doe
9. TIME : TIME
     Example: DAY : NIGHT :: sunrise : sunset
10. DEGREE : DEGREE
     Example: HAPPY : ECSTATIC :: warm : hot
11. OBJECT : TOOL
     Example: STENCIL : TYPEWRITER :: thread : needle
12. USER : TOOL
     Example: FARMER : HOE :: dentist : drill
13. CREATOR : CREATION
     Example: ARTIST : PICTURE :: poet : poem
14. CATEGORY : TYPE
     Example: RODENT : SQUIRREL :: fish : flounder
15. PERSON (ANIMAL,ETC.) : CHARACTERISTIC
     Example: MONSTER : FEROCITY :: baby : helplessness
16. OBJECT : CHARACTERISTIC
     Example: PICKLE : SOUR :: sugar : sweet
17. PERSON : FUNCTION
     Example: TEACHER : EDUCATION :: doctor : health
18. INSTRUMENT : FUNCTION
     Example: CAMERA : PHOTOGRAPHY :: ruler : measurement
19. WORD : GRAMMATICAL FORM
     Example: WE : I :: they : he
20. SYMBOL : ATTITUDE
     Example: SALUTE : PATRIOTISM :: prayer : religion
21. REWARD : ACTION
     Example: MEDAL : BRAVERY :: trophy : championship
22. OBJECT : ASSISTS
     Example: WATER : THIRST :: food : hunger
23. OBJECT : HINDERS
     Example: NOISE : STUDY :: rut : car
24. PERSON : RELATIONSHIP
     Example: FATHER : SON :: uncle : nephew
25. OBJECT : LOCALE
     Example: SHIP : WATER :: airplane : air
26. OBJECT : METHOD
     Example: DOOR : KEY :: safe : combination
27. QUALITY : PROFUSION
     Example: WIND : TORNADO :: water : flood
28. QUALITY : ABSENCE
     Example: FORTITUDE : COWARDICE :: carefully : casually
29. SIZE : SIZE
     Example: BOAT : SHIP :: lake : sea
30. GENUS : SPECIES
     Example: RODENT : RAT :: canine : wolf

There are other relationships, but these will suffice to show some
of those more frequently occurring.

————

4

SUGGESTIONS FOR ANSWERING THE VERBAL ANALOGY QUESTION (APTITUDE)

1. Always keep in mind that a verbal analogy is a relationship of like-ness between two things, consisting in the resemblances not, usually, of the things themselves but of two or more of their attributes, func-tions, circumstances, or effects. Therefore, in the one-blank or two-blank questions, you are not looking so much for similarity in struc-ture (although this may prove to be a factor, too), as you are for a relationship in the _functioning_ of the subject words.

2. How do we proceed to answer the verbal-analogy type question? *First,* discover for yourself in a meaningful way the exact relationship ex-isting between the subject words. Whether you are able to label or tag this relationship is not so important (as we have said before) as to _understand_ the relationship that exists. The logical *second* and *final* step is to examine the possible answers given and to ascertain which of these possibilities, on the basis of *meaning, order,* and *form,* bears a similar relationship to the subject pair.

3. For the analogy in question, the subject words (i.e., the question words given in the first part of the analogy) need not be of the same class, type, order, or species as the object words (i.e., the answer-words or fill-ins). For example, in the analogy, BUCCANEER:SAILOR :: fungus : plant, the subject words (in capital letters) are types of people, the object words (in small letters) refer to types of things. However, the analogy that exists is on the basis of a descriptive re-lationship between these two different sets of words. (The first word in each pair constitutes the depredatory or despoiling form of the se-cond, which is the general category name.) Thus, it is actually the _total_ effect of the *first pair* on each other that is being compared with the _total_ effect of the *second pair* on each other: *this is what really counts,* and not the individual components of each pair.

4. The order of the object words must be in the same sequence as the or-der of the subject words. For example, the analogy, INAUGURATION : PRESIDENT :: ordination : priest, is correct. But, INAUGURATION : PRESIDENT :: priest : ordination, would be incorrect. Watch for this _reversal_ of order in word sequence; it is a common source of entrap-ment for the uninitiated.

5. Likewise, it is necessary to check to see that the parts of speech used in the analogy are the same, and occur in the same sequence. For example, if the subject pair contains a noun and an adjective in that order, the object pair _must_ contain a noun and an adjective in *that* order. Thus, MOTHER : GOOD :: murderer : bad, is correct. But, MOTHER : GOOD :: murderer : badly, is incorrect.

6. The best way to answer the analogy question -- one-blank or two-blanks -- is to study intensively the relationship contained in the given pair. Having fully comprehended this relationship and, perhaps, having "labeled" it, proceed to scan the possible answers, choosing the most likely one. This will save time, and avoid needless trial and error.

———

VERBAL ANALOGIES – 2 BLANKS
EXAMINATION SECTION

DIRECTIONS FOR THIS SECTION:
Each question in this part consists of two capitalized words which have a certain relationship to each other, followed by five lettered pairs of words in small letters. Choose the letter of the pair of words which are related to each other in the SAME way as the words of the capitalized pair are related to each other. *PRINT THE LETTER OF THE CORRECT ANSWER IN THE SPACE AT THE RIGHT.*

TEST 1

1. DISEASE : IMMUNITY :: _____ : _____   1. ...
    A. crime : pardon   B. custom : practice
    C. debt : bankruptcy   D. tax : exemption
    E. travel : deduction

2. RESPONSIBILITY : RELEASE :: _____ : _____   2. ...
    A. duty : refrain   B. promise : renege   C. debt : honor
    D. blame : vindicate   E. position : retract

3. PENDULUM : SWING :: _____ : _____   3. ...
    A. pulley : ladder   B. hand : clock   C. lever : crowbar
    D. balance : seesaw   E. weight : fulcrum

4. NADIR : ZENITH :: _____ : _____   4. ...
    A. depression : recovery   B. perigee : apogamy
    C. earth : sky   D. appanage : station
    E. threshold : lintel

5. ROB : CONFISCATE :: _____ : _____   5. ...
    A. punish : revenge   B. walk : trespass   C. insult : offend
    D. murder : execute   E. take : accept

6. WORKER : UNEMPLOYED :: _____ : _____   6. ...
    A. crop : barren   B. property : useless
    C. purchase : unnecessary D. visitor : unwelcome
    E. field : fallow

7. PROFUSION : AUSTERITY :: _____ : _____   7. ...
    A. capitalism : socialism   B. erudition : reprise
    C. logic : irrationality   D. affluence : frugality
    E. effluence : confluence

8. REPERTOIRE : OPERA :: _____ : _____   8. ...
    A. suits : closet   B. team : baseball   C. melody : harmony
    D. wardrobe : costume   E. chest : drawers

9. DISDAIN : AFFRONT :: _____ : _____   9. ...
    A. perjury : boos   B. pleasure : pain
    C. approval : applause   D. age : wrinkle   E. grimace : awry

10. SALES : ADVERTISING :: _____ : _____   10. ...
    A. votes : campaigning   B. savings : banking
    C. liquor : drinking   D. troops : leading
    E. weakness : strength

11. ATTACK : MURDER :: _____ : _____   11. ...
    A. filial : fraternal   B. mind : body
    C. paroxysm : parricide   D. sudden : poison
    E. diseased : dead

12. BALTIC : INDIAN :: _____ : _____   12. ...
    A. Mediterranean : Pacific   B. Atlantic : Caribbean
    C. Arctic : Gulf of Mexico   D. Black Sea : Persian Gulf
    E. Antarctic : Andaman Sea

13. PROFESSION : STRUGGLE :: _____ : _____   13. ...
    A. strong : weak   B. métier : melee   C. mixed : confusion
    D. vocation : trade   E. expert : novice

1

14. ALLOYS : ATMOSPHERE :: _____ : _____   14. ...
    A. weight : measure   B. metallurgy : meteorology
    C. technology : science   D. archaic : present
    E. metal : meteor

15. GRAM : KILOGRAM :: _____ : _____   15. ...
    A. millimeter : centimeter B. dekameter : decimeter
    C. mile : kilometer   D. micron : microbe
    E. Centigrade : Fahrenheit

16. PRESIDENT : FRANCE :: _____ : _____   16. ...
    A. Queen Elizabeth : England B. king : Belgium
    C. president : United States D. governor : state
    E. king : Italy

17. HAND : DIAL :: _____ : _____   17. ...
    A. time : number B. light : lamp C. ticking : talking
    D. clock : radio E. time : space

18. ANNEX : BUILDING :: _____ : _____   18. ...
    A. pin : clasp B. stone : setting C. cell : prison
    D. branch : tree   E. island : mainland

19. FLOOR : PARQUET :: _____ : _____   19. ...
    A. elevator : escalator   B. functional : ornamental
    C. filigree : scroll   D. wreath : nosegay
    E. head : hair

20. DEVIL : DRUGGIST :: _____ : _____   20. ...
    A. demon : farmer   B. demonology : pharmacology
    C. medieval : primitive   D. dispensed : compounded
    E. Faustian : Freudian

21. ELECTRICITY : GAS :: _____ : _____   21. ...
    A. lighter : match B. current : flow C. fire : flame
    D. conductor : ignition   E. train : automobile

22. - : HYPHEN :: _____ : _____   22. ...
    A. x : division   B. $: pound   C. symbol : word
    D. y : geometry   E. & : sum

23. WILD : DOMESTICATED :: _____ : _____   23. ...
    A. jungle : forest   B. atavistic : masochistic
    C. cave : dwelling   D. animal : man
    E. primitive : civilized

24. INEPT : TACTLESS :: _____ : _____   24. ...
    A. right : left B. evil : sinful C. clever : stupid
    D. depraved : foolish   E. maladroit : gauche

25. INTERVENE : INTERCEDE :: _____ : _____   25. ...
    A. interfere : impute   B. interpose : intrude
    C. arbitrate : argue   D. meditate : mediate
    E. space : species

TEST 2

1. PITHY : BOMBASTIC :: _____ : _____   1. ...
    A. verbose : taciturn   B. garrulous : pompous
    C. meagre : replete   D. laconic : grandiloquent
    E. concise : precise

2. MANAGER : TEAM :: _____ : _____   2. ...
    A. President : Congress B. Speaker : Senate
    C. captain : crew   D. minister : hierarchy
    E. principal : P.T.A.

3. STEEPLE : LEDGE :: _____ : _____   3. ...
    A. citadel : tower   B. spire : dungeon   C. warp : woof
    D. peak : summit   E. cone : roof
4. CREDULOUS : UNCTUOUS :: _____ : _____   4. ...
    A. ingenious : artful   B. ingenuous : urbane
    C. naive : provincial   D. benign : benignant
    E. cantankerous : peevish
5. PHILIPPIC : ABUSE :: _____ : _____   5. ...
    A. eulogy : mirth B. tirade : tears C. sycophancy : music
    D. encomium : praise   E. intrepidity : fear
6. CUMULATIVE : ACCRETIVE :: _____ : _____   6. ...
    A. indigenous : spontaneous B. reticence : verbosity
    C. philately : numismatics   D. indigence : poverty
    E. culvert : bridge
7. UNCONSTRAINED : IMPROVISED :: _____ : _____   7. ...
    A. unrehearsed : prepared   B. simultaneous : pithy
    C. premeditated : unpremeditated
    D. extemporaneous : contemporaneous
    E. spontaneous : impromptu
8. INORDINACY : EXCESSIVE :: _____ : _____   8. ...
    A. applause : approval   B. anomaly : irregular
    C. remuneration : payable   D. provocation : irritate
    E. emulation : insidious
9. PLEBEIAN : PATRICIAN :: _____ : _____   9. ...
    A. Democrat : Republican   B. Communist : Conservative
    C. serf : fief   D. vassal : lord
    E. common man : elite
10. FLEETING : EPHEMERAL :: _____ : _____   10. ...
    A. permanent : temporary   B. casual : persistent
    C. transient : evanescent   D. temporary : permanent
    E. passing : perceptible
11. INSTRUMENTALIST : ORGANIST :: _____ : _____   11. ...
    A. harmonist : contrapuntist B. quartet : counterpoint
    C. lute : lutanist   D. singer : composition
    E. cello : violoncello
12. ADULTERATE : COMPOUND :: _____ : _____   12. ...
    A. fusion : blend   B. commingle : miscellany
    C. interpretation : commingling
    D. interpolate : amalgamate E. mix : potpourri
13. QUIESCENCE : INDOLENCE :: _____ : _____   13. ...
    A. lurk : abeyance   B. concealed : potential
    C. latency : dormancy   D. escape : observation
    E. suppress : inertia
14. BROGUE : JARGONIST :: _____ : _____   14. ...
    A. patois : neologist   B. empathy : psychiatrist
    C. dialect : Anglicism   D. country : patriot
    E. gazette : journalist
15. DENIAL : DISCLAIMER :: _____ : _____   15. ...
    A. veto : ignore   B. contradiction : convention
    C. cancel : canker   D. disavowal : negation
    E. gainsay : contradict
16. FATE : PREDESTINATION :: _____ : _____   16. ...
    A. doom : destiny B. appointed : office C. elect : fated
    D. exigency : inevitability   E. lot : choice

3

17. LETHARGY : EXHAUSTION :: _____ : _____   17. ...
    A. laziness : weariness   B. continence : ennui
    C. enfeebled : haggard   D. exertion : tiredness
    E. lassitude : fatigue

18. QUALM : IRRESOLUTION :: _____ : _____   18. ...
    A. fear : diffidence   B. fright : stampede
    C. awe : trust   D. sanguine : apprehensive
    E. nightmare : alarm

19. WAR : SURRENDER :: _____ : _____   19. ...
    A. victor : accede   B. grant : scholarship
    C. election : concede   D. state : cede
    E. prison : confess

20. BALD EAGLE : GROUSE :: _____ : _____   20. ...
    A. termite : cockroach   B. chanticleer : rooster
    C. falcon : pheasant   D. peacock : hen
    E. vulture : hawk

21. ORANGUTAN : BRONCHO :: _____ : _____   21. ...
    A. antelope : trotter   B. Wales : United States
    C. caribou : marmoset   D. ewe : ram
    E. steeplechaser : pacer

22. UNITED STATES : FRANCE :: _____ : _____   22. ...
    A. official : citizen   B. policeman : gendarme
    C. officer : attendant   D. New York : Louisiana
    E. west : east

23. SEOUL : SOUTH KOREA :: _____ : _____   23. ...
    A. Estopil : Portugal   B. Pnom Penh : Laos
    C. Barcelona : Spain   D. London : England
    E. Venezuela : Caracas

24. PERSECUTION : PARANOIA :: _____ : _____   24. ...
    A. altruism : megalomania   B. neurosis : psychosis
    C. dichotomy : schizophrenia
    D. extraversion : claustrophobia   E. disease : symptom

25. ONE : TWO :: _____ : _____   25. ...
    A. century : millennium   B. planet : astronomy
    C. year : twenty   D. month : year   E. decade : score

TEST 3

1. CHAFFER : BARGAIN :: _____ : _____   1. ...
    A. scarify : cleanse   B. hector : befriend
    C. propitiate : placate   D. improvise : intercalate
    E. decollate : decode

2. SPANIEL : FAWNING PERSON :: _____ : _____   2. ...
    A. cameo : miniature   B. nonage : minority
    C. pediment : obstacle   D. flacon : flag
    E. marasca : wine

3. SEMINAL : ORIGINATIVE :: _____ : _____   3. ...
    A. sullied : inflamed   B. beleaguered : besieged
    C. viable : moribund   D. amorphous : remanent
    E. quintan : fourth

4. SLAKE : ALLAY :: _____ : _____   4. ...
    A. comport : frolic B. beset : assail C. parry : join
    D. revet : review E. remonstrate : concur

5. SALAAM : OBEISANCE :: _____ : _____   5. ...
    A. jape : hiatus B. ethos : fundamental spirit of a culture

4

C. gravamen : greeting   D. chanticleer : fox

E. ablation : inhalation

6. SLATTERNLY : SLOVENLY :: _____ : _____   6. ...

A. complaisant : priggish   B. myopic : farsighted

C. awry : convex

D. oblate : flattened at the poles   E. slavish : sleazy

7. PREEN : SLEEK :: _____ : _____   7. ...

A. extrapolate : disengage   B. discountenance : disconcert

C. bandy : banter   D. cense : ascribe

E. cite : proscribe

8. SATRAP : EXECUTIVE :: _____ : _____   8. ...

A. rigmarole : prolix talk   B. apostasy : denunciation

C. apogee : perigee   D. allotrophy : allusion

E. chaldron : chalice

9. INCHOATE : NASCENT :: _____ : _____   9. ...

A. extirpative : invective   B. contumacious : headstrong

C. disinterested : prejudiced

D. veracious : mendacious   E. abandoned : manumitted

10. RAIL : REVILE :: _____ : _____   10. ...

A. abjure : appeal to   B. vouchsafe : contemplate

C. execrate : curse   D. exorcise : criticize

E. ablactate : abominate

11. ANTONYM : OPPOSITE :: _____ : _____   11. ...

A. antonym : unlike   B. metaphor : poetry

C. triangle : pyramid   D. synonym : same

E. metonymy : versification

12. READER: PUNCTUATION :: _____ : _____   12. ...

A. telegraph operator : Morse code   B. vocabulary : alphabet

C. English : pronunciation   D. bicyclist : roadblock

E. motorist : road sign

13. OCEAN : ROAD :: _____ : _____   13. ...

A. ship : hurricane   B. canal : road

C. storm : accident   D. buoy : detour

E. warning : signal

14. MATTER : ESSENCE :: _____ : _____   14. ...

A. play : outcome   B. matter : particle   C. molecule : atom

D. paragraph : gist   E. epitome : paraphrase

15. PENURIOUS : SLUM :: _____ : _____   15. ...

A. captive : jail   B. parched : desert

C. withered : plant   D. inundated : flood

E. glum : outlook

16. DEMEANOR : CHARACTER :: _____ : _____   16. ...

A. personality : qualities   B. aspect : appearance

C. vestibule : apartment   D. facade : building

E. front : affront

17. HAIR : TRIM :: _____ : _____   17. ...

A. beard : shave   B. lawn : mow   C. wool : shear

D. shrub : prune   E. scissors : cut

18. WORK : PUTTER :: _____ : _____   18. ...

A. bum : thief   B. late : laggard   C. regress : ingress

D. diligent : tardy   E. wait : loiter

19. EXILE : SANCTUARY :: _____ : _____   19. ...

A. child : bed   B. refugee : haven   C. berth : stowaway

D. fish : bowl   E. prisoner : dungeon

20. CAR : HORN :: _____ : _____   20. ...

A. air raid : siren   B. swimmer : bell buoy

5

C. singer : tune   D. train : whistle   E. ship : anchor
21. SETTING : DIAMOND :: _____ : _____   21. ...
    A. sash : window   B. frame : picture   C. shell : egg
    D. painting : canvas   E. border : exile
22. AFFECTION : PASSION :: _____ : _____   22. ...
    A. storm : sea   B. contraction : dilation
    C. atmospheric pressure : clear day
    D. breeze : gale   E. wind : gale
23. TEAR : CUT :: _____ : _____   23. ...
    A. wrinkle : fold B. paper : refuse C. wrinkle : smooth
    D. steal : lose   E. sprinkle : rub
24. FIGHTER : BELL :: _____ : _____   24. ...
    A. butterfly hunter : net   B. fencer : sword
    C. writer : pen   D. dog : whistle
    E. sprinter : gun
25. PLANT : FUNGUS :: _____ : _____   25. ...
    A. transient : permanent   B. mate : captain
    C. sailor : pirate D. police : thief   E. wolf : prey

TEST 4

1. EVENING : MORNING :: _____ : _____   1. ...
    A. coming : going B. ten : five   C. sunset : sunrise
    D. spring : autumn E. despair : hope
2. RUNG : RING :: _____ : _____   2. ...
    A. arisen : arise B. drunk : drink   C. stroke : strike
    D. sang : sing   E. clang : cling
3. ENTHUSIASTIC : APPROVING :: _____ : _____   3. ...
    A. disliking : liking B. pink : red C. frigid : cool
    D. bitter : sour   E. apathetic : disapproving
4. MOLECULE : ATOM :: _____ : _____   4. ...
    A. kennel : dog   B. shelf : book   C. sea : fish
    D. regiment : soldier   E. star : galaxy
5. ACT : PLAY :: _____ : _____   5. ...
    A. notes : staff   B. harmony : counterpoint
    C. melody : harmony   D. key : piano
    E. movement : symphony
6. APIARY : BEES :: _____ : _____   6. ...
    A. dog : kennel B. fish : aquarium C. mortuary : people
    D. corral : cattle   E. breviary : priest
7. STRANDS : ROPE :: _____ : _____   7. ...
    A. sugar : cane   B. warp : woof   C. links : chain
    D. train : cars   E. rivers : ocean
8. BODY : SKIN :: _____ : _____   8. ...
    A. window : door B. ink : crayon   C. book : cover
    D. write : compose E. spelling : grammar
9. PENCIL : LEAD :: _____ : _____   9. ...
    A. lighter : fluid B. keys : typewriter C. cup : coffee
    D. book : page   E. razor : blade
10. AIRPLANE : LOCOMOTION :: _____ : _____   10. ...
    A. statement : contention   B. canoe : paddle
    C. hero : worship   D. spectacles : vision
    E. hay : horse
11. STREAM : RIVER :: _____ : _____   11. ...
    A. land : water B. village : suburb C. cape : continent

6

D. sea : ocean   E. city : country

12. RECTANGLE : SQUARE :: _____ : _____   12. ...
    A. line : perimeter   B. triangle : square
    C. square : diamond D. circle : square E. oval : circle

13. EMOLUMENT : INCENTIVE :: _____ : _____   13. ...
    A. deed : crime   B. play : plot   C. criminal : reward
    D. dance : movement   E. reward : capture

14. WOLF : PROWL :: _____ : _____   14. ...
    A. rat : gnaw   B. monkey : mimic   C. reader : browse
    D. trooper : lurk   E. gang : highjack

15. FOND : INFATUATION :: _____ : _____   15. ...
    A. affectionate : adumbration   B. calm : listless
    C. eager : sentimentality   D. glib : fluency
    E. enthusiastic : fervor

16. CONCORD : DISCORD :: _____ : _____   16. ...
    A. alliance : organization   B. treaty : covenant
    C. conciliation : revolution
    D. entreaty : parity   E. pact : feud

17. EXTENUATE : CRIME :: _____ : _____   17. ...
    A. condone : error   B. placate : pardon   C. expiate : sin
    D. moderate : tone   E. reprisal : retaliation

18. APPENDIX : PREFACE :: _____ : _____   18. ...
    A. glossary : index   B. preface : table of contents
    C. progeny : proletariat   D. footnote : emendation
    E. epilogue : prologue

19. SUBSEQUENT : COINCIDENTAL :: _____ : _____   19. ...
    A. posthumous : following   B. now : there
    C. consecutive : ensuing   D. posterior : simultaneous
    E. prolonged : before

20. MUNDANE : SPIRITUAL :: _____ : _____   20. ...
    A. scientist : missionary   B. secular : altruistic
    C. municipal : ecclesiastical
    D. pecuniary : musical   E. student : teacher

21. UNSCRUPULOUS : QUALMS :: _____ : _____   21. ...
    A. remorseless : compassion B. intrepid : rashness
    C. opportunist : opportunity
    D. querulous : lamentation E. impenitent : sin

22. SOPHISTRY : LOGIC :: _____ : _____   22. ...
    A. discretion : improvidence B. spirit : spiritualism
    C. reason : rationalization   D. feeling : intuition
    E. wisdom : sophistication

23. TRESPASSER : BARK :: _____ : _____   23. ...
    A. snake : hiss B. burglar : alarm   C. crossing : bell
    D. air raid : siren   E. ship : buoy

24. RESEARCH : FELLOWSHIP :: _____ : _____   24. ...
    A. honor : medal   B. merit : scholarship
    C. student : bonus D. matrimony : dowry E. study : grant

25. IMPEND : CATASTROPHE :: _____ : _____   25. ...
    A. loom : disaster   B. question : puzzle
    C. imminent : eminent D. howl : storm   E. hurt : penalty

TEST 5

1. DEATH : DEMISE :: _____ : _____   1. ...
    A. frightful : horrid   B. resistance : invasion
    C. asylum : insane D. life : breath   E. might : right

2. DRAGON : DINOSAUR :: _____ : _____   2. ...
   A. descendant : ancestor   B. medieval : prehistoric
   C. fabulous : real   D. creditable : veritable
   E. amphibian : reptile

3. SHIP : NAVIGATOR :: _____ : _____   3. ...
   A. promoter : event   B. victory : leader
   C. conduct : conscience   D. state : army
   E. nation : patriotism

4. GUFFAW : LAUGH :: _____ : _____   4. ...
   A. lament : cry   B. wail : whimper   C. face : mouth
   D. chuckle : snicker   E. smirk : simper

5. ANARCHY : CHAOS :: _____ : _____   5. ...
   A. government : order   B. beast : beauty
   C. government : law   D. rule : order
   E. totalitarian : mob

6. INFINITE : FINITE :: _____ : _____   6. ...
   A. second : minute   B. hour : minute   C. era : decade
   D. month : day   E. immortality : mortality

7. WATER : BOAT :: _____ : _____   7. ...
   A. locomotive : steam   B. wagon : horse   C. air : dirigible
   D. lion : tiger   E. gasoline : taxi

8. INAUGURATION : PRESIDENT :: _____ : _____   8. ...
   A. promulgation : list   B. matriculation : student
   C. election : candidate   D. promotion : officer
   E. ordination : priest

9. OMNIPOTENT : VASSAL :: _____ : _____   9. ...
   A. soldier : civilian   B. policeman : prisoner
   C. master : slave   D. captain : tar   E. native : alien

10. SAME : SYNONYM :: _____ : _____   10. ...
   A. bell : bellows   B. false : pseudonym   C. same : homonym
   D. botanist : biologist   E. opposite : antonym

KEYS (CORRECT ANSWERS)

TEST 1	TEST 2	TEST 3	TEST 4	TEST 5
1. D	1. D	1. C	1. C	1. A
2. D	2. C	2. B	2. B	2. C
3. C	3. C	3. B	3. D	3. C
4. E	4. B	4. B	4. E	4. B
5. D	5. D	5. B	5. E	5. A
6. E	6. D	6. D	6. D	6. E
7. D	7. E	7. B	7. C	7. C
8. D	8. B	8. A	8. C	8. E
9. C	9. E	9. B	9. E	9. C
10. A	10. C	10. C	10. D	10. E
11. C	11. A	11. D	11. D	
12. A	12. D	12. E	12. E	
13. B	13. C	13. D	13. E	
14. B	14. A	14. D	14. E	
15. A	15. D	15. B	15. E	
16. C	16. A	16. D	16. E	
17. D	17. E	17. D	17. A	
18. D	18. A	18. E	18. E	
19. B	19. C	19. B	19. D	
20. B	20. C	20. D	20. B	
21. B	21. A	21. B	21. A	
22. C	22. B	22. E	22. D	
23. E	23. D	23. A	23. B	
24. E	24. C	24. E	24. E	
25. B	25. E	25. C	25. A	

VERBAL ANALOGIES — 2 BLANKS
EXAMINATION SECTION

DIRECTIONS FOR THIS SECTION:
Each question in this part consists of two capitalized words which have a certain relationship to each other, followed by five lettered pairs of words in small letters. Choose the letter of the pair of words which are related to each other in the SAME way as the words of the capitalized pair are related to each other. *PRINT THE LETTER OF THE CORRECT ANSWER IN THE SPACE AT THE RIGHT.*

TEST 1

1. DISCRETE : ABRIDGED :: _____ : _____
   A. quotes : parentheses B. decimal : fraction
   C. separation : partition D. hyphenated : abbreviated
   E. separated : slang
                      1. ...

2. COURT : DESERT :: _____ : _____
   A. boar : camel B. diversion : pachyderm C. fig : forest
   D. droll : dromedary   E. plant : person
                      2. ...

3. RECORDS : FILE :: _____ : _____
   A. stipend : income B. wall : plug C. socket : bulb
   D. stocks : bonds E. savings : bank
                      3. ...

4. FURROW : PLOW :: _____ : _____
   A. sign : street B. route : avenue C. orbit : earth
   D. ring : bull E. crash : aeroplane
                      4. ...

5. FAMILY : CHILDREN :: _____ : _____
   A. party : guests B. clan : crest C. flag : country
   D. club : members E. feline : cat
                      5. ...

6. RECIDIVISTIC : PRUDENT :: _____ : _____
   A. period : proper B. cadence : credo
   C. impoverished : wealthy D. depraved : respectful
   E. decadent : circumspect
                      6. ...

7. PARTITION : SERIES :: _____ : _____
   A. enclosing : parietal B. division : rescission
   C. septum : spectrum D. wall : ghastly
   E. fencing : parading
                      7. ...

8. SEISMOGRAPH : EARTHQUAKE :: _____ : _____
   A. barometer : temperature B. thermometer : pressure
   C. fluoroscope : tuberculosis
   D. lubritorium : laboratory E. x-ray : pulsation
                      8. ...

9. ELECTRICITY : ILLUMINATION :: _____ : _____
   A. gravity : force B. water : power C. sieve : straining
   D. stroke : brush E. atomic : bomb
                      9. ...

10. DEMEANOR : CHARACTER :: _____ : _____
   A. innate : temperament B. distinguished : personified
   C. singer : song D. tenor : type E. aspect : acuity
                      10. ...

11. INSTINCT : BEAST :: _____ : _____
   A. reason : rationale B. mind : brain C. thought : process
   D. intelligence : man E. rattle : snake
                      11. ...

12. ROMANTIC : PRACTICAL :: _____ : _____
   A. weak : strong B. inspired : clumsy C. quixotic : realistic
   D. light : heavy E. surface : depth
                      12. ...

13. REPRESSION : AWARENESS :: _____ : _____
   A. passivity : activity B. sleep : dream
   C. forget : remember D. coma : comatose
   E. unconscious : conscious
                      13. ...

14. PREDISPOSITION : RELATIONSHIP :: _____ : _____
   A. prepossession : prediction B. atom : combination
                      14. ...

C. impartiality : partiality D. predilection : affinity
E. affiliation : preponderance

15. STORM : HURRICANE :: _____ : _____   15. ...
A. disease : germ B. fear : panic C. ship : sank
D. courage : hero E. solitude : hermit

16. SUPPLY : DEMAND :: _____ : _____   16. ...
A. cost : market B. price : value C. wholesale : retail
D. net : worth E. tax : article

17. CAMOUFLAGE : GUERRILLA :: _____ : _____   17. ...
A. radar : instrument B. painter : anonymity
C. cocoon : butterfly D. costume : masquerader
E. color : ship

18. LENS : CAMERA :: _____ : _____   18. ...
A. toe : foot B. beacon : lighthouse C. eye : mind
D. head : body E. vision : thought

19. CRUTCHES : MOVEMENT :: _____ : _____   19. ...
A. windows : houses B. defect : myopic
C. glasses : vision D. teeth : braces
E. telescope : astronomer

20. MILES : AUTOMOBILES :: _____ : _____   20. ...
A. sea : fathoms B. suits : divers C. knots : ships
D. gasoline : aeroplane E. milligram : gram

21. NOMINATION : CONVENTION :: _____ : _____   21. ...
A. judge : sentence B. panel : member C. verdict : jury
D. criminal : crime E. policeman : arrest

22. FACET : GEM :: _____ : _____   22. ...
A. intelligence : test B. father : son
C. brilliance : genius D. heredity : environment
E. constellation : star

23. ABSTRUSE : OBTUSE :: _____ : _____   23. ...
A. concave : convex B. erudition : profundity
C. dull : translucent D. abstract : realistic
E. recondite : opaque

24. TURNSTILE : SUBWAY :: _____ : _____   24. ...
A. ticket : aeroplane B. price : goods C. desk : office
D. door : taxicab E. porthole : ship

25. CAGE : CANARY :: _____ : _____   25. ...
A. walls : jail B. warden : prison C. cell : inmate
D. jungle : lion E. patient : hospital

TEST 2

1. PSEUDONYM : ASSUMED NAME :: _____ : _____   1. ...
A. nomenclature : title B. appellation : given name
C. nom de plume : pen name D. surname : first name
E. title : aristocrat

2. PECK : BUSHEL :: _____ : _____   2. ...
A. dram : ton B. rod : pound C. gill : fathom
D. gallon : cord E. ounce : inch

3. ABDICATE : KING :: _____ : _____   3. ...
A. track : train B. derail : engineer C. execute : warden
D. crash : aeroplane E. revolution : anarchist

4. SECURE : WITHDRAW :: _____ : _____   4. ...
A. anchor : anchorite B. ship : mausoleum C. sailor : salacious
D. secrete : drop E. article : manufacturer

2

5. MATHEMATICAL : VERBAL :: _____ : _____   5. ...
    A. numbers : equation   B. quotient : proportion
    C. ratio : analogy   D. fraction : word
    E. computation : anagram

6. SEASONING : THYME :: _____ : _____   6. ...
    A. space : season B. hybrid : herb C. measure : mite
    D. predict : plant E. time : season

7. VOLATILE : TACITURN :: _____ : _____   7. ...
    A. planet : position   B. mercurial : saturnine
    C. Mercury : Saturn D. mood : fluid C. undependable : stolid

8. HEAD : AX :: _____ : _____   8. ...
    A. pine : cone B. close : call C. cylinder : engine
    D. chair : rung E. angle : line

9. BEAM : SEARCHLIGHT :: _____ : _____   9. ...
    A. tank : oil B. flame : welder C. torch : fire
    D. film : projector   E. forest : timber

10. CONSPIRE : CABAL :: _____ : _____   10. ...
    A. scheme : expedite   B. contrivance : contrive
    C. machinate : plot   D. conspiracy : intrigue
    E. object : plan

11. LAW : PROMULGATION :: _____ : _____   11. ...
    A. voting : election   B. interview : census
    C. decision : declaration D. battle : war E. idea : action

12. MEMBER : SOCIETY :: _____ : _____   12. ...
    A. molecule : amoeba   B. growth : osmosis
    C. cell : organism D. disease : parasite E. leg : foot

13. HIPPOCRATIC OATH : PHYSICIAN :: _____ : _____   13. ...
    A. fealty : fief   B. citizenship : alien
    C. allegiance : citizen   D. contract : marriage
    E. covenant : treaty

14. SKIS : SNOW :: _____ : _____   14. ...
    A. cork : water B. rain : umbrellas C. clouds : sky
    D. shoes : feet E. parachutes : air

15. TASTE : SMELL :: _____ : _____   15. ...
    A. touch : hand B. sight : hearing C. ears : eyes
    D. hearing aid : eyeglasses   E. aural : oral

16. SORCERY : PRESTIDIGITATOR :: _____ : _____   16. ...
    A. magic : demonology   B. witchcraft : entomologist
    C. conjure : spirit   D. astrology : astrologist
    E. fetishism : palmist

17. YOUTH : IMPULSIVE :: _____ : _____   17. ...
    A. juvenile : puerile   B. characteristic : degree
    C. adolescence : childhood D. soil : erosion
    E. age : senile

18. SATISFACTION : DISQUIETUDE :: _____ : _____   18. ...
    A. chaos : satisfaction   B. doubt : security
    C. dissatisfaction : friction
    D. civilization : jungle E. complacent : restive

19. GASLIGHT : ELECTRICITY :: _____ : _____   19. ...
    A. jet : aeroplane B. fiction : science C. loud : gift
    C. obsolete : extant   E. horse : carriage

20. HYPOTHETICAL : FORMULATED :: _____ : _____   20. ...
    A. method : science   B. irrational : deranged
    C. insanity : sanity   D. vagary : rationality
    E. animal : machine

21. OATH : PERJURY :: _____ : _____   21. ...
    A. truth : oath B. perfidy : imposture C. promise : renege
    D. inviolability : swear E. inaccuracy : falsity
                                                                         22. ...
22. PROSAIC : AESTHETIC :: _____ : _____
    A. dull : beautiful B. lethargic : ambitious
    C. behavior : feeling D. humorous : brilliant
    E. judicious : sensitivity
23. OPERATION : SURGEON :: _____ : _____   23. ...
    A. philately : necromancer B. student : study
    C. pyromaniac : fire D. embezzlement : thief
    E. murderer : homicide
24. BEIGE : BROWN :: _____ : _____   24. ...
    A. primary : secondary B. hue : value
    C. shade : color D. yellow : gold E. red : pink
25. CLOTH : DESIGNER :: _____ : _____   25. ...
    A. clay : model B. statue : sculptor C. brush : palette
    D. paint : artist E. painting : canvas

TEST 3

1. RUPEE : INDIA :: _____ : _____   1. ...
    A. peseta : Cuba B. drachma : Hong Kong
    C. escudo : Spain D. franc : France
    E. krona : Czechoslavakia
2. REDUCTION : REMOVAL :: _____ : _____
    A. abate : abstruse B. dwindle : inattentive
    C. decree : summarize D. diminution : difficult
    E. contraction : abstraction
3. STYLIZED : FACTUAL :: _____ : _____   3. ...
    A. question : fact B. abstract : equation
    C. rhetorical : pragmatical D. florid : dogma
    E. doctrinaire : philosophy
4. REFLECTOR : SIGHT :: _____ : _____   4. ...
    A. color wheel : rotation B. vision : eyeglasses
    C. mirror : image D. compendium : exhibit
    E. spectrum : spectacles
5. GENE : GENDER :: _____ : _____   5. ...
    A. corporeal : body B. paper : wood
    C. factor : characteristic D. composition : author
    E. ventricle : heart
6. STRONGHOLD : MUNICIPALITY :: _____ : _____   6. ...
    A. state : capital B. citadel : city C. fortress : command
    D. protected : protector E. strategic : locale
7. HYDROGEN : WATER :: _____ : _____   7. ...
    A. organic : compound B. dextrose : glucose
    C. coal : carbon D. liquid : solid E. pure : impure
8. ARRAY : MEDITATION :: _____ : _____   8. ...
    A. image : idea B. spectrum : speculation
    C. varying : thought D. sequence : continuous
    E. reflecting : reflect
9. BUDDHISM : MOHAMMEDANISM :: _____ : _____   9. ...
    A. Islamic : Utopia B. Hindu : Arabian
    C. heaven : center D. nirvana : mecca E. fantasy : reality
10. NOTICE : APPEASE :: _____ : _____   10. ...
    A. pacific : pacify B. placard : placate

  C. poster : propaganda   D. agreement : compromise
  E. place : please

11. WEEK : MONTH :: _____ : _____   11. ...
    A. month : day   B. foot : inch   C. hour : clock
    D. vacation : holiday   E. Sunday : July

12. CANOE : RIVER :: _____ : _____   12. ...
    A. element : vehicle B. ride : winter C. ice : skate
    D. sleigh : snow   E. hounds : ranger

13. MINERAL : REPTILE :: _____ : _____   13. ...
    A. lizard : lair B. ocean : amphibian C. stone : snake
    D. mummy : body   E. water : goldfish

14. MAN : BEE :: _____ : _____   14. ...
    A. domestic : habitat   B. abode : hiatus
    C. domicile : hive D. ant : hill E. sanctuary : wilderness

15. PATIENT : PHYSICIAN :: _____ : _____   15. ...
    A. jury : judge B. audience : actor C. client : attorney
    D. customer : store   E. adviser : advised

16. PIANO : SCALE :: _____ : _____   16. ...
    A. violin : music   B. range : singer
    C. instrument : octave D. one : seven E. stanza : poem

17. MAN : BROTHER :: _____ : _____   17. ...
    A. death : dishonor B. homicide : fratricide
    C. father : son   D. murder : man   E. child : murder

18. ARM : HEAD :: _____ : _____   18. ...
    A. leg : temple   B. brain : foot   C. hole : bullet
    D. head : neck   E. break : concussion

19. SEW : CLOTH :: _____ : _____   19. ...
    A. staple : machine   B. sharpener : pencil
    C. stamp : letter D. clip : paper   E. stamp : mail

20. PAPER : BODY :: _____ : _____   20. ...
    A. break : crack B. arm : cast   C. bruise : heal
    D. tear : wound   E. rip : mend

21. PLUCK : CHICKEN :: _____ : _____   21. ...
    A. wood : fire   B. goat : milk   C. skin : snake
    D. fur : bear   E. feather : ostrich

22. SAIL : BOAT :: _____ : _____   22. ...
    A. pinwheel : toy B. pilot : controls C. wing : aeroplane
    D. fender : automobile E. ski shoes : skis

23. VIBRATION : LIGHT :: _____ : _____   23. ...
    A. sound : reflection   B. symphony : color wheel
    C. intensity : pitch   D. music : color
    E. rhyme : harmony

24. REBELLION : GOVERNMENT :: _____ : _____   24. ...
    A. motion : meeting   B. discord : partisan
    C. dissent : group   D. disbanding : party
    E. commitment : withdrawl

25. GREGARIOUSNESS : ASCETICISM :: _____ : _____   25. ...
    A. denial : acceptance   B. austere : sensuous
    C. monastery : monk   D. conviviality : seclusion
    E. secluded : remote

TEST 4

1. BURY : DISINTER :: _____ : _____   1. ...
    A. inhale : exhale   B. inhume : exhume

C. corporeal : spirit   D. autopsy : funeral
E. burial : cremation

2. INVOLUNTARY : VOLUNTARY :: _____ : _____   2. ...
   A. criminal : soldier B. export : import C. illegal : legal
   D. deportation : expatriation E. punishment : crime

3. IGNITE : FIRE :: _____ : _____   3. ...
   A. water : flood B. ax : tree   C. incite : revolt
   D. mass : riot E. flame : gasoline

4. LEDGER : BOOKKEEPER _____ : _____   4. ...
   A. fort : cavalry   B. compass : direction
   C. log : captain   D. deck : crew
   E. biography : historian

5. SPACE : TIME :: _____ : _____   5. ...
   A. locale : situation   B. geography : history
   C. navigation : course   D. individual : ancestry
   E. dimension : depth

6. STRAITS : GIBRALTAR :: _____ : _____   6. ...
   A. island : coast B. ocean : Atlantic C. peninsula : Malta
   D. cape : Africa E. Danube : river

7. HERD : CATTLE :: _____ : _____   7. ...
   A. sled : snow   B. team : dogs   C. race : horse
   D. people : group E. sheep : flock

8. ELECT : GOVERNOR :: _____ : _____   8. ...
   A. office : appoint   B. administer : administration
   C. position : order   D. inauguration : president
   E. deputize : deputy

9. COMBINATION : SAFE :: _____ : _____   9. ...
   A. raise : window B. key : door   C. nail : picture
   D. hanger : coat E. latch : key

10. SALT : SHAKER :: _____ : _____   10. ...
    A. minute : time B. bottle : milk C. sand : hourglass
    D. sun dial : sun E. ship : ocean

11. STORY : SENTENCE :: _____ : _____   11. ...
    A. poem : rhyme   B. chant : paean   C. hymn : note
    D. brushstroke : painting   E. song : music

12. LOOSE : DISCIPLINE :: _____ : _____   12. ...
    A. lazy : perfect   B. individual : political
    C. dinner : banquet   D. order : disorder
    E. lax : protocol

13. CREST : CLAN :: _____ : _____   13. ...
    A. judge : robe   B. road : sign   C. insignia : army
    D. fairy : wand   E. king : scepter

14. PENULTIMATE : ULTIMATE :: _____ : _____   14. ...
    A. among : between   B. first : second
    C. perfect : excellent   D. better : best
    E. more : many

15. WORSEN : WITHDRAW :: _____ : _____   15. ...
    A. regress : egress B. down : up C. fantasy : reality
    D. swing : gate   E. retrogress : digress

16. CEREMONY : CORRECT :: _____ : _____   16. ...
    A. manner : might B. rite : right C. kinsman : kind
    C. inauguration : irate   E. sworn : swerve

17. CHALLENGE : CONTEST :: _____ : _____   17. ...
    A. sprint : pistol B. fencing : sport C. hat : ring
    D. insult : duel   E. sword : rapier

6

18. WORM : SNAKE :: _____ : _____
    A. shark : whale B. lion : tamer   C. cat : mouse
    D. cat : panther E. shark : carnivorous

19. INDIFFERENCE : UNDERSTANDING :: _____ : _____
    A. sympathy : identification B. peasant : worker
    C. apathy : empathy   D. peon : peonage
    E. happiness : sadness

20. INCIPIENT : RUDIMENTARY :: _____ : _____
    A. disappearing : appearing B. plant : seed
    C. inchoate : embryonic   D. unknown : unseen
    E. death : birth

21. SEASONING : HERB :: _____ : _____
    A. saccharine : sugar   B. candy : dextrose
    C. condiment : thyme   D. synthetic : genuine
    E. natural : manufactured

22. SIMULATED : GENUINE :: _____ : _____
    A. semi-precious : precious B. bullion : gold
    C. pretense : fraud   D. rhinestone : diamond
    E. private : general

23. FLOWER : PETAL :: _____ : _____
    A. sprout : potato B. seed : plant C. tree : branch
    D. root : earth   E. moss : stone

24. DESERT : OCEAN :: _____ : _____
    A. illness : death B. parch : thirst C. abundance : surfeit
    D. suffocation : evaporation   E. dehydrate : drown

25. STANZA : CHAPTER :: _____ : _____
    A. art : fiction B. meter : rhyme C. narration : style
    D. poetry : prose E. clause : sentence

TEST 5

1. DOGMATIC : VACILLATORY :: _____ : _____
    A. absolute : relative B. all : few C. certain : decisive
    D. affinity : infinity   E. pure : contaminated

2. LINE : CURVE :: _____ : _____
    A. perimeter : parallel B. hypotenuse : rectangle
    C. earth : equator   D. diameter : circumference
    E. semi-circle : circle

3. BOWL : BALL :: _____ : _____
    A. up : down   B. hemisphere : globe
    C. concave : convex   D. earth : cave
    E. bulging and curved : hollow and curved

4. WIND : CYCLONE :: _____ : _____
    A. river : ocean B. exhaust : fume C. suffocate : drown
    D. water : deluge   E. pressure : atmosphere

5. LION : JUNGLE :: _____ : _____
    A. faun : deer   B. plant : flower C. fauna : flora
    D. seaweed : octopus   E. cow : milk

6. SUBTERRANEAN : SURFACE :: _____ : _____
    A. road : sea B. league : fathom C. ship : car
    D. depth : distance   E. diver : driver

7. IMPASSIVE : INFLATED :: _____ : _____
    A. pain : noise   B. enthusiasm : exuberance
    C. stoical : bombastic   D. mediocre : outstanding
    E. hermit : pedant

7

8. PRODUCT : MULTIPLICATION :: _____ : _____   8. ...
    A. multiplication : table B. add : arithmetic
    C. part : whole D. words : sentence E. sum : addition
9. DECIMAL : COMMA :: _____ : _____   9. ...
    A. sum : fraction B. number : word C. letter : fraction
    D. period : sentence E. clause : ratio
10. ANARCHIST : PATRIOT :: _____ : _____   10. ...
    A. iconoclast : chauvinist B. agnostic : heretic
    C. soldier : revolutionary D. topple : government
    E. Loyalist : Tory
11. SPEED : SOUND :: _____ : _____   11. ...
    A. linear : dimension B. fathom : ocean C. time : hour
    D. velocity : light E. force : gravity
12. SUBURB : CITY :: _____ : _____   12. ...
    A. peasant : peon B. prince : pauper
    C. provincial : urban D. capital : state
    E. town : country
13. VELOCITY : WIND :: _____ : _____   13. ...
    A. economy : gross national product
    B. element : temperament C. variable : constant
    D. same : change E. fluctuation : rate
14. WIRE : TELEPHONE :: _____ : _____   14. ...
    A. refrigerator : freezer B. bookcase : book
    C. telephone : dial D. bureau : drawer
    E. ribbon : typewriter
15. TRAIN : DEPOT :: _____ : _____   15. ...
    A. cow : barn B. traveler : destination
    C. baseball : home plate D. bus : terminal
    E. field : hangar

KEYS (CORRECT ANSWERS)

TEST 1		TEST 2		TEST 3		TEST 4		TEST 5	
1.	D	1.	C	1.	D	1.	B	1.	A
2.	D	2.	A	2.	E	2.	D	2.	D
3.	E	3.	B	3.	C	3.	C	3.	C
4.	C	4.	A	4.	E	4.	C	4.	D
5.	D	5.	C	5.	C	5.	B	5.	C
6.	E	6.	E	6.	B	6.	B	6.	E
7.	C	7.	B	7.	B	7.	B	7.	C
8.	C	8.	C	8.	B	8.	E	8.	E
9.	B	9.	D	9.	D	9.	B	9.	B
10.	D	10.	C	10.	B	10.	C	10.	A
11.	D	11.	C	11.	E	11.	C	11.	D
12.	C	12.	C	12.	D	12.	E	12.	C
13.	E	13.	C	13.	C	13.	C	13.	C
14.	D	14.	E	14.	C	14.	D	14.	E
15.	B	15.	B	15.	C	15.	A	15.	D
16.	B	16.	D	16.	C	16.	B		
17.	D	17.	E	17.	B	17.	D		
18.	C	18.	E	18.	E	18.	D		
19.	C	19.	D	19.	D	19.	C		
20.	C	20.	D	20.	D	20.	C		
21.	C	21.	C	21.	C	21.	C		
22.	C	22.	A	22.	C	22.	D		
23.	E	23.	D	23.	D	23.	C		
24.	D	24.	C	24.	C	24.	E		
25.	C	25.	D	25.	D	25.	D		

READING COMPREHENSION
PROBLEM SOLVING TECHNIQUES

1. Identify the type of question
   A. Basic information questions (easy)
   B. Inferential questions (hard)
   C. Vocabulary in context (easy)

2. Underline or circle key words in question.

   The author's main purpose is apparently to
      A. <u>criticize</u> present methods of helping the poor
      B. <u>discuss</u> various types of power and how they can be used by the poor
      C. <u>describe</u> the various causes of poverty
      D. <u>propose</u> a way in which the poor can be more effectively helped
      E. <u>describe</u> the psychological and social effects of power

   The primary purpose of the passage is to
      A. <u>expose</u> those who support government anti-poverty programs
      B. <u>distinguish</u> between the pre- and post-Second World War poor
      C. <u>argue</u> for social investment by the federal government to alleviate poverty
      D. <u>reveal</u> the practices of society that perpetuate poverty
      E. <u>distinguish</u> among the first, second, and third New Deal approaches to reducing unemployment

   The information in the passage suggests that the author is most likely
      A. <u>an historian</u> who is concerned about the validity of his sources
      B. <u>a Chicano</u> who is interested in bringing the Chicanos together
      C. a literary <u>critic</u> who questions the conclusions of historians
      D. <u>an educator</u> primarily concerned with the future of Chicano children
      E. <u>a researcher</u> who is interested in discovering new facts about the Mexican Indians

3. With two word answers, focus on the second word
   Example:

   The author's attitude toward Aristotle's writings is best described as one of
      A. unqualified <u>endorsement</u>   B. apologetic <u>approval</u>
      C. analytical <u>objectivity</u>   D. skeptical <u>reserve</u>
      E. scholarly <u>dissatisfaction</u>

The tone of Josephy's statement about the location of
Aztlan can best be described as one of
   A. apologetic <u>regret</u>   B. disguised <u>irony</u>
   C. cautious <u>speculation</u>   D. <u>dramatic revelation</u>
   E. philosophical <u>resignation</u>

4. Mark up the passage underlining important sections, words or
    sentences so that you can look back at the circled markings
    as you answer the questions. Be careful not to mark up too
    much or it will not help.

5. You should skim the questions and select the ones you can
    answer quickly. Then go back to find the ones you still want
    to answer. Do not jump from passage to passage because you
    will waste time rereading the passage in order to answer
    questions.

6. Choose the reading selection you are most comfortable with
    to do first. Be careful about matching your answers with the
    number on the answer sheet. Remember this is especially
    important when you skip questions.

7. Notes on some types of questions
    A. ATTITUDE - Answer will be usually positive or negative
    B. TONE - Ethnic passages are almost always inspirational or
       positive
    C. GENERAL STYLE - Never choose answers with these words:
       indifferent, apathetic, ambivalent, dogmatic
    D. MAIN IDEAS FOR FACTUAL PASSAGE - to discuss; to describe
    E. MAIN IDEAS FOR OPINION PASSAGE - to argue; to urge; to
       present; to propose
    F. MAIN IDEAS FOR FICTION PASSAGE - to portray; to present;
       to describe

Recognizing Inference Questions

    This exercise has a series of inference questions following
a reading passage. Read the passage and answer the questions that
follow. Circle the letter of the BEST response, and then write,
in the space provided, the supporting evidence that led you to that
answer.

       A flash of bright blue in the green depths of the
     piney woods caught the eye of wildlife biologist Hilbert
     Siegler of the Texas Game Commission. Then a second spot
     of blue stirred as another jay sailed on silent wings to
(5)   the same branch. The newcomer, holding a morsel of food
     in its beak, hopped closer to the first bird. Turning
     eagerly, the first jay lifted its crested head and accepted
     hungrily the gift its visitor poked down into its throat.
       Siegler was astonished. In fledgling season, young
(10) birds often continue coaxing food from their parents even
     after they have grown up; in courting season bird swains

often bestow dainties upon the females they are wooing. But this wasn't the season for fledglings, nor was it courting time. This was the dead of winter.

Hastily the wildlife expert raised his binoculars and got the answer. The recipient of the bounty was an adult jay, a grizzled veteran. The lower mandible of its beak had been broken off nearly at the base. It had no way to pick up its food.

(20)   This impulse to share and cooperate is familiarly awakened in creatures of the wild by members of their immediate families. But here seemed to be something close to the human ideal of sharing.

Nature's creatures often exhibit impulses of self-
(25) assertion and competition. But all through life's vast range, these instincts are balanced by another kind of drive. Nature does not implant in her children just the single message: *Take care of yourself*. There is a second ancient and universal injunction: *Get together*.
(30) It is as vital as the breath of life.

1. What do you think made Hilbert Siegler go into the piney woods with his binoculars?
      A. He liked walking.
      B. It was a nice day.
      C. It was part of his job.
      D. He wanted to get away.

    Supporting evidence:_____

2. It can be inferred from the information in the second paragraph that Siegler
      A. is familiar with the habits of wildlife
      B. thinks jays are interesting to watch
      C. is hopelessly puzzled by the actions of birds
      D. has little curiosity

    Supporting evidence:_____

3. The fourth paragraph suggests that the author of the passage
      A. disapproves of the birds' behavior described in the first paragraph
      B. thinks blue jays have little regard for each other
      C. regards most interpretations of animal behavior with suspicion
      D. admires what Hilbert Siegler saw the birds doing

    Supporting evidence:_____

4. From the incident described, the author concludes that
      A. nature is based on competition
      B. the laws of nature are not yet fully understood
      C. the laws of nature allow for competition and cooperation
      D. nature favors the strongest

    Supporting evidence:_____

READING COMPREHENSION
UNDERSTANDING AND INTERPRETING WRITTEN MATERIAL

STRATEGIES

Surveying Passages, Sentences as Cues

While individual readers develop unique reading styles and skills, there are some known strategies which can assist any reader in improving his or her reading comprehension and performance on the reading subtest. These strategies include understanding how single paragraphs and entire passages are structured, how the ideas in them are ordered, and how the author of the passage has connected these ideas in a logical and sequential way for the reader.

The section that follows highlights the importance of reading a passage through once for meaning, and provides instruction on careful reading for context cues within the sentences before and after the missing word.

SURVEY THE ENTIRE PASSAGE

To get a sense of the topic and the organization of ideas in a passage, it is important to survey each passage initially in its entirety and to identify the main idea. (The first sentence of a paragraph usually states the main idea.) Do not try to fill in the blanks initially. The purpose of surveying a passage is to prepare for the more careful reading which will follow. You need a sense of the big picture before you start to fill in the details; for example, a quick survey of the passage on page 12, indicates that the topic is the early history of universities. The paragraphs are organized to provide information on the origin of the first universities, the associations formed by teachers and students, the early curriculum, and graduation requirements.

READ PRECEDING SENTENCES CAREFULLY

The missing words in a passage cannot be determined by reading and understanding only the sentences in which the deletions occur. Information from the sentences which precede or follow can provide important cues to determine the correct choice. For example, if you read the first sentence from the passage about universities which contains a blank, you will notice that all the alternatives make sense if this one sentence is read in isolation:

Nobody actually _____ them.

8. A. started
    C. blamed
    E. remembered

    B. guarded
    D. compared

The only way that you can make the correct word choice is to read the preceding sentences. In the excerpt below, notice that the first sentence tells the reader what the passage will be about: how universities developed. A key word in the first sentence is *emerged*, which is closely related in meaning to one of the five choices for the first blank. The second sentence explains the key word, *emerged*, by pointing out that we have no historical record of a decree or a date indicating when the first university was established. Understanding the ideas in the first two sentences makes it possible to select the correct word for the blank. Look at the sentence with the deleted word in the context of the preceding sentences and think about why you are now able to make the correct choice.

The first universities emerged at the end of the 11th century and beginning of the 12th. These institutions were not founded on any particular date or created by any formal action. Nobody actually _____ them.

8. A. started   B. guarded
    C. blamed   D. compared
    E. remembered

Started is the best choice because it fits the main idea of the passage and is closely related to the key word *emerged*.

READ THE SENTENCE WHICH FOLLOWS TO VERIFY YOUR CHOICE

The sentences which follow the one from which a word has been deleted may also provide cues to the correct choice. For example, look at an excerpt from the passage about universities again, and consider how the sentence which follows the one with the blank helps to reinforce the choice of the word, *started*.

The first universities emerged at the end of the 11th century and the beginning of the 12th. These institutions were not founded on any particular date or created by any formal action. Nobody actually _____ them. Instead, they developed gradually in places like Paris, Oxford, and Bologna, where scholars had long been teaching students.

1. A. started   B. guarded
    C. blamed   D. compared
    E. remembered

The words, *developed gradually*, mean the same as the key word, *emerged*. The signal word, *instead*, helps to distinguish the difference between starting on a specific date as a result of some particular act or event and emerging over a period of time as a result of various factors.

Here is another example of how the sentence which follows the one from which a word is deleted might help you decide which of two good alternatives is the correct choice. This excerpt is from the practice passage about bridges (page 11).

> Bridges are built to allow a continuous flow of highway and railway traffic across water lying in their paths. But engineers cannot forget that river traffic, too, is essential to our economy. The role of _____ is important. To keep these vessels moving freely, bridges are built big enough, when possible, to let them pass underneath.

   1. A. wind   B. boats
        C. weight   D. wires
        E. experiences

After the first two sentences, the reader may be uncertain about the direction the writer intended to take in the rest of the paragraph. If the writer intended to continue the paragraph with information concerning how engineers make choices about the relative importance and requirements of land traffic and river traffic, *experience* might be the appropriate choice for the missing word. However, the sentence following the one in which the deletion occurs makes it clear that *boats* is the correct choice. It provides the synonym *vessels*, which in the noun phrase *these vessels* must refer back to the previous sentence or sentences. The phrase *to let them pass underneath* also helps make it clear that *boats* is the appropriate choice. *Them* refers back to *these vessels* which, in turn, refers back to *boats* when the word *boats* is placed in the previous sentence. Thus, the reader may use these cohesive ties (the pronoun referents) to verify the final choice.

Even when the text following a sentence with a deletion is not necessary to choose the best alternative, it may be helpful in other ways. Specifically, complete sentences provide important transitions into a related topic which is developed in the rest of the paragraph or in the next paragraph of the same passage. For example, the first paragraph in the passage about universities ends with a sentence which introduces the term *guilds*: *But, over time, they joined together to form guilds.* Prior to this sentence, information about the slow emergence of universities and about how independently scholars had acted was introduced. The next paragraph begins with two sentences about guilds in general. Someone who had not read the last sentence in the first paragraph might have missed the link between guilds and scholars and universities and, thus, might have been unnecessarily confused.

Cohesive Ties As Cues

Sentences in a paragraph may be linked together by several devices called cohesive ties. Attention to these ties may provide further cues about missing words. This section will describe the different types of cohesive ties and show how attention to them can help you to select the correct word.

PERSONAL PRONOUNS

Personal pronouns (e.g., he, she, they, it, its) are often used in adjoining sentences to refer back to an already mentioned person, place, thing, or idea. The word to which the pronoun refers is called the antecedent.

Tools used in farm work changed very slowly from ancient times to the eighteenth century, and the changes were minor. Since the eighteenth century *they* have changed quickly and dramatically.

The word *they* refers back to *tools* in the example above.

In the examination reading subtest, a deleted word sometimes occurs in a sentence in which the sentence subject is a pronoun that refers back to a previously mentioned noun. You must correctly identify the referent for the particular pronoun in order to interpret the sentence and select the correct answer. Here is an example from the passage about bridges.

An ingenious engineer designed the bridge so that it did not have to be raised above traffic. Instead it was _____.

7. A. burned   B. emptied
    C. secured   D. shared
    E. lowered

Q. What is the antecedent of *it* in both cases in the example?

A. The antecedent, of course, is *bridge*.

DEMONSTRATIVE PRONOUNS

Demonstrative pronouns (e.g., this, that, these) are also used to refer to a specific, previously mentioned noun. They may occur alone as noun replacements, or they may accompany and modify nouns.

I like jogging, swimming, and tennis. *These* are the only sports I enjoy.

In the sentence above, the word *these* is a replacement noun. However, demonstrative pronouns may also occur as adjectives modifying nouns.

I like jogging, swimming, and tennis. *These* sports are the only ones I enjoy.

The word *these* in the example above is an adjective modifier. The word *these* in each of the two previous examples refers to *jogging*, *swimming*, and *tennis*.

Here is an example from the passage about universities on page 12.

Undergraduates took classes in Greek philosophy, Latin grammar, arithmetic, music, and astronomy. These were the only _____ available.

12.　A. rooms　　　　　B. subjects
　　　C. clothes　　　　D. pens
　　　E. company

Q.　Which word is a noun replacement?
A.　The word *these* is the replacement noun for *Greek philosophy, Latin grammar, arithmetic, music,* and *astronomy.*

Here is another example from the same passage.

The concept of a fixed program of study leading to a degree first evolved in Medieval Europe. This _____ had not appeared before.

14.　A. idea　　　　　B. desk
　　　C. library　　　D. capital

Q.　What is the antecedent of *this*?
A.　The antecedent is *the concept of a fixed program of study leading to a degree.*

COMPARATIVE ADJECTIVES AND ADVERBS

When comparative adjectives or adverbs (e.g., so, such, better, more) occur, they refer to something else in the passage, otherwise a comparison could not be made.

The hotels in the city were all full; so were the motels and boarding houses.

Q.　To what in the first sentence does the word *so* refer?
A.　*So* tells us to compare the *motels* and *boarding houses* to the *hotels in the city.*

Q.　In what way are the *hotels, motels,* and *boarding houses* similar to each other?
A.　The *hotels, motels,* and *boarding houses* are similar in that they were all *full.*

Look at an example from the passage about universities.

Guilds were groups of tradespeople, somewhat akin to modern trade unions. In the Middle Ages, all the crafts had such _____.

3.　A. taxes　　　　　B. secrets
　　　C. products　　　D. problems
　　　E. organizations

Q. To what in the first sentence does the word *such* refer?
A. *Such* refers to *groups of tradespeople*.

SUBSTITUTIONS

Substitution is another form of cohesive tie. A substitution occurs when one linguistic item (e.g., a noun) is replaced by another. Sometimes the substitution provides new or contrasting information. The substitution is not identical to the original, or antecedent, idea. A frequently occurring substitution involves the use of *one*. A noun substitution may involve another member of the same class as the original one.

My car is falling apart. I need a new one.

Q. What in the first sentence is replaced in the second sentence with *one*?
A. *One* is a substitute for the specific car mentioned in the first sentence. The contrast comes from the fact that the *new one* isn't the writer's current car.

The substitution may also pinpoint a specific member of a general class.

1. There are many unusual courses available at the university this summer. The *one* I am taking is called *Death and Dying*.

2. There are many unusual courses available at the university this summer. *Some* have never been offered before.

Q. In these examples, what is the general class in the first sentence that is replaced by *one* and by *some*?
A. In both cases the words *one* and *some* replace *many unusual courses*.

SYNONYMS

Synonyms are words that have similar meaning. In the examination reading subtest, a synonym of a deleted word is sometimes found in one of the sentences before and/or after the sentence with the deletion. Examine the following excerpt from the passage about bridges again.

But engineers cannot forget that river traffic, too, is essential to our economy. The role of _____ is important. To keep these vessels moving freely, bridges are built high enough, when possible, to let them pass underneath.

8. A. wind   B. boats
     C. weight   D. wires
     E. experience

Q. Can you identify synonyms in the sentences, before and after the sentence containing the deletion, which are cues to the correct deleted word?

A. If you identified the correct words, you probably noticed that *river traffic* is not exactly a synonym, since it is a slightly more general term than the word *boats* (the correct choice). But the word *vessels* is a direct synonym. Demonstrative pronouns (this, that, these, those) are sometimes used as modifiers for synonymous nouns in sentences which follow those containing deletions. The word *these* in *these vessels* is the demonstrative pronoun (modifier) for the synonymous noun *vessels*.

ANTONYMS

Antonyms are words of opposite meaning. In the examination reading subtest passages, antonyms may be cues for missing words. A contrasting relationship, which calls for the use of an antonym, is often signaled by the connective words *instead, however, but,* etc. Look at an excerpt from the passage about bridges.

An ingenious engineer designed the bridge so that it did not have to be raised above traffic. Instead it was _____.

    7. A. burned   B. emptied
        C. secured   D. shared
        E. lowered

Q. Can you identify an antonym in the first sentence for one of the five alternatives?

A. The word *raised* is an antonym for the word *lowered*.

SUPERORDINATE-SUBORDINATE WORDS

In the examination reading subtest, a passage sometimes contains a general term which provides a cue that a more specific term is the appropriate alternative. At other times, the passage may contain a specific term which provides cues that a general term is the appropriate alternative for a particular deletion. The general and more specific words are said to have superordinate-subordinate relationships.

Look at example 1 below. The more specific word *boy* in the first sentence serves as the antecedent for the more general word *child* in the second sentence. In example 2, the relationship is reversed. In both examples, the words *child* and *boy* reflect a superordinate-subordinate relationship.

    1. The *boy* climbed the tree. Then the *child* fell.
    2. The *child* climbed the tree. Then the *boy* fell.

In the practice passage about bridges on page 11, the phrase *river traffic* is a general term that is superordinate to the alternative *boats* (item 1). Later in the passage about bridges the following sentences also contain superordinate-subordinate words:

A lift bridge was desired, but there were wartime shortages of steel and machinery needed for the towers. It was hard to find enough _____.

6.   A. work   B. material
      C. time   D. power
      E. space

Q. Can you identify two words in the first sentence that are specific examples for the correct response in the second sentence?

A. Of course, the words *steel* and *machinery* are the specific examples for the more general term *material*.

WORDS ASSOCIATED BY ENTAILMENT

Sometimes the concept described by one word within the context of the passage entails, or implies, the concept described by another word. For example, consider again item 7 in the practice passage about bridges. Notice how the follow-up sentence to item 7 provides a cue to the correct response.

An ingenious engineer designed the bridge so that it did not have to be raised above traffic. Instead it was _____. It could be submerged seven meters below the surface of the river.

7.   A. burned   B. emptied
      C. secured   D. shared
      E. lowered

Q. What word in the sentence after the blank implies the concept of an alternative?

A. *Submerged* implies *lowered*. The concept of submerging something implies the idea of lowering the object beneath the surface of the water.

WORDS ASSOCIATED BY PART-WHOLE RELATIONSHIPS

Words may be related because they involve part of a whole and the whole itself; for example, *nose* and *face*. Words may also be related because they involve two parts of the same whole; for example, *radiator* and *muffler* both refer to parts of a car.

The captain of the ship was nervous. The storm was becoming worse and worse. The hardened man paced the _____.

      A. floor   B. hall
      C. deck   D. court

Q. Which choice has a part-whole relationship with a word in the sentences above?

A. A *deck* is a part of a *ship*. Therefore, *deck* has a part-whole relationship with *ship*.

CONJUNCTIVE AND CONNECTIVE WORDS AND PHRASES

Conjunctions or connectives are words or phrases that connect parts of sentences or parts of a passage to each other. Their purpose is to help the reader understand the logical and conceptual relationships between ideas and events within a passage. Examples of these words and phrases include coordinate conjunctions (e.g., and, but, yet), subordinate conjunctions (e.g., because, although, since, after), and other connective words and phrases (e.g, too, also, on the other hand, as a result).

Listed below are types of logical relationships expressed by conjunctive, or connective words. Also listed are examples of words used to cue relationships to the reader.

Additive and comparative words and phrases: and, in addition to, too, also, furthermore, similarly

Adversative and contrastive words and phrases: yet, though, only, but, however, instead, rather, on the other hand, in contrast, conversely

Causal words or phrases: so, therefore, because, as a result, if...then, unless, except, in that case, under the circumstances

Temporal words and phrases: before, after, when, while, initially, lastly, finally, until.

Examples

1. I enjoy fast-paced sports like tennis and volleyball, but my brother prefers _____ sports.

   A. running   B. slower
   C. team   D. active

Q. What is the connective word that tells you to look for a contrast relationship between the two clauses?
A. The connective word *but* signals that a contrast relationship exists between the two parts of the sentence.

Q. Of the four options, what is the best choice for the blank?
A. The word *slower* is the best response here.

2. The child stepped too close to the edge of the brook. As a result, he _____ in.
   A. fell   B. waded
   C. ran   D. jumped

Q. What is the connective phrase that links the two sentences?
A. The connective phrase *as a result* links the two sentences.

Q. Of the four relationships of words and phrases listed previously, what kind of relationship between the two sentences does the connective phrase in the example signal to the reader?

A. The phrase *as a result* signals that a cause and effect relationship exists between the two sentences.

Q. Identify the correct response which makes the second sentence reflect the cause and effect relationship.

A. The correct response is *fell*.

Understanding connectives is very important to success on the examination reading subtest. Sentences with deletions are often very closely related to adjacent sentences in meaning, and the relationship is often signaled by connective words or phrases. Here is an example from the practice passage about universities.

At first, these tutors had not been associated with one another. Rather, they had been _____. But, over time, they joined together to form guilds.

A. curious   B. poor
C. religious   D. ready
E. independent

Q. Identify the connective and contrastive words and phrases in the example.

A. *At first* and *over time* are connective phrases that set up temporal progression. *Rather* and *but* are contrastive items. The use of *rather* in the sentence with the deletion tells the reader that the missing word has to convey a meaning in contrast to *associated with one another*. (Notice also that *rather* occurs after a negative statement.) The use of *but* in the sentence after the one with the deletion indicates that the deleted word in the previous sentence has to reflect a meaning that contrasts with *joined together*. Thus, the reader is given two substantial cues to the meaning of the missing word. *Independent* is the only choice that meets the requirement for contrastive meaning.

SAMPLE QUESTIONS

DIRECTIONS: There are two passages on the following pages. In each passage some words are missing. Wherever a word is missing, there is a blank line with a number on it. Below the passage you will find the same number and five words. Choose the word that makes the best sense in the blank.

You may not be sure of the answer to a question until you read the sentences that come after the blank, so be sure to read enough to answer the questions. As you work on these passages, you will find that the second passage is harder to read than the first. Answer as many questions as you can.

Bridges are built to allow a continuous flow of highway and railway traffic across water lying in their paths. But engineers cannot forget that river traffic, too, is essential to our economy. The role of _____1_____ is important. To keep these vessels moving freely, bridges are built high enough, when possible, to let them pass underneath. Sometimes, however, channels must accommodate very tall ships. It may be uneconomical to build a tall enough bridge. The _____2_____ would be too high. To save money, engineers build movable bridges.

In the swing bridge, the middle part pivots or swings open. When the bridge is closed, this section joins the two ends of the bridge, blocking tall vessels. But this section _____3_____. When swung open, it is perpendicular to the ends of the bridge, creating two free channels for river traffic. With swing bridges, channel width is limited by the bridge's piers. The largest swing bridge provides only a 75-meter channel. Such channels are sometimes too _____4_____. In such cases, a bascule bridge may be built.

Bascule bridges are drawbridges with two arms that swing upward. They provide an opening as wide as the span. They are also versatile. These bridges are not limited to being fully opened or fully closed. They can be _____5_____ in many ways. They can be fixed at different angles to accommodate different vessels.

In vertical lift bridges, the center remains horizontal. Towers at both ends allow the center to be lifted like an elevator. One interesting variation of this kind of bridge was built during World War II. A lift bridge was desired, but there were wartime shortages of the steel and machinery needed for the towers. It was hard to find enough _____6_____. An ingenious engineer designed the bridge so that it did not have to be raised above traffic. Instead it was _____7_____. It could be submerged seven meters below the surface of the river. Ships sailed over it.

1. A. wind   B. boats   C. weight
   D. wires   E. experience

2. A. levels   B. cost   C. standards
   D. waves   E. deck

3. A. stands   B. floods   C. wears
   D. turns   E. supports

4. A. narrow   B. rough   C. long
   D. deep   E. straight

5. A. crossed   B. approached   C. lighted
   D. planned   E. positioned

6. A. work   B. material   C. time
   D. power   E. space

7. A. burned   B. emptied   C. secured
   D. shared   E. lowered

The first universities emerged at the end of the 11th century and beginning of the 12th. These institutions were not founded on any particular date or created by any formal action. Nobody actually ____8____ them. Instead, they developed gradually in places like Paris, Oxford, and Bologna, where scholars had long been teaching students. At first, these tutors had not been associated with one another. Rather, they had been ____9____. But, over time, they joined together to form guilds.

Guilds were groups of tradespeople, somewhat akin to modern unions. In the Middle Ages, all the crafts had such ____10____. The scholars' guilds built school buildings and evolved an administration which charged fees and set standards for the curriculum. It set prices for members' services and fixed requirements for entering the profession.

Professors were not the only schoolpeople forming associations. In Italy, students joined guilds to which teachers had to swear obedience. The students set strict rules, fining professors for beginning class a minute late. Teachers had to seek their students' permission to marry, and such permission was not always granted. Sometimes the students ____11____. Even if they said yes, the teacher got only one day's honeymoon.

Undergraduates took classes in Greek philosophy, Latin grammar, arithmetic, music, and astronomy. These were the only ____12____ available. More advanced study was possible in law, medicine, and theology, but one could not earn such postgraduate degrees quickly. It took a long time to ____13____. Completing the requirements in theology, for example, took at least 13 years.

The concept of a fixed program of study leading to a degree first evolved in medieval Europe. This ____14____ had not appeared before. In earlier academic settings, notions about *meeting requirements* and *graduating* had been absent. Since the Middle Ages, though, we have continued to view education as a set curriculum culminating in a degree.

8. A. started   B. guarded   C. blamed
    D. compared   E. remembered

9. A. curious   B. poor   C. religious
    D. ready   E. independent

10. A. taxes   B. secrets   C. products
    D. problems   E. organizations

11. A. left   B. copied   C. refused
    D. paid   E. prepared

12. A. rooms   B. subjects   C. clothes
    D. pens   E. markets

13. A. add   B. answer   C. forget
    D. finish   E. travel

14. A. idea   B. desk   C. library
    D. capital   E. company

———

KEY (CORRECT ANSWERS)

1. B   8. A
2. B   9. E
3. D   10. E
4. A   11. C
5. E   12. B
6. B   13. D
7. E   14. A

———

READING COMPREHENSION

COMMENTARY

Questions on reading comprehension -- the ability to understand and interpret written materials -- are now universal, staple parts of almost all aptitude and achievement tests, as well as tests of general and mental ability.

By its very nature, the reading comprehension question is the most difficult of the question-types to cope with successfully, and, accordingly, it is usually weighted more heavily (assigned more credits) than other questions.

Generally, tests of aptitude and/or achievement derive their reading selections ("passages")from the several disciplines -- art, biology, chemistry, economics, education, engineering, history, literature, mathematics, music, philosophy, physics, political science, psychology, and sociology. Thus, the student or applicant is *not* being tested for specific knowledge of, or proficiency in, these areas. Rather, he is being tested on his understanding and comprehension of the meaning of the materials contained in the specific passages presented, the theory being that his mental ability will be *best* tested by his reading power, not by his training or acquired knowledge in the different fields,since it may be reasonably expected that such training and/or knowledge will differ among the candidates for a variety of reasons. The great equalizing element is the reading comprehension test. Therefore, all the information and material needed for answering the questions are imbedded in the passages themselves. *The power or skill or ability of the testee, then, is to be shown in the extent and degree to which he succeeds in making the correct answers to the questions in the reading passages.*

Historically, many colleges and universities, leaning on the theory of transfer of training, regard the reading comprehension factor as, perhaps the most important of all criteria in measuring scholastic aptitude since, according to this view, the ability to read with understanding and to go on from this point, is basic to all academic professional, graduate, and research work.

Let us examine just what reading comprehension means in the context described above and analyze its basic components.

The factor of reading abiluty is a complex one which may be tested and measured at several discrete levels of ability.

Comparatively, the easiest type of reading question is that which tests understanding of the material to be read -- to list facts or details as described in the passage, to explain the meanings of words or phrases used, to clarify references, etc.

1

The next level of difficulty is reached when the student is confronted with questions designed to show his ability to interpret and to analyze the material to be read, e.g., to discover the central thought of the passage, to ascertain the mood or point of view of the author, to note contradictions, etc.

The third stage consists of the ability to apply the principles and/or opinions expressed in the article, e.g., to surmise the recommendations that the writer may be expected to make later on or to formulate his stand on related issues.

The final and highest point is attained when the student is called upon to evaluate what he has read -- to agree with or to differ with the point of view of the writer, to accept or to refute the evidences or methods employed, to judge the efficacy or the inappropriateness of different proposals, etc.

All these levels will be broached and tested in this reading section.

SAMPLE PASSAGE - QUESTIONS AND ANSWERS
PASSAGE

(1) Our ignorance of the complex subject of social insurance was and remains colossal. (2) For years American business leaders delighted in maligning the British social insurance schemes. (3) Our industrialists condemned them without ever finding out what they were about. (4) Even our universities displayed no interest. (5) Contrary to the interest in this subject taken by organized labor abroad, our own labor movement bitterly opposed the entire program of social insurance up to a few years ago. (6) Since the success of any reform depends largely upon a correct public understanding of the principles involved, the adoption of social insurance measures presented peculiar difficulties for the United States under our Federal type of government of limited powers, our constitutional and judicial handicaps, our long conditioning to individualism, the traditional hostility to social reform by both capital and labor, the general inertia, and our complete lack of trained administrative personnel without which even the best law can be ineffective. (7) Has not bitter experience taught us that far more important than the passage of a law, which is at best only a declaration of intention, is a ready public opinion prepared to enforce it?

1. According to this writer, what attitude have we shown in this country toward social insurance?
   A. We have been extremely doubtful that it will work, but have been willing to give it a chance.
   B. We have opposed it on the grounds of a careful study of its defects.
   C. We have shown an unintelligent and rather blind antagonism toward it.
   D. We have been afraid that it would not work under our type of government.
   E. We have resented it because of the extensive propaganda in favor of it.

2

2. To what does the phrase, "our long conditioning to individualism," refer?
   A. Our habit of depending upon ourselves
   B. Our increasing dependence on the Federal Government
   C. Our long established distrust of "big business"
   D. Our policies of high protective tariff
   E. Our unwillingness to accept reforms

3. Which of these ideas is expressed in this passage?
   A. The surest way to cure a social evil is to get people to pass a law against it.
   B. Legislation alone cannot effect social reforms.
   C. The American people are seriously uninformed about all social problems.
   D. Our type of government makes social reform practically impossible.
   E. Capital and labor retard social progress.

ANALYSIS

These are the steps you must take to answer the questions:

First, scan the passage quickly, trying to gather at a glance the general import.

Then, read the passage carefully and critically, <u>underlining with a pencil, what are apparently leading phrases and concepts</u>.

Next, read each question carefully, and seek the answer in definite parts -- sentences, clauses, phrases, figures of speech, adverbs, adjectives, etc. -- in the text of the passage.

Finally, select the one answer which *best* answers the question, that is, it *best* matches what the paragraph says or is *best* supported by something in the passage.

The passage is concerned with the advent of social insurance to the United States. The author makes several points in this connection:
   1. Our gross ignorance of, and lack of interest in, the subject.
   2. The bitter opposition to social insurance in this country, particularly, of organized labor.
   3. Special and augmented difficulties in the United States in respect to this area; enumeration of these factors.
   4. The ultimate, certain method of achieving reform.

Having firmly encompassed the central meaning and basic contents of the passage, let us now proceed to examine each of the stated questions and proposed answers.

<u>Question 1</u>. According to this writer, what attitude have we shown in this country toward social insurance?
   A. We have been extremely doubtful that it will work, but have been willing to give it a chance.
      Sentences 1,2,3,4,5 drastically negate the second clause of this statement ("but we have been willing to give it a chance").

B. We have opposed it on the grounds of a careful study of its defects.

This statement is completely refuted by sentences 2 and 3.

C. We have shown an unintelligent and rather blind antagonism toward it.

Just as A is fully denied by sentences 1-5, so these sentences fully affirm the validity of this statement.

D. We have been afraid that it would not work under our type of government.

This is one -- and only one -- of the several difficulties facing the success of social insurance. Thus, this answer is only *partially* true.

E. We have resented it because of the extensive propaganda in favor of it.

Quite the contrary. Again, see sentences 1-5.

———

Looking back, you now see that the one suggested answer of the five (5) offered that *BEST* answers the question is item C., We have shown an unintelligent and rather blind antagonism toward it. The CORRECT answer, then, is C.

Question 2. To what does the phrase, "our long conditioning to individualism," refer?
A. Our habit of depending upon ourselves.

When a phrase is quoted from the text, as in this question, we should immediately locate it, review the context, and then consider it *in the light of the meaning of the passage as a whole.*

We find the quoted phrase in long sentence 6, beginning "Since the success ..."

A is clearly the answer to question 2.

Items B, C, D, E have little or no merit with reference to the meaning of the quoted phrase within the passage, and are, therefore, to be discarded as possible answers.

Question 3. Which of these ideas is expressed in this passage?
A. The surest way to cure a social evil is to get people to pass a law against it.

This is clearly refuted by the last sentence, "Has not bitter experience ...... it?"
B. Legislation alone cannot effect social reforms.

This is just as clearly supported by this same last sentence.
C. The American people are seriously uninformed about all social problems.

There is no evidence in the passage to support this statement.
D. Our type of government makes social reform practically impossible.

Our democratic form of government does present serious handi-

caps to social reform, as stated in the next-to-last sentence,
but does *not* make social reform "practically impossible."
E. Capital and labor retard social progress.
   American business leaders and the labor movement both opposed
social *insurance*. They did not, however, retard social *progress*.

SUGGESTIONS FOR ANSWERING THE READING COMPREHENSION QUESTION

1. Be sure to answer the questions *only* on the basis of the passage,
   and not from any other source, unless specifically directed to do
   otherwise.
2. Note that the answers may not be found directly in the text. For
   the more difficult reading questions, answers are generally to be
   inferred or *derived* from the sense of one or more sentences,
   clauses, and even paragraphs.
3. Do not expect to find the bases for the answers in sequential parts
   of the textual material. The difficulty of questions is increased
   when the candidate is required to skip from one part of the passage
   to another without any order, i.e., Question 1 may have its root
   in the last sentence of the paragraph, let us say, and Question 5
   may be based upon the second sentence, for example. This is a method of increasing the difficulty of the research and investigation required of the candidate.
4. When the question refers to a specific line, sentence, paragraph,
   or quotation, be sure to find this reference and to re-read it
   thoroughly. <u>The answer to such a question is almost certain to be
   found in or near this reference in the passage</u>.
5. Time for the reading question is limited, as it is for the examination as a whole. In other words, one must work speedily as well
   as effectively. The candidate, in seeking the answers to the reading questions, is not expected to go through all of the items in
   the thorough way presented in the sample questions above. That is,
   he has only to suit himself. It suffices, in order to attain to
   the right answer, to note <u>mentally</u> the basis for the answer in the
   text. There is no need to <u>annotate</u> your answer or to <u>write out</u>
   reasons for your answer. What we have attempted to do in the sam-
   ples is to show that there is a definite and logical attack on this
   type of question, which, principally, consists of careful, critical
   reading, research and investigation, and evaluation of the material.
   One must learn to arrive at the correct answer through this process
   rather than through hit-or-miss tactics or guessing. There is no
   reading comprehension question, logically or fairly devised, which
   cannot be answered by the candidate provided he goes about this
   task in a systematic, sustained manner.
6. The candidate may be assisted by this advanced technique. Often,
   the general sense of the passage when fully captured, <u>rather than
   specific parts in the passage,</u> will lead to the correct answer.
   Therefore, it is most important that the candidate read the passage
   for total meaning first. This type of general understanding will
   be most helpful in answering those questions which have no specific
   background in the text but, rather, must be inferred from what has
   been read.

7. Beware of the following pitfalls:
     A. The categorical statement. -- You can almost be sure that any answer which uses the words <u>solely</u>, <u>wholly</u>, <u>always</u>, <u>never</u>, <u>at all times</u>, <u>forever</u>, etc., is wrong.
     B. The too-easy answer. -- When the question appears to be so simple that it can be answered almost word for word by reference to the text, be particularly on your guard. You will, probably, find that the language of the question may have been inverted or changed or that some important word has been added or omitted, so that you are being tested for alertness and attention to details. For example, if, in a passage, a comparison is made between Country A and Country B, and you are told that Country A has twice the area of Country B, and the question contains an item which states that "it is clear that the area of Country B is greater than Country A," note how easily you can be beguiled into accepting this statement as true.
     C. Questions requiring that the candidate show his understanding of the main point of a passage, e.g., to state the central theme, or to suggest a worthy title, must be answered on that basis alone. You may be sure that other worthy possibilities are available, but you should examine your choice from the points of view of both appropriateness and breadth. For the most part, answers that are ruled out will contain one, but not both of these characteristics.
     D. Make up your mind now that some, but not all, of the material in the various passages in the reading comprehension questions will be useful for finding the answer. Sometimes, passages are made purposely long to increase the difficulty and to further confuse the harried candidates. However, do not disregard any of the textual material without first having given it a thorough reading.
     E. If the question requires that you give the writer's opinion or feelings on possible future action, do just that, and do not substitute your own predilections or antidotes. Similarly, do not make inferences if there exists in the text a clear-cut statement of facts. Base your answer, preferably, on the facts; make inferences or assumptions when they are called for, or as necessary.
     F. Do not expect the passages to deal with your subject field(s) alone. The passages offered will illustrate all the academic areas. While interest is a major factor in attaining to success, resolve now that you are going to wade through all the passages, in a thorough way, be they science or mathematics or economics or art. Unfamiliarity with a subject is no excuse on this type of test since the answers are to be based upon the reading passage <u>alone</u>.
     In corollary fashion, should you encounter a passage dealing with a field with which you are familiar, do not permit your special knowledge to play a part in your answer. <u>Answer only on the</u> basis of the passage, as <u>directed.</u>
     G. The hardest type of reading question is the one in which the fifth choice presented is "none of these." Should this phrase prove to be the correct answer, it would require a thorough, albeit rapid, examination of ALL the possibilities. This, of course, is time consuming and often frustrating.

H. A final word of advice at this point. On the Examination, leave the more difficult reading questions for the end. Try to answer those of lesser difficulty first. In this way, you will leave yourself maximum time for the _really_ difficult part of the Examination

———

In accordance with the special challenge of the reading comprehension question, ten (10) selected passages, varying in subject matter, style, length, and form, are presented for solution by the candidate. However, the passages are all alike in one respect: they extend to the highest ranges of difficulty.

———

EXAMINATION SECTION

TEST 1

DIRECTIONS: Each question or incomplete statement is followed by
several suggested answers or completions. Select the one
that *BEST* answers the question or completes the statement.
*PRINT THE LETTER OF THE CORRECT ANSWER IN THE SPACE AT THE
RIGHT.*

PASSAGE

It is a common belief that a thing is desirable because it is
scarce and thereby has ostentation value. The notion that such a
standard of value is an inescapable condition of settled social
existence rests on one of two implicit assumptions. The first is
that the attempt to educate the human race so that the desire to
display one's possessions is not a significant feature of man's
social behavior, is an infringement against personal freedom. The
greatest obstacle to lucid discourse in these matters is the psychological anti-vaccinationist who uses the word freedom to signify the
natural right of men and women to be unhappy and unhealthy through
scientific ignorance instead of being healthy and happy through the
knowledge which science confers. Haunted by a perpetual fear of the
dark, the last lesson which man learns in the difficult process of
growing up is "ye shall know the truth, and the truth shall make
you free." The professional economist who is too sophisticated to
retreat into the obscurities of this curious conception of liberty
may prefer to adopt the second assumption, that the truth does not
and cannot make us free because the need for ostentation is a universal species characteristic, and all attempts to eradicate the
unconscionable nuisance and discord which arise from overdeveloped
craving for personal distinction artificially fostered by advertise-
ment propaganda and so-called good breeding are therefore destined
to failure. It may be earnestly hoped that those who entertain this
view have divine guidance. No rational basis for it will be found
in textbooks of economics. Whatever can be said with any plausi-
bility in the existing state of knowledge rests on the laboratory
materials supplied by anthropology and social history.

1. According to the writer, the second assumption   1.____
   A. is fostered by propaganda and so-called good breeding
   B. is basically opposite to the view of the psychological
      anti-vaccinationist
   C. is not so curious a conception of liberty as is the
      first assumption
   D. is unsubstantiated
   E. is a religious explanation of an economic phenomenon

2. The author's purpose in writing this paragraph is *MOST*   2.____
   probably to
   A. denounce the psychological anti-vaccinationists
   B. demonstrate that the question under discussion is
      an economic rather than a psychological problem
   C. prove the maxim "ye shall know the truth, and the
      truth shall make you free"
   D. prove that ostentation is not an inescapable pheonomenon
      of settled social existence
   E. prove the inability of economics to account for ostentation

8

3. The writer implies that   3.___
    A. neither the psychological anti-vaccinationist nor the
       professional economist recognizes the undesirability
       of ostentation
    B. our cultural standards are at fault in enhancing
       ostentation value
    C. scarcity as a criterion of value is an inexplicable
       concept
    D. his main objection is to the inescapable standard of
       values
    E. the results of studies of ostentation in anthropology
       and social history are irrational

4. The writer believes that both assumptions   4.___
    A. are invalid because they ignore the lesson "ye shall
       know the truth, and the truth shall make you free"
    B. are fallacious because they agree that a thing is
       desirable because it is scarce
    C. arise from overdeveloped craving for personal distinction
    D. are implicit in the conception of ostentation value
    E. dispute the efficacy of education in eliminating
       ostentation

5. In his reference to divine guidance, the writer is   5.___
    A. being ironic
    B. implying that only divine guidance can solve the problem
    C. showing how the professional economist is opposing
       divine laws
    D. referring to opposition which exists between religion
       and science
    E. indicating that the problem is not a matter for
       divine guidance

6. The writer believes that personal freedom is   6.___
    A. less important than is scientific knowledge
    B. a requisite for the attainment of truth
    C. attained by eradicating false beliefs
    D. no concern of the professional economist
    E. an unsophisticated concept

7. We may infer that this writer does *NOT* believe that   7.___
    A. education can solve the problem
    B. people have any "natural rights"
    C. science can solve the problem
    D. the psychological anti-vaccinationist is more than
       a lipservant of the cause of freedom
    E. people can be happy under the present value system

8. The writer would consider as *MOST* comparable to the effect of
   a vaccination on the body, the effect of   8.____
      A. fear upon personality
      B. science upon the supposed need for ostentation
      C. truth upon the mind
      D. knowledge upon ignorance
      E. knowledge upon happiness

———

TEST 2

DIRECTIONS: Each question or incomplete statement is followed by
several suggested answers or completions. Select the one
that *BEST* answers the question or completes the statement.
*PRINT THE LETTER OF THE CORRECT ANSWER IN THE SPACE AT THE
RIGHT*.

PASSAGE

In any country the wages commanded by laborers who have comparable skills but who work in various industries are determined by the productivity of the least productive unit of labor, i.e., that unit of labor which works in the industry which has the greatest economic disadvantage. We will represent the various opportunities of employment in a country like the United States by symbols: A, standing for a group of industries in which we have exceptional economic advantages over foreign countries; B, for a group in which our advantages are less; C, one in which they are still less; D, the group of industries in which they are least of all.

When our population is so small that all our labor can be engaged in the group represented by A, productivity of labor (and therefore wages) will be at their maximum. When our population increases so that some of the labor will have to be set to work in group B, the wages of all labor must decline to the level of the productivity in that group. But no employer, without government aid, will yet be able to afford to hire labor to exploit the opportunities represented by C and D, unless there is a further increase in population.

But suppose that the political party in power holds the belief that we should produce everything that we consume, that the opportunities represented by C and D should be exploited. The commodities that the industries composing C and D will produce have been hitherto obtained from abroad in exchange for commodities produced by A and B. The government now renders this difficult by placing high duties upon the former class of commodities. This means that workers in A and B must pay higher prices for what they buy, but do not receive higher prices for what they sell.

After the duty has gone into effect and the prices of commodities that can be produced by C and D have risen sufficiently, enterprisers will be able to hire labor at the wages prevailing in A and B, and establish industries in C and D. So far as the remaining laborers in A and B buy the products of C and D, the difference between the price which they pay for those products and the price that they would pay if they were permitted to import those products duty-free is a tax paid not to the government, but to the producers in C and D, to enable the latter to remain in business. It is an uncompensated deduction from the natural earnings of the laborers in A and B. Nor are the workers in C and D paid as much, estimated in purchasing power, as they would have received if they had been allowed to remain in A and B under the earlier conditions.

11

1. When C and D are established, workers in these industries   1.___
    A. receive higher wages than do the workers in A and B
    B. receive lower wages than do the workers in A and B
    C. must be paid by government funds collected from the
       duties on imports
    D. are not affected so adversely by the levying of duties
       as are workers in A and B
    E. receive wages equal to those workers in A and B

2. We cannot exploit C and D *UNLESS*   2.___
    A. the productivity of labor in all industries is increased
    B. the prices of commodities produced by A and B are raised
    C. we export large quantities of commodities produced
       by A and B
    D. the producers in C and D are compensated for the
       disadvantages under which they operate
    E. we allow duties to be paid to the producers in C and
       D rather than to the government

3. "No employer, without government aid, will yet be able to   3.___
   afford to hire labor to exploit the opportunities represented
   by C and D" because
    A. productivity of labor is not at the maximum
    B. we cannot produce everything we consume
    C. the population has increased
    D. enterprisers would have to pay wages equivalent to
       those obtained by workers in A and B, while producing
       under greater economic disadvantages
    E. productivity would drop correspondingly with the wages
       of labor

4. The government, when it places high duties on imported   4.___
   commodities of classes C and D,
    A. raises the price of commodities produced by A and B
    B. is, in effect, taxing the workers in A and B
    C. raises the wages of workers in C and D at the expense
       of the workers in A and B
    D. does not affect the productivity of the workers in A
       and B, although the wages of these workers are reduced
    E. is adopting a policy made necessary by the stability
       of the population

5. The author's *MAIN* point is that   5.___
    A. it is impossible to attain national self-sufficiency
    B. the varying productivity of the various industries leads
       to the inequalities in wages of workers in these industries
    C. a policy that draws labor from the fields of greater
       natural productiveness to fields of lower natural pro-
       ductiveness tends to reduce purchasing power
    D. wages ought to be independent of international trade
    E. the government ought to subsidize C and D

6. The author's arguments in this passage could *BEST* be used to   6.___
    A. refute the belief that it is theoretically possible
       for us to produce everything that we consume
    B. disprove the theory that national self-sufficiency
       can be obtained by means of protective tariffs
    C. advocate the levying of duties on imported goods
    D. advocate equal wages for workers who have comparable
       skills but who work in various industries
    E. advocate free trade

7. When could C and D, as here defined, be exploited without the   7.___
    assistance of an artificially boosted price and without
    resultant lowering of wage levels?
    A. When a duty is placed on competing products from
       other countries
    B. When the products of C and D are exchanged in trade
       for other commodities
    C. When the country becomes economically self-sufficient
    D. When there is a favorable balance of trade
    E. At no time

8. In the last sentence in the selection, the statement is made: 8.___
    "Nor are the workers in C and D paid as much, estimated in
    purchasing power, as they would have received if they had been
    allowed to remain in A and B under the earlier conditions."
    This is because
    A. they must pay higher prices for commodities produced
       by C and D
    B. C and D cannot pay so high wages as can A and B
    C. products of C and D do not command sufficiently high
       prices
    D. there has not been an increase in population
    E. wages in all groups have declined

_____

TEST 3

DIRECTIONS: Each question or incomplete statement is followed by several suggested answers or completions. Select the one that *BEST* answers the question or completes the statement. *PRINT THE LETTER OF THE CORRECT ANSWER IN THE SPACE AT THE RIGHT.*

PASSAGE

In the Federal Convention of 1787, the members were fairly well agreed as to the desirability of some check on state laws; but there was sharp difference of opinion whether this check should be political in character as in the form of a congressional veto, or whether the principle of judicial review should be adopted.

Madison was one of the most persistent advocates of the congressional veto and in his discussion of the subject he referred several times to the former imperial prerogative of disallowing provincial statutes. In March, 1787, he wrote to Jefferson, urging the necessity of a federal negative upon state laws. He referred to previous colonial experience in the suggestion that there should be "some emanation" of the federal prerogative "within the several states, so far as to enable them to give a temporary sanction to laws of immediate necessity." This had been provided for in the imperial system through the action of the royal governor in giving immediate effect to statutes, which nevertheless remained subject to royal disallowance. In a letter to Randolph a few weeks later, Madison referred more explicitly to the British practice, urging that the national government be given "a negative, in all cases whatsoever, on the Legislative acts of the States, as the King of Great Britain heretofore had." Jefferson did not agree with Madison; on practical grounds rather than as a matter of principle, he expressed his preference for some form of judicial control.

On July 17, Madison came forward with a speech in support of the congressional veto, again supporting his contention by reference to the royal disallowance of colonial laws: "Its utility is sufficiently displayed in the British System. Nothing could maintain the harmony and subordination of the various parts of the empire, but the prerogative by which the Crown stifles in the birth every Act of every part tending to discord or encroachment. It is true the prerogative is sometimes misapplied thro' ignorance or a partiality to one particular part of the empire: but we have not the same reason to fear such misapplications in our System." This is almost precisely Jefferson's theory of the legitimate function of an imperial veto.

This whole issue shows that the leaders who wrestled with confederation problems during and after the war understood, in some measure at least, the attitude of British administrators when confronted with the stubborn localism of a provincial assembly.

1. Madison was advocating   1.____
   - A. royal disallowance of state legislation
   - B. a political check on state laws
   - C. the supremacy of the states over the federal government
   - D. the maintenance of a royal governor to give immediate effect to statutes
   - E. discord and encroachment among the states

2. From this passage there is *NO* indication   2.____
   - A. of what the British System entailed
   - B. of Jefferson's stand on the question of a check on state laws
   - C. that the royal negative had been misapplied in the past
   - D. that Jefferson understood the attitude of British administrators
   - E. of what judicial review would entail

3. According to this passage, Madison believed that the federal government   3.____
   - A. ought to legislate for the states
   - B. should recognize the sovereignty of the several states
   - C. ought to exercise judicial control over state legislation
   - D. should assume the king's veto power
   - E. was equivalent to a provincial assembly

4. Madison's conception of a congressional veto   4.____
   - A. was opposed to Jefferson's conception of a congressional veto
   - B. developed from fear that the imperial negative might be misused
   - C. was that the federal prerogative should be exercised in disallowing state laws
   - D. was that its primary function was to give temporary sanction to laws of immediate necessity
   - E. was that its primary function was to prevent such injustices as "taxation without representation"

5. Madison believed that   5.____
   - A. the congressional veto would not be abused
   - B. the royal prerogative ought to have some form of check to correct misapplications
   - C. the review of state legislation by the federal government ought to remain subject to a higher veto
   - D. the imperial veto had not been misused
   - E. utility rather than freedom is the criterion for governmental institutions

6. Jefferson believed that   6.___
    A. the congressional veto would interfere with states'
       rights
    B. Madison's proposal smacked of imperialism
    C. the veto of state legislation was outside the limits of
       the federal prerogative
    D. the British System would be harmful if applied in the
       United States
    E. an imperial veto should include the disallowance of all
       legislation leading to discord

7. Madison's *MAIN* principle was that   7.___
    A. the national interest is more important than the
       interests of any one state
    B. the national government should have compulsive power
       over the states
    C. the king can do no wrong
    D. the United States should follow the English pattern
       of government
    E. the veto power of the royal governor should be included
       in the federal prerogative

8. Madison thought of the states as   8.___
    A. emanations of the federal government
    B. comparable to provinces of a colonial empire
    C. incapable of creating sound legislation
    D. having no rights specifically delegated to them
    E. incapable of applying judicial review of their legislation

9. Which of the following is the *BEST* argument which could be 9.___
  made against Madison's proposition?
    A. The United States has no king.
    B. The federal government is an entity outside the juris-
       diction of the states.
    C. Each state has local problems concerning which repre-
       sentatives from other states are not equipped to pass
       judgment.
    D. The federal prerogative had been misused in the past.
    E. It provides no means of dealing with stubborn localism.

TEST 4

DIRECTIONS: Each question or incomplete statement is followed by several suggested answers or completions. Select the one that *BEST* answers the question or completes the statement. *PRINT THE LETTER OF THE CORRECT ANSWER IN THE SPACE AT THE RIGHT.*

PASSAGE

The nucleus of its population is the local businessmen, whose interests constitute the municipal policy and control its municipal administration. These local businessmen are such as the local bankers, merchants of many kinds and degrees, real estate promoters, local lawyers, local clergymen. . . The businessmen, who take up the local traffic in merchandising, litigation, church enterprise and the like, commonly begin with some share in the real estate speculation. This affords a common bond and a common ground of pecuniary interest, which commonly masquerades under the name of local patriotism, public spirit, civic pride, and the like. This pretense of public spirit is so consistently maintained that most of these men come presently to believe in their own professions on that head. Pecuniary interest in local land values involves an interest in the continued growth of the town. Hence any creditable misrepresentation of the town's volume of business traffic, population, tributary farming community, or natural resources, is rated as serviceable to the common good. And any member of this business-like community will be rated as a meritorious citizen in proportion as he is serviceable to this joint pecuniary interest of these "influential citizens."

1. The tone of the paragraph is   1.____
   A. bitter   B. didactic
   C. complaining   D. satirical
   E. informative

2. The foundation for the "influential citizens'" interest in
   their community is   2.____
   A. their control of the municipal administration
   B. their interests in trade and merchandising
   C. their natural feeling of civic pride
   D. a pretense of public spirit
   E. ownership of land for speculation

3. The "influential citizens'" type of civic pride may be compared
   with the patriotism of believers in   3.____
   A. a balance of power in international diplomacy
   B. racial superiority
   C. laissez faire
   D. a high tariff
   E. dollar diplomacy

4. The *IMPORTANT* men in the town   4.____
   A. are consciously insincere in their local patriotism
   B. are drawn together for political reasons
   C. do not scruple to give their community a false boost
   D. regard strict economy as a necessary virtue
   E. are extremely jealous of their prestige

5. The writer considers that the influential men of the town   5.___
    A. are entirely hypocritical in their conception of their
       motives
    B. are blinded to facts by their patriotic spirit
    C. have deceived themselves into thinking they are altruistic
    D. look upon the welfare of their community as of paramount
       importance
    E. form a closed corporation devoted to the interests of the
       town

6. *PROBABLY* the author's own view of patriotism is that it   6.___
    A. should be a disinterested passion untinged by commercial
       motives
    B. is found only among the poorer classes
    C. is usually found in urban society
    D. grows out of a combination of the motives of self-
       interest and altruism
    E. consists in the main of a feeling of local pride

_____

TEST 5

DIRECTIONS: Each question or incomplete statement is followed by several suggested answers or completions. Select the one that *BEST* answers the question or completes the statement. *PRINT THE LETTER OF THE CORRECT ANSWER IN THE SPACE AT THE RIGHT.*

PASSAGE

Negative thinking and lack of confidence in oneself or in the pupils are probably the greatest hindrances to inspirational teaching. Confronted with a new idea, one teacher will exclaim: "Oh, my children couldn't do that! They're too young." Another will mutter, "If I tried that stunt, the whole class would be in an uproar." Such are the self-justifications for mediocrity.

Here and there it is good to see a teacher take a bold step away from the humdrum approach. For example, Natalie Robinson Cole was given a class of fourth-year pupils who could hardly speak English. Yet in her book, THE ARTS IN THE CLASSROOM, she describes how she tried clay work, creative writing, interpretive dancing and many other exciting activities with them. Did her control of the class suffer? Were the results poor? Was morale adversely affected? The answer is *NO* on all three counts.

But someone may point out that what Mrs. Cole could do on the fourth-grade could not be done in the primary grades. Wrong again! The young child is more malleable than his older brother. Furthermore, his radiant heritage of originality has not been enveloped in clouds of self-consciousness. Given the proper encouragement, he will paint an interesting design on the easel, contribute a sparkling expression to the "class poem" as it takes shape on the blackboard, make a puppet speak his innermost thoughts, and react with sensitivity in scores of other ways.

All teachers on all grade levels need to think positively and act confidently. Of course, any departure from the commonplace must be buttressed by careful preparation, firm handling of the situation, and consistent attention to routines. Since these assets are within the reach of all teachers there should be no excuse for not putting some imagination into their work.

1. The central idea of the above passage is *BEST* conveyed by the   1.____
    A. first sentence in the first paragraph
    B. last sentence in the first paragraph
    C. first sentence in the second paragraph
    D. last sentence in the passage
    E. third sentence in the third paragraph

2. If the concepts of this passage were to be expanded into a   2.____
   book, the one of the following titles which would be *MOST*
   suitable is
    A. THE ARTS IN THE CLASSROOM
    B. THE POWER OF POSITIVE THINKING
    C. THE HIDDEN PERSUADERS
    D. KIDS SAY THE DARNDEST THINGS
    E. ARMS AND THE MAN

19

Test 5

3. Of the following reasons for uninspired teaching, the one   3.___
   which is *NOT* given explicitly in the passage is
       A. negative thinking
       B. teachers' underestimation of pupils' ability or stability
       C. teachers' failure to broaden themselves culturally
       D. teachers' lack of self-assurance
       E. teachers' rationalizations

4. From reading the passage one can gather that Natalie R. Cole
       A. teaches in New York City   4.___
       B. has been married
       C. is an expert in art
       D. teaches in the primary grades
       E. is a specialist in child psychology

5. An activity for children in the primary grades which is *NOT*
   mentioned in the passage is   5.___
       A. creative expression
       B. art work
       C. puppetry
       D. constructing with blocks
       E. work on the blackboard

6. A basic asset of the inspirational teacher *NOT* mentioned in
   the passage is   6.___
       A. a pleasant, outgoing personality
       B. a firm hand
       C. a thorough, careful plan
       D. consistent attention to routines
       E. acting confidently

20

TEST 6

DIRECTIONS: Each question or incomplete statement is followed by several suggested answers or completions. Select the one that *BEST* answers the question or completes the statement. *PRINT THE LETTER OF THE CORRECT ANSWER IN THE SPACE AT THE RIGHT.*

PASSAGE

Of all the areas of learning the most important is the development of attitudes. Emotional reactions as well as logical thought processes affect the behavior of most people. "The burnt child fears the fire" is one instance; another is the rise of despots like Hitler. Both these examples also point up the fact that attitudes stem from experience. In the one case the experience was direct and impressive; in the other it was indirect and cumulative. The Nazis were indoctrinated largely by the speeches they heard and the books they read.

The classroom teacher in the elementary school is in a strategic position to influence attitudes. This is true partly because children acquire attitudes from these adults whose word they respect. Another reason it is true is that pupils often delve somewhat deeply into a subject in school that has only been touched upon at home or has possibly never occurred to them before. To a child who had previously acquired little knowledge of Mexico, his teacher's method of handling such a unit would greatly affect his attitude toward Mexicans.

The media through which the teacher can develop wholesome attitudes are innumerable. Social studies (with special reference to races, creeds and nationalities), science, matters of health and safety, the very atmosphere of the classroom ... these are a few of the fertile fields for the inculcation of proper emotional reactions.

However, when children come to school with undesirable attitudes, it is unwise for the teacher to attempt to change their feelings by cajoling or scolding them. She can achieve the proper effect by helping them obtain constructive experiences. To illustrate, first-grade pupils afraid of policemen will probably alter their attitudes after a classroom chat with the neighborhood officer in which he explains how he protects them. In the same way, a class of older children can develop attitudes through discussion, research, outside reading and all-day trips.

Finally, a teacher must constantly evaluate her own attitude because her influence can be deleterious if she has personal prejudices. This is especially true in respect to controversial issues and questions on which children should be encouraged to reach their own decisions as a result of objective analysis of all the facts.

1. The central idea conveyed in the above passage is that   1.___
    A. attitudes affect our actions
    B. teachers play a significant role in developing or changing pupils' attitudes
    C. by their attitudes, teachers inadvertently affect pupils' attitudes
    D. attitudes can be changed by some classroom experiences
    E. attitudes are affected by experience

2. The author implies that   2.___
    A. children's attitudes often come from those of other
       children
    B. in some aspects of social studies a greater variety
       of methods can be used in the upper grades than in
       the lower grades
    C. the teacher should guide all discussions by revealing
       her own attitude
    D. people usually act on the basis of reasoning rather than
       on emotion
    E. parents' and teachers' attitudes are more often in
       harmony than in conflict

3. A statement *NOT* made or implied in the passage is that   3.___
    A. attitudes cannot easily be changed by rewards and
       lectures
    B. a child can develop in the classroom an attitude about
       the importance of brushing his teeth
    C. attitudes can be based on the learning of falsehoods
    D. the attitudes of children are influenced by all the
       adults in their environment
    E. the children should accept the teacher's judgment in
       controversial matters

4. The passage *SPECIFICALLY* states that   4.___
    A. teachers should always conceal their own attitudes
    B. whatever attitudes a child learns in school have
       already been introduced at home
    C. direct experiences are more valuable than indirect ones
    D. teachers can sometimes have an unwholesome influence
       on children
    E. it is unwise for the teacher to attempt to change
       children's attitudes

5. The first and fourth paragraphs have all the following points
  in common *EXCEPT*   5.___
    A. how reading affects attitudes
    B. the importance of experience in building attitudes
    C. how attitudes can be changed in the classroom
    D. how fear sometimes governs attitudes
    E. how differences in approach change attitudes

TEST 7

DIRECTIONS: Each question or incomplete statement is followed by
several suggested answers or completions. Select the one
that *BEST* answers the question or completes the statement.
*PRINT THE LETTER OF THE CORRECT ANSWER IN THE SPACE AT THE
RIGHT*.

PASSAGE

The word geology refers to the study of the composition, structure,
and history of the earth. The term is derived from the Latin,
geologia, coined by Bishop Richard de Bury in 1473 to distinguish
lawyers who study "earthy things" from theologians. It was first
consistently used in its present sense in the latter part of the 17th
centry. The great mass of detail that constitutes geology is clas-
sified under a number of subdivisions which, in turn, depend upon the
fundamental sciences, physics, chemistry and biology.

The principal subdivisions of geology are: mineralogy, petrology,
structural geology, physiography (geomorphology), usually grouped
under physical or dynamical geology; and paleontology, stratigraphy
and paleogeography, grouped under historical geology. The term
economic geology usually refers to the study of valuable mineral "ore"
deposits, including coal and oil. The economic aspects of geology
are, however, much more embracive, including many subjects associated
with civil engineering, economic geography, and conservation. Some
of the more important of these subjects are: meteorology, hydrology,
agriculture, and seismology. Subjects which are also distinctly
allied to geology are geophysics, geochemistry, and cosmogony.

1. The statement that geology treats of the history of the   1.____
   earth and its life, especially as recorded in the rocks, is
   A. contrary to the paragraph
   B. made in the paragraph
   C. neither made nor implied in the paragraph
   D. not made, but implied in the paragraph
   E. unclear from the passage

2. The statement that the principal branches or phases of   2.____
   geology are dynamical geology and historical geology are
   A. contrary to the paragraph
   B. made in the paragraph
   C. neither made nor implied in the paragraph
   D. not made, but implied in the paragraph
   E. unclear from the passage

3. The statement that mining geology is a subdivision of   3.____
   geophysics is
   A. contrary to the paragraph
   B. made in the paragraph
   C. neither made nor implied in the paragraph
   D. not made, but implied in the paragraph
   E. unclear from the passage

4. The statement that the study of both the exterior of the
   earth and its inner constitution constitutes the funda-
   ental subject matter of geology is
       A. contrary to the paragraph
       B. made in the paragraph
       C. neither made nor implied in the paragraph
       D. not made, but implied in the paragraph
       E. unclear from the passage

    4. ____

5. The statement that geology utilizes the principles of
   astronomy, zoology, and botany is
       A. contrary to the paragraph
       B. made in the paragraph
       C. neither made nor implied in the paragraph
       D. not made, but implied in the paragraph
       E. unclear from the passage

    5. ____

6. The statement that geology is synonymous with the study of
   the attributes of rocks, rock formation, or rock attributes
   is
       A. contrary to the paragraph
       B. made in the paragraph
       C. neither made nor implied in the paragraph
       D. not made, but implied in the paragraph
       E. unclear from the passage

    6. ____

————

TEST 8

DIRECTIONS: Each question or incomplete statement is followed by several suggested answers or completions. Select the one that *BEST* answers the question or completes the statement. *PRINT THE LETTER OF THE CORRECT ANSWER IN THE SPACE AT THE RIGHT.*

PASSAGE

```
 1      Schiller was the first to ring a change on this state of things
 2   by addressing himself courageously to the entire population of his
 3   country in all its social strata at one time.  He was the great popu-
 4   larizer of our theatre, and remained for almost a century the guiding
 5   spirit of the German drama of which Schiller's matchless tragedies
 6   are still by many people regarded as the surpassing manifestoes.
 7   Schiller's position, while it demonstrates a whole people's gratitude
 8   to those who respond to its desires, does not however furnish a
 9   weapon of self-defense to the "popularizers" of drama, or rather its
10   diluters.  Schiller's case rather proves that the power of popular
11   influence wrought upon a poet may be vastly inferior to the strength
12   that radiates from his own personality.  Indeed, whereas the secret
13   of ephemeral power is only too often found in paltriness or mediocrity,
14   an influence of enduring force such as Schiller exerts on the Germans
15   can only emanate from a strong and self-assertive character.  No poet
16   lives beyond his day who does not exceed the average in mental sta-
17   ture, or who, through a selfish sense of fear of the general, allows
18   himself to be ground down to the conventional size and shape.
19   Schiller, no less than Ibsen, forced his moral demands tyrannically
20   upon his contemporaries.  And in the long run your moral despot, pro-
21   vided he be high-minded, vigorous, and able, has a better chance of
22   fame than the pliant time-server.  However, there is a great differ-
23   ence between the two cases.  For quite apart from the striking dis-
24   similarities between the poets themselves, the public, through the
25   gradual growth of social organization, has become greatly altered.
```

1. Schiller's lasting popularity may be attributed to   1.____
    A. his meeting the desires of a whole people, not just
       a segment of the people
    B. his abiding by his inmost convictions
    C. his mediocrity and paltriness
    D. his courageous facing up to the problems of his day
    E. his ability to popularize the unknown

2. In the first line, "on this state of things" refers to   2.____
    A. romantic drama
    B. the French play of contrived construction
    C. drama directed to the rich and well-born
    D. the popularizers of the theatre of today
    E. the ruling class

3. In the second sentence from the last, "the two cases" refer   3.____
   to
   A. pliant time-server and moral despot
   B. the one who exceeds the average in mental stature and the
      one who allows himself to be ground down to conventional
      size
   C. the popularizer and the poet of enduring fame
   D. Ibsen and Schiller
   E. the man of character and the man of wealth

4. We may assume that the author   4.____
   A. is no believer in the democratic processes
   B. has no high opinions of the "compact majority"
   C. regards popularity with the people as a measure of
      enduring success
   D. is opposed to the aristocracy
   E. has no fixed opinions

5. A word used in an ambiguous sense (having 2 or more possible
   meanings) in this passage is   5.____
   A. "poet" (lines 11,15,24)
   B. "power" (lines 10,13)
   C. "people" (lines 6,7)
   D. "popularizer" (lines 3,9)
   E. "moral" (lines 19,20)

TEST 9

DIRECTIONS: Each question or incomplete statement is followed by several suggested answers or completions. Select the one that *BEST* answers the question or completes the statement. *PRINT THE LETTER OF THE CORRECT ANSWER IN THE SPACE AT THE RIGHT.*

PASSAGE

In one sense, of course, this is not a new insight: all our great social and philosophical thinkers have been keenly aware of the fact of individual differences. It has remained, however, for psychologists to give the insight scientific precision.

What all this adds up to is more than just a working body of information about this and that skill. It adds up to a basic recognition of one important factor in the maturing of the individual. If each individual has a certain uniqueness of power, his maturing will best be accomplished along the line of that power. To try to develop him along lines that go in directions contrary to that of his major strength is to condition him to defeat. Thus, the non-mechanical person who is arbitrarily thrust into a mechanical occupation cannot help but do his work poorly and reluctantly, with some deep part of himself in conscious or unconscious rebellion.

He may blame himself for the low level of his accomplishment or for his persistent discontent;but not all his self-berating, nor even all his efforts to become more competent by further training, can make up for the original aptitude-lack. Unless he discovers his aptitude-lack, he may be doomed to a lifetime of self-blame, with a consequent loss of self-confidence and a halting of his psychological growth.

Or he may take refuge in self-pity — finding reason to believe that his failure is due to one or another bad break, to the jealousy of a superior, to lack of sympathy and help at home, to an initial bad start, to a lack of appreciation of what he does. If he thus goes the way of self-pity, he is doomed to a lifetime of self-commiseration that makes sound growth impossible.

The characteristic of the mature person is that he affirms life. To affirm life he must be involved, heart and soul, in the process of living. Neither the person who feels himself a failure nor the person who consciously or unconsciously resents what life has done to him can feel his heart and soul engaged in the process of living. That experience is reserved for the person whose full powers are enlisted. This, then, is what this fourth insight signifies: to mature, the individual must know what his powers are and must make them competent for life.

1. It is the author's view that   1.___
    A. "all men are created equal"
    B. "each man in his life plays many parts"
    C. "all comes to him who waits"
    D. "no kernel of nourishing corn can come to one but
       through his toil bestowed on that plot of ground
       given to him to till ...."
    E. "that is what it is not to be alive. To move about
       in a cloud of ignorance ... to live with envy ... in
       quiet despair ... to feel oneself sunk into a common
       grey mass ..."

2. Ignorance of this fourth insight   2.___
    A. may very likely cause one to take refuge in self-
       pity or conscious or unconscious rebellion
    B. constitutes a failure to understand that each indi-
       vidual is different and must cultivate his special
       powers in socially rewarding ways
    C. is a major deterrent to a growth to maturity
    D. means unawareness of the fact that each must use all
       his energy and powers to the best of his ability to
       make him competent for life
    E. may becloud the use of scientific precision

3. Two possible maladjustments of a man thrust into a position   3.___
he is unfitted for may be summed up in the phrase,
    A. conscious and unconscious rebellion
    B. guilt-feelings and scapegoating
    C. halting of psychological growth and blaming the "breaks"
    D. "Peccavi - I have sinned" and "all the world is made
       except thee and me and I am not so sure of thee"
    E. light and darkness

4. We will expect a person placed in a job he is unequal to, to   4.___
    A. strike out for himself as an extrepreneur
    B. display quick angers and fixed prejudices
    C. show a great love of life outside of his work
    D. engage in labor union activities
    E. join political and social movements

TEST 10

DIRECTIONS: Each question or incomplete statement is followed by several suggested answers or completions. Select the one that *BEST* answers the question or completes the statement. *PRINT THE LETTER OF THE CORRECT ANSWER IN THE SPACE AT THE RIGHT.*

PASSAGE

1   "For the ease and pleasure of treading the old road, accepting
2 the fashions, the education, the religion of society, he takes the
3 cross of making his own, and, of course, the self-accusation, the
4 faint heart, the frequent uncertainty and loss of time, which are the
5 nettles and tangling vines in the way of the self-relying and self-
6 directed; and the state of virtual hositility in which he seems to
7 stand to society, and especially to educated society. For all this
8 loss and scorn, what offset? He is to find consolation in exercising
9 the highest functions of human nature. He is one who raises himself
10 from private consideration and breathes and lives on public and
11 illustrious thoughts. He is the world's eye. He is the world's
12 heart. He is to resist the vulgar prosperity that retrogrades ever
13 to barbarism, by preserving and communicating heroic sentiments,
14 noble biographies, melodious verse, and the conclusions of history.
15 Whatsoever oracles the human heart, in all emergencies, in all solemn
16 hours, has uttered as its commentary on the world of actions -- these
17 he shall receive and impart. And whatsoever new verdict Reason from
18 her inviolable seat pronounces on the passing men and events of
19 today -- this he shall hear and promulgate.   .

20   "These being his functions, it becomes him to feel all confidence
21 in himself, and to defer never to the popular cry. He and he only
22 knows the world. The world of any moment is the merest appearance.
23 Some great decorum, some fetish of a government, some ephemeral
24 trade, or war, or man, is cried up by half mankind and cried down by
25 the other half, as if all depended on this particular up or down.
26 The odds are that the whole question is not worth the poorest thought
27 which the scholar has lost in listening to the controversy. Let him
28 not quit his belief that a popgun is a popgun, though the ancient and
29 honorable of the earth affirm it to be the crack of doom. In silence,
30 in steadiness, in severe abstraction, let him hold by himself; add
31 observation to observation, patient of neglect, patient of reproach,
32 and bide his own time -- happy enough if he can satisfy himself alone
33 that this day he has seen something truly. Success treads on every
34 right step. For the instinct is sure, that prompts him to tell his
35 brother what he thinks. He then learns that in going down into the
36 secrets of his own mind he has descended into the secrets of all
37 minds. He learns that he who has mastered any law in his private
38 thoughts, is master to the extent of all translated. The poet, in
39 utter solitude remembering his spontaneous thoughts and recording
40 them, is found to have recorded that which men in crowded cities
41 find true for them also. The orator distrusts at first the fitness
42 of his frank confessions, his want of knowedge of the persons he
43 addresses, until he finds that he is the complement of his hearers --
44 that they drink his words because he fulfills for them their own
45 nature; the deeper he delves into his privatest, secretest presentiment,
46 to his wonder he finds this is the most acceptable, most public, and

47 universally true. The people delight in it; the better part of every
48 man feels. This is my music; this is myself."

1. It is a frequent criticism of the scholar that he lives by   1.__
himself, in an "ivory tower," remote from the problems and
business of the world. Which of these below constitutes the
BEST refutation by the writer of the passage to the criticism
here noted?

    A. The world's concern being ephemeral, the scholar does
       well to renounce them and the world.
    B. The scholar lives in the past to interpret the present.
    C. The scholar at his truest is the spokesman of the people.
    D. The scholar is not concerned with the world's doing
       because he is not selfish and therefore not engrossed in
       matters of importance to himself and neighbors.
    E. The scholar's academic researches of today are the
       businessman's practical products of tomorrow.

2. The scholar's road is rough, according to the passage.   2.__
Which of these is his *GREATEST* difficulty?
    A. He must renounce religion.
    B. He must pioneer new approaches.
    C. He must express scorn for, and hostility to, society.
    D. He is uncertain of his course.
    E. There is a pleasure in the main-traveled roads in
       education, religion, and all social fashions.

3. When the writer speaks of the "world's eye" and the "world's
heart," he means   3.__
    A. the same thing
    B. culture and conscience
    C. culture and wisdom
    D. a scanning of all the world's geography and a deep
       sympathy for every living thing
    E. mind and love

4. By the phrase, "nettles and tangling vines," the author   4.__
PROBABLY refers to
    A. "self-accusation" and "loss of time"
    B. "faint heart" and "self accusation"
    C. "the slings and arrows of outrageous fortune"
    D. a general term for the difficulties of a scholar's life
    E. "self-accusation" and "uncertainty"

5. The various ideas in the passage are *BEST* summarized in   5.___
which of these groups?
   1. (a) truth versus society
      (b) the scholar and books
      (c) the world and the scholar

   2. (a) the ease of living traditionally
      (b) the glory of a scholar's life
      (c) true knowledge versus trivia

   3. (a) the hardships of the scholar
      (b) the scholar's function
      (c) the scholar's justifications for disregarding the
         world's business

   A. 1 and 3 together
   B. 3 only
   C. 1 and 2 together
   D. 1 only
   E. 1, 2, and 3 together

6. "seems to stand" (lines 6 and 7) means   6.___
   A. is
   B. gives the false impression of being
   C. ends probably in becoming
   D. is seen to be
   E. the quicksands of time

7. "public and illustrious thoughts" (lines 10 and 11) means   7.___
   A. what the people think
   B. thoughts for the good of mankind
   C. thoughts in the open
   D. thoughts transmitted by the people
   E. the conclusions of history

KEY (CORRECT ANSWERS)

TEST 1		TEST 2		TEST 3		TEST 4		TEST 5	
1.	D	1.	E	1.	B	1.	B	1.	A
2.	D	2.	D	2.	E	2.	E	2.	B
3.	B	3.	D	3.	D	3.	E	3.	C
4.	D	4.	B	4.	C	4.	C	4.	B
5.	A	5.	C	5.	A	5.	C	5.	D
6.	C	6.	E	6.	D	6.	A	6.	A
7.	E	7.	B	7.	B				
8.	C	8.	E	8.	B				
				9.	C				

TEST 6		TEST 7		TEST 8		TEST 9		TEST 10	
1.	B	1.	D	1.	B	1.	D	1.	C
2.	B	2.	B	2.	C	2.	B	2.	B
3.	D	3.	C	3.	D	3.	B	3.	C
4.	D	4.	D	4.	B	4.	B	4.	E
5.	C	5.	D	5.	D			5.	B
		6.	A					6.	B
								7.	B

32

READING COMPREHENSION
UNDERSTANDING AND INTERPRETING WRITTEN MATERIAL
EXAMINATION SECTION

DIRECTIONS: Each question or incomplete statement is followed by
several suggested answers or completions. Select the
one that BEST answers the question or completes the
statement. *PRINT THE LETTER OF THE CORRECT ANSWER IN
THE SPACE AT THE RIGHT.*

1. The National Assessment of Educational Progress recently   1.___
released the results of the first statistically valid
national sampling of young adult reading skills in the
United States. According to the survey, ninety-five
percent of United States young adults (aged 21-25) can
read at a fourth-grade level or better. This means they
can read well enough to apply for a job, understand a
movie guide or join the Army. This is a higher literacy
rate than the eighty to eighty-five percent usually
estimated for all adults. The study also found that
ninety-nine percent can write their names, eighty percent
can read a map or write a check for a bill, seventy percent can understand an appliance warranty or write a
letter about a billing error, twenty-five percent can
calculate the amount of a tip correctly, and fewer than
ten percent can correctly figure the cost of a catalog
order or understand a complex bus schedule.
Which statement about the study is BEST supported by the
above passage?
   A. United States literacy rates among young adults are
      at an all-time high.
   B. Forty percent of young people in the United States
      cannot write a letter about a billing error.
   C. Twenty percent of United States teenagers cannot
      read a map.
   D. More than ninety percent of United States young
      adults cannot correctly calculate the cost of a
      catalog order.

2. It is now widely recognized that salaries, benefits, and   2.___
working conditions have more of an impact on job satisfaction than on motivation. If they aren't satisfactory,
work performance and morale will suffer. But even when
they are high, employees will not necessarily be motivated
to work well. For example, THE WALL STREET JOURNAL
recently reported that as many as forty or fifty percent
of newly hired Wall Street lawyers (whose salaries start
at upwards of $50,000) quit within the first three years,
citing long hours, pressures, and monotony as the prime
offenders. It seems there's just not enough of an
intellectual challenge in their jobs. An up and coming
money-market executive concluded: *Whether it was $1
million or $100 million, the procedure was the same.*

Except for the tension, a baboon could do my job. When money and benefits are adequate, the most important additional determinants of job satisfaction are: more responsibility, a sense of achievement, recognition, and a chance to advance. All of these factors have a more significant influence on employee motivation and performance. As a footnote, several studies have found that the absence of these non-monetary factors can lead to serious stress-related illnesses.

Which statement is BEST supported by the above passage?
 A. A worker's motivation to perform well is most affected by salaries, benefits, and working conditions.
 B. Low pay can lead to high levels of job stress.
 C. Work performance will suffer if workers feel they are not paid well.
 D. After satisfaction with pay and benefits, the next most important factor is more responsibility.

3. The establishment of joint labor-management production committees occurred in the United States during World War I and again during World War II. Their use was greatly encouraged by the National War Labor Board in World War I and the War Production Board in 1942. Because of the war, labor-management cooperation was especially desired to produce enough goods for the war effort, to reduce conflict, and to control inflation. The committees focused on how to achieve greater efficiency, and consulted on health and safety, training, absenteeism, and *people* issues in general. During the second world war, there were approximately five thousand labor-management committees in factories, affecting over six million workers. While research has found that only a few hundred committees made significant contributions to productivity, there were additional benefits in many cases. It became obvious to many that workers had ideas to contribute to the running of the organization, and that efficient enterprises could become even more so. Labor-management cooperation was also extended to industries that had never experienced it before. Directly after each war, however, few United States labor-management committees were in operation.

3.___

Which statement is BEST supported by the above passage?
 A. The majority of United States labor-management committees during the second world war accomplished little.
 B. A major goal of United States labor-management committees during the first and second world wars was to increase productivity.
 C. There were more United States labor-management committees during the second world war than during the first world war.
 D. There are few United States labor-management committees in operation today.

4. Studies have found that stress levels among employees who   4.___
have a great deal of customer contact or a great deal of
contact with the public can be very high. There are
many reasons for this. Sometimes stress results when the
employee is caught in the middle - an organization wants
things done one way, but the customer wants them done
another way. The situation becomes even worse for the
employee's stress levels when he or she knows ways to
more effectively provide the service, but isn't allowed
to,by the organization. An example is the bank teller
who is required to ask a customer for two forms of identification before he or she can cash a check, even though
the teller knows the customer well. If organizational
mishaps occur or if there are problems with job design,
the employee may be powerless to satisfy the customer,
and also powerless to protect himself or herself from
the customer's wrath. An example of this is the waitress
who is forced to serve poorly prepared food. Studies
have also found, however, that if the organization and
the employee design the positions and the service
encounter well, and encourage the use of effective stress
management techniques, stress can be reduced to levels
that are well below average.
Which statement is BEST supported by the above passage?
   A. It is likely that knowledgeable employees will
      experience greater levels of job-related stress.
   B. The highest levels of occupational stress are found
      among those employees who have a great deal of
      customer contact.
   C. Organizations can contribute to the stress levels of
      their employees by poorly designing customer contact
      situations.
   D. Stress levels are generally higher in banks and
      restaurants.

5. It is estimated that approximately half of the United   5.___
States population suffers from varying degrees of adrenal
malfunction. When under stress for long periods of time,
the adrenals produce extra cortisol and norepinephrine.
By producing more hormones than they were designed to
comfortably manufacture and secrete, the adrenals can
burn out over time and then decrease their secretion.
When this happens, the body loses its capacity to cope
with stress, and the individual becomes sicker more
easily and for longer periods of time. A result of
adrenal malfunction may be a diminished output of cortisol.
Symptoms of diminished cortisol output include any of the
following: craving substances that will temporarily
raise serum glucose levels such as caffeine, sweets, soda,
juice, or tobacco; becoming dizzy when standing up too
quickly; irritability; headaches; and erratic energy
levels. Since cortisol is an anti-inflammatory hormone,
a decreased output over extended periods of time can make

one prone to inflammatory diseases such as arthritis, bursitis, colitis, and allergies. (Many food and pollen allergies disappear when adrenal function is restored to normal.) The patient will have no reserve energy, and infections can spread quickly. Excessive cortisol production, on the other hand, can decrease immunity, leading to frequent and prolonged illnesses.

Which statement is BEST supported by the above passage?
   A. Those who suffer from adrenal malfunction are most likely to be prone to inflammatory diseases such as arthritis and allergies.
   B. The majority of Americans suffer from varying degrees of adrenal malfunction.
   C. It is better for the health of the adrenals to drink juice instead of soda.
   D. Too much cortisol can inhibit the body's ability to resist disease.

6. Psychologist B.F. Skinner pointed out long ago that gambling is reinforced, either by design or accidentally, by what he called a variable ratio schedule. A slot machine, for example, is cleverly designed to provide a payoff after it has been played a variable number of times. Although the person who plays it and wins while playing receives a great deal of monetary reinforcement, over the long run the machine will take in much more money than it pays out. Research on both animals and humans has consistently found that such variable reward schedules maintain a very high rate of repeat behavior, and that this behavior is particularly resistant to extinction.

Which statement is BEST supported by the above passage?
   A. Gambling, because it is reinforced by the variable ratio schedule, is more difficult to eliminate than most addictions.
   B. If someone is rewarded or wins consistently, even if it is not that often, he or she is likely to continue that behavior.
   C. Playing slot machines is the safest form of gambling because they are designed so that eventually the player will indeed win.
   D. A cat is likely to come when called if its owner has trained it correctly.

6.___

7. Paper entrepreneurialism is an offshoot of scientific management that has become so extreme that it has lost all connection to the actual workplace. It generates profits by cleverly manipulating rules and numbers that only in theory represent real products and real assets. At its worst, paper entrepreneurialism involves very little more than imposing losses on others for the sake of short-term profits. The others may be taxpayers, shareholders who end up indirectly subsidizing other shareholders, consumers, or investors. Paper entrepreneurialism

7.___

has replaced product entrepreneurialism, is seriously threatening the United States economy, and is hurting our necessary attempts to transform the nation's industrial and productive economic base. An example is the United States company that complained loudly in 1979 that it did not have the $200 million needed to develop a video-cassette recorder, though demand for them had been very high. The company, however, did not hesitate to spend $1.2 billion that same year to buy a mediocre finance company. The video recorder market was handed over to other countries, who did not hesitate to manufacture them. Which statement is BEST supported by the above passage?

    A. Paper entrepreneurialism involves very little more than imposing losses on others for the sake of short-term profits.

    B. Shareholders are likely to benefit most from paper entrepreneurialism.

    C. Paper entrepreneurialism is hurting the United States economy.

    D. The United States could have made better video-cassette recorders than the Japanese but we ceded the market to them in 1979.

8. The *prisoner's dilemma* is an almost 40-year-old game-theory model psychologists, biologists, economists, and political scientists use to try to understand the dynamics of competition and cooperation. Participants in the basic version of the experiment are told that they and their *accomplice* have been caught red-handed. Together, their best strategy is to cooperate by remaining silent. If they do this, each will get off with a 30-day sentence. But either person can do better for himself or herself. If you double-cross your partner, you will go scott free while he or she serves ten years. The problem is, if you each betray the other, you will both go to prison for eight years, not thirty days. No matter what your partner chooses, you are logically better off choosing betrayal. Unfortunately, your partner realizes this too, and so the odds are good that you will both get eight years. That's the dilemma. (The length of the prison sentences is always the same for each variation.) Participants at a recent symposium on behavioral economics at Harvard University discussed the many variations on the game that have been used over the years. In one standard version, subjects are paired with a supervisor who pays them a dollar for each point they score. Over the long run, both subjects will do best if they cooperate every time. Yet in each round, there is a great temptation to betray the other because no one knows what the other will do. The best overall strategy for this variation was found to be *tit for tat*, doing unto your opponent as he or she has just done unto you. It is a simple strategy, but very

    8.___

effective. The partner can easily recognize it and
respond. It is retaliatory enough not to be easily ex-
ploited, but forgiving enough to allow a pattern of mutual
cooperation to develop.
Which statement is BEST supported by the above passage?
  A. The best strategy for playing *prisoner's dilemma* is
     to cooperate and remain silent.
  B. If you double-cross your partner, and he or she does
     not double-cross you, your partner will receive a
     sentence of eight years.
  C. When playing prisoner's dilemma, it is best to
     double-cross your partner.
  D. If you double-cross your partner, and he or she
     double-crosses you, you will receive an eight-year
     sentence.

9. After many years of experience as the vice president and
   general manager of a large company, I feel that I know
   what I'm looking for in a good manager. First, the
   manager has to be comfortable with himself or herself,
   and not be arrogant or defensive. Secondly, he or she has
   to have a genuine interest in people. There are some
   managers who love ideas - and that's fine - but to be a
   manager, you must love people, and you must make a hobby
   of understanding them, believing in them and trusting
   them. Third, I look for a willingness and a facility to
   manage conflict. Gandhi defined conflict as a way of
   getting at the truth. Each person brings his or her own
   grain of truth and the conflict washes away the illusion
   and fantasy. Finally, a manager has to have a vision, and
   the ability and charisma to articulate it. A manager
   should be seen as a little bit crazy. Some eccentricity
   is an asset. People don't want to follow vanilla leaders.
   They want to follow chocolate-fudge-ripple leaders.
   Which statement is BEST supported by the above passage?
     A. It is very important that a good manager spend time
        studying people.
     B. It is critical for good managers to love ideas.
     C. Managers should try to minimize or avoid conflict.
     D. Managers should be familiar with people's reactions
        to different flavors of ice cream.

9.___

10. Most societies maintain a certain set of values and assump-
    tions that make their members feel either good or bad
    about themselves, and either better or worse than other
    people. In most developed countries, these values are
    based on the assumption that we are all free to be what
    we want to be, and that differences in income, work, and
    education are a result of our own efforts. This may make
    us believe that people with more income, work that is more
    skilled, more education, and more power are somehow *better*
    people. We may view their achievements as proof that they

10.___

have more intelligence, more motivation, and more initiative than those with *lower* status. The myth tells us that power, income, and education are freely and equally available to all, and that our failure to achieve them is due to our own personal inadequacy. This simply is not the case.

The possessions we own may also seem to point to our real worth as individuals. The more we own, the more worthy of respect we may feel we are. Or, the acquisition of possessions may be a way of trying to fulfill ourselves, to make up for the loss of community and/or purpose. It is a futile pursuit because lost community and purpose can never be compensated for by better cars or fancier houses. And too often, when these things fail to satisfy, we believe it is only because we don't have enough money to buy better quality items, or more items. We feel bad that we haven't been successful enough to get all that we think we need. No matter how much we do have, goods never really satisfy for long. There is always something else to acquire, and true satisfaction eludes many, many of us.

Which statement is BEST supported by the above passage?
   A. The author would agree with the theory of *survival of the fittest*.
   B. The possessions an individual owns are not a proper measure of his or her real worth.
   C. Many countries make a sincere attempt to ensure equal access to quality education for their citizens.
   D. The effect a society's value system has on the lives of its members is greatly exaggerated.

11. *De nihilo nihil* is Latin for *nothing comes from nothing*.   11.___
In the first century, the Roman poet Persius advised that if anything is to be produced of value, effort must be expended. He also said, *In nihilum nil posse revorti* - anything once produced cannot become nothing again. It is thought that Persius was parodying Lucretius, who expounded the 500-year-old physical theories of Epicurus. *De nihilo nihil* can also be used as a cynical comment, to negatively comment on something that is of poor quality produced by a person of little talent. The implication here is: *What can you expect from such a source?*

Which statement is BEST supported by the above passage?
   A. *In nihilum nil posse revorti* can be interpreted as meaning *if anything is to be produced of value, then effort must be expended*.
   B. *De nihilo nihil* can be understood in two different ways.
   C. Lucretius was a great physicist.
   D. Persius felt that Epicurus put in little effort while developing his theories.

12. A Cornell University study has found that less than one
    percent of the billion pounds of pesticides used in this
    country annually strike their intended targets. The
    study found that the pesticides, which are somewhat hap-
    hazardly applied to 370 million acres, or about sixteen
    percent of the nation's total land area, end up polluting
    the environment and contaminating almost all 200,000
    species of plants and animals, including humans. While
    the effect of indirect contamination on human cancer
    rates was not estimated, the study found that approximate-
    ly 45,000 human pesticide poisonings occur annually,
    including about 3,000 cases admitted to hospitals and
    approximately 200 fatalities.
    Which statement about the study is BEST supported by the
    above passage?
       A. It is likely that indirect pesticide contamination
          affects human health.
       B. Pesticides are applied to over one-quarter of the
          total United States land area.
       C. If pesticides were applied more carefully, fewer
          pesticide-resistant strains of pests would develop.
       D. Human cancer rates in this country would drop con-
          siderably if pesticide use was cut in half.

    12.___

13. The new conservative philosophy presents a unified,
    coherent approach to the world. It offers to explain
    much of our experience since the turbulent 1960's, and
    it shows what we've learned since about the dangers of
    indulgence and permissiveness. But it also warns that
    the world has become more ruthless, and that as indivi-
    duals and as a nation, we must struggle for survival.
    It is necessary to impose responsibility and discipline
    in order to defeat those forces that threaten us. This
    lesson is dramatically clear, and can be applied to a
    wide range of issues.
    Which statement is BEST supported by the above passage?
       A. The 1970's were a time of permissiveness and indul-
          gence.
       B. The new conservative philosophy may help in imposing
          discipline and a sense of responsibility in order to
          meet the difficult challenges facing this country.
       C. The world faced greater challenges during the second
          world war than it faces at the present time.
       D. More people identify themselves today as conservative
          in their political philosophy.

    13.___

14. One of the most puzzling questions in management in recent
    years has been how usually honest, compassionate, intel-
    ligent managers can sometimes act in ways that are dis-
    honest, uncaring, and unethical. How could top-level
    managers at the Manville Corporation, for example, suppress
    evidence for decades that proved beyond all doubt that

    14.___

asbestos inhalation was killing their own employees?
What drove the managers of a midwest bank to continue to
act in a way that threatened to bankrupt the institution,
ruin its reputation, and cost thousands of employees and
investors their jobs and their savings? It's been
estimated that about two out of three of America's five
hundred largest corporations have been involved in some
form of illegal behavior. There are, of course, some
common rationalizations used to justify unethical conduct:
believing that the activity is in the organization's or
the individual's best interest, believing that the
activity is not *really* immoral or illegal, believing that
no one will ever know, or believing that the organization
will sanction the behavior because it helps the organization. Ambition can distort one's sense of *duty*.
Which statement is BEST supported by the above passage?
- A. Top-level managers of corporations are currently
  involved in a plan to increase ethical behavior
  among their employees.
- B. There are many good reasons why a manager may act
  unethically.
- C. Some managers allow their ambitions to override their
  sense of ethics.
- D. In order to successfully compete, some organizations
  may have to indulge in unethical or illegal behavior
  from time to time.

15. Some managers and supervisors believe that they are   15.___
leaders because they occupy positions of responsibility
and authority. But leadership is more than holding a
position. It is often defined in management
literature as *the ability to influence the opinions,
attitudes, and behaviors of others*. Obviously, there are
some managers that would not qualify as leaders, and
some leaders that are not *technically* managers. Research
has found that many people overrate their own leadership
abilities. In one recent study, seventy percent of those
surveyed rated themselves in the top quartile in leadership abilities, and only two percent felt they were below
average as leaders.
Which statement is BEST supported by the above passage?
- A. In a recent study, the majority of people surveyed
  rated themselves in the top twenty-five percent in
  leadership abilities.
- B. Ninety-eight percent of the people surveyed in a
  recent study had average or above-average leadership skills.
- C. In order to be a leader, one should hold a management position.
- D. Leadership is best defined as the ability to be
  liked by those one must lead.

KEY (CORRECT ANSWERS)

1. D	6. B	11. B
2. C	7. C	12. A
3. B	8. D	13. B
4. C	9. A	14. C
5. D	10. B	15. A

READING COMPREHENSION
EXAMINATION SECTION

DIRECTIONS FOR THIS SECTION:

Each question or incomplete statement is followed by several suggested answers or completions. Select the one that *BEST* answers the question or completes the statement. *PRINT THE LETTER OF THE CORRECT ANSWER IN THE SPACE AT THE RIGHT.*

TEST 1

In its current application to art, the term "primitive" is as vague and unspecific as the term "heathen" is in its application to religion. A heathen sect is simply one which is not affiliated with one or another of three or four organized systems of theology. Similarly, a primitive art is one which flourishes outside the small number of cultures which we have chosen to designate as civilizations. Such arts differ vastly and it is correspondingly difficult to generalize about them. Any statements which will hold true for such diverse aesthetic experiences as the pictographs of the Australians, the woven designs of the Peruvians, and the abstract sculptures of the African Negroes must be of the broadest and simplest sort. Moveover, the problem is complicated by the meaning attached to the term "primitive" in its other uses. It stands for something simple, undeveloped, and, by implication, ancestral to more evolved forms. Its application to arts and cultures other than our own is an unfortunate heritage from the nineteenth-century scientists who laid the foundations of anthropology. Elated by the newly enunciated doctrines of evolution, these students saw all cultures as stages in a single line of development and assigned them to places in this series on the simple basis of the degree to which they differed from European culture, which was blandly assumed to be the final and perfect flower of the evolutionary process. This idea has long since been abandoned by anthropologists, but before its demise it diffused to other social sciences and became a part of the general body of popular misinformation. It still tinges a great deal of the thought and writing about the arts of non-European peoples and has been responsible for many misunderstandings.

1. The *MAIN* purpose of the passage is to   1. ...
   - A. explain the various definitions of the term "primitive"
   - B. show that the term "primitive" can be applied validly to art
   - C. compare the use of the term "primitive" to the use of the term "heathen"
   - D. deprecate the use of the term "primitive" as applied to art
   - E. show that "primitive" arts vary greatly among themselves
2. The nineteenth-century scientists believed that the theory   2. ... of evolution
   - A. could be applied to the development of culture
   - B. was demonstrated in all social sciences
   - C. was substantiated by the diversity of "primitive" art
   - D. could be applied only to European culture
   - E. disproved the idea that some arts are more "primitive" than others
3. With which of the following would the author agree?   3. ...
   - A. The term "primitive" is used only by the misinformed.

1

B. "Primitive" arts may be as highly developed as "civilized" arts.
C. The arts of a culture often indicated how advanced that culture was.
D. Australian, Peruvian, and African Negro arts are much like the ancestral forms from which European art evolved.
E. A simple culture is likely to have a simple art.

4. According to the author, many misunderstandings have been   4. ...
caused by the belief that
A. most cultures are fundamentally different
B. inferior works of art in any culture are "primitive" art
C. "primitive" arts are diverse
D. non-European arts are diverse
E. European civilization is the final product of the evolutionary process

---

TEST 2

One of the ways the intellectual *avant-garde* affects the technical intelligentsia is through the medium of art, and art is, if only implicitly, a critique of experience. The turning upon itself of modern culture in the forms of the new visual art, the utilization of the detritus of daily experience to mock that experience, constitutes a mode of social criticism. Pop art, it is true, does not go beyond the surface of the visual and tactile experience of an industrial (and a commercialized) culture. Dwelling on the surface, it allows its consumers to mock the elements of their daily life, without abandoning it. Indeed, the consumption of art in the organized market for leisure serves at times to encapsulate the social criticism of the *avant-garde*. However, the recent engagement of writers, artists and theater people in contemporary issues suggests that this sort of containment may have begun to reach its limits.

In an atmosphere in which the intellectually dominant group insists on the contradictions inherent in daily experience, the technical intelligentsia will find it difficult to remain unconscious of those contradictions. The technical intelligentsia have until now avoided contradictions by accepting large rewards for their expertise. As expertise becomes increasingly difficult to distinguish from ordinary service on the one hand, and merges on the other with the change of the social environment, the technical intelligentsia's psychic security may be jeopardized. Rendering of labor services casts it back into spiritual proletarianization; a challenge to the social control exercised by elites, who use the technical intelligentsia's labor power, pushes it forward to social criticism and revolutionary politics. That these are matters, for the moment, of primarily spiritual import does not diminish their ultimate political significance. A psychological precondition for radical action is usually far more important than an "objectively" revolutionary situation -- whatever that may be.

The chances for a radicalization of the technical intelligentsia, thus extending the student revolt, cannot be even approximated. I believe I have shown there is a chance.

2

1. It may be *inferred* that the technical intelligentsia are: 1. ...
      I. The executives and employers in society
     II. Critics of *avant-garde* art
    III. Highly skilled technical workers
    The *CORRECT* answer is:
      A. I *only*   B. I and III   C. I, II, and III
      D. III *only*   E. I and II

2. The engagement of the intellectual *avant-garde* in con-   2. ...
   temporary issues
      A. indicates that people tire of questioning the contra-
         dictions inherent in day-to-day living
      B. indicates that the technical intelligentsia are close
         to the point where they will rebel against the *avant-
         garde*
      C. could cause a challenge to the social control of the
         elites
      D. could cause the public to become more leisure-oriented
      E. could cause an increase in the consumption of art in
         the organized market for leisure services

3. The *possible* effect of the intellectual *avant-garde* on   3. ...
   the technical intelligentsia is that
      A. the intellectual *avant-garde* makes the technical
         intelligentsia conscious of society's contradictions
      B. rapid curtailment of large rewards for expertise will
         result
      C. it may cause a strong likelihood of a radicalization
         of the technical intelligentsia
      D. the *avant-garde* will replace the employment of the
         technical intelligentsia in contemporary issues
      E. the rendering of labor services will be eliminated

4. If it is assumed that the technical intelligentsia become   4. ...
   fully aware of the contradictions of modern life, it is
   the author's position that
      A. revolution will result
      B. the technical intelligentsia may refuse to perform
         manual labor
      C. the technical intelligentsia will be pushed forward
         to social criticism and revolutionary politics
      D. the technical intelligentsia will experience some
         psychic dislocation
      E. ordinary service will replace technical expertise

5. According to the author,   5. ...
      A. the state of mind of a particular group may have more
         influence on its action than the effect of environmental
         factors
      B. the influence of art will often cause social upheaval
      C. matters of primarily spiritual import necessarily lack
         political significance
      D. the detritus of day-to-day living should be mocked by
         the intellectual *avant-garde*
      E. the technical intelligentsia can only protect their
         psychic security by self-expression through art

3

6. *With which* of the following would the author *agree?*   6. ...
    I. As contradictions are less contained, the psychic security of all members of the working class would be jeopardized.
   II. The expertise of the technical intelligentsia evolved from the ownership and management of property.
  III. The technical intelligentsia are not accustomed to rendering labor services.
The *CORRECT* answer is:
    A. I only   B. III only   C. I and III
    D. II only   E. None of the above

7. The *MAIN* purpose of the passage is to   7. ...
    A. discuss the influence of the *avant-garde* art form on the expertise of the technical intelligentsia
    B. discuss the effect of the intellectual *avant-garde* on the working classes
    C. discuss the social significance of the technical intelligentsia
    D. discuss the possible effects of the deencapsulation of *avant-garde* social criticism
    E. point out that before a change psychological preconditions are first established

TEST 3

Turbulent flow over a boundary is a complex phenomenon for which there is no really complete theory even in simple laboratory cases. Nevertheless, a great deal of experimental data has been collected on flows over solid surfaces, both in the laboratory and in nature, so that, from an engineering point of view at least, the situation is fairly well understood. The force exerted on a surface varies with the roughness of that surface and approximately with the square of the wind speed at some fixed height above it. A wind of 10 meters per second (about 20 knots, or 22 miles per hour) measured at a height of 10 meters will produce a force of some 30 tons per square kilometer on a field of mown grass or of about 70 tons per square kilometer on a ripe wheat field. On a really smooth surface, such as glass, the force is only about 10 tons per square kilometer.

When the wind blows over water, the whole thing is much more complicated. The roughness of the water is not a given characteristic of the surface but depends on the wind itself. Not only that, the elements that constitute the roughness - the waves - themselves move more or less in the direction of the wind. Recent evidence indicates that a large portion of the momentum transferred from the air into the water goes into waves rather than directly into making currents in the water; only as the waves break, or otherwise lose energy, does their momentum become available to generate currents, or produce Ekman layers. Waves carry a substantial amount of both energy and momentum (typically about as much as is carried by the wind in a layer about one wavelength thick), and so the wave-generation process is far from negligible.

A violently wavy surface belies its appearance by acting, as far as the wind is concerned, as though it were very smooth. At 10 meters per second, recent measurements seem to agree, the force on the surface is quite a lot less than the force over mown grass and scarcely more than it is over glass; some observations in light winds of two or three meters per second indicate that the force on the wavy surface is less than it is on a surface as smooth as glass. In some way the motion of the waves seems to modify the airflow so that air slips over the surface even more freely than it would without the waves. This seems not to be the case at higher wind speeds, above about five meters per second, but the force remains strikingly low compared with that over other natural surfaces.

One serious deficiency is the fact that there are no direct observations at all in those important cases in which the wind speed is greater than about 12 meters per second and has had time and fetch (the distance over water) enough to raise substantial waves. The few indirect studies indicate that the apparent roughness of the surface increases somewhat under high-wind conditions, so that the force on the surface increases rather more rapidly than as the square of the wind speed.

Assuming that the force increases at least as the square of the wind speed, it is evident that high-wind conditions produce effects far more important than their frequency of occurrence would suggest. Five hours of 60-knot storm winds will put more momentum into the water than a week of 10-knot breezes. If it should be shown that, for high winds, the force on the surface increases appreciably more rapidly than as the square of the wind speed, then the transfer of momentum to the ocean will turn out to be dominated by what happens during the occasional storm rather than by the long-term average winds.

1. According to the passage, several hours of storm winds   1. ...
   (60 miles per hour) over the ocean would
      A. be similar to the force exerted by light winds for
         several hours over glass
      B. create an ocean roughness which reduces the force
         exerted by the high winds
      C. have proved to be more significant in creating ocean
         momentum than light winds
      D. create a force not greater than 6 times the force of
         a 10-mile-per-hour wind
      E. eventually affect ocean current
2. According to the passage, a rough-like ocean surface   2. ...
      A. is independent of the force of the wind
      B. has the same force exerted against it by high and
         light winds
      C. is more likely to have been caused by a storm than
         by continuous light winds
      D. nearly always allows airflow to be modified so as to
         cause the force of the wind to be less than on glass
      E. is a condition under which the approximate square of
         wind speed can never be an accurate figure in measur-
         ing the wind force

5

3. The author indicates that, where a hurricane is followed   3. ...
    by light winds of 10 meters per second or less,
     I. ocean current will be unaffected by the light winds
     II. ocean current will be more affected by the hurricane
       winds than the following light winds
   III. the force of the light winds on the ocean would be
       less than that exerted on a wheat field
    The *CORRECT* combination is:
     A. I only   B. III only   C. II and III
     D. I and III   E. II only

4. The *MAIN* purpose of the passage is to discuss   4. ...
     A. oceanic momentum and current
     B. turbulent flow of wind over water
     C. wind blowing over water as related to causing tidal
       flow
     D. the significance of high wind conditions on ocean
       momentum
     E. experiments in wind force

5. The author would be *incorrect* in concluding that the   5. ...
    transfer of momentum to the ocean is dominated by the
    occasional storm if
     A. air momentum went directly into making ocean current
     B. high speed winds slipped over waves as easily as low
       speed winds
     C. waves did not move in the direction of wind
     D. the force exerted on a wheat field was the same as
       on mown grass
     E. the force of wind under normal conditions increased
       as the square of wind speed

6. A wind of 10 meters per second measured at a height of   6. ...
    10 meters will produce a force close to 30 tons per square
    mile on *which* of the following?
     A. Unmown grass   B. Mown grass   C. Glass
     D. Water   E. A football field

TEST 4

Political scientists, as practitioners of a negligibley formalized
discipline, tend to be accommodating to formulations and suggested
techniques developed in related behavioral sciences. They even tend,
on occasion, to speak of psychology, sociology and anthropology as
"hard core sciences." Such a characterization seems hardly justified.
The disposition to uncritically adopt into political science non-
indigenous sociological and general systems concepts tends, at times,
to involve little more than the adoption of a specific, and sometimes
barbarous, academic vocabulary which is used to redescribe reasonably
well-confirmed or intuitively-grasped low-order empirical generalizations.

At its worst, what results in such instances is a runic explanation, a redescription in a singular language style, i.e., no explanation at all. At their best, functional accounts as they are
found in the contemporary literature provide explanation sketches,
the type of elliptical explanation characteristic of historical and

psychoanalytic accounts. For each such account there is an in-
determinate number of equally plausible ones, the consequence of
either the complexity of the subject matter, differing perspectives,
conceptual vagueness, the variety of sometimes mutually exclusive
empirical or quasi-empirical generalizations employed, or syntactical
obscurity, or all of them together.

Functional explanations have been most reliable in biology and
physiology (where they originated) and in the analysis of servo-
mechanical and cybernetic systems (to which they have been effectively extended). In these areas we possess a well-standardized body
of lawlike generalizations. Neither sociology nor political science
has as yet the same resource of well-confirmed lawlike statements.
Certainly sociology has few more than political science. What passes
for functional explanation in sociology is all too frequently para-
sitic upon suggestive analogy and metaphor, trafficking on our
familiarity with goal directed-systems.

What is advanced as "theory" in sociology is frequently a non-
theoretic effort at classification or "codification," the search
for an analytic conceptual schema which provides a typology or a
classificatory system serviceable for convenient storage and ready
retrieval of independently established empirical regularities. That
such a schema takes on a hierarchic and deductive character, impart-
ing to the collection of propositions a *prima facie* theoretical
appearance, may mean no more than that the terms employed in the
high-order propositions are so vague that they can accommodate almost any inference and consequently can be made to any conceivable
state of affairs.

1. The author *implies* that, when the political scientist is   1. ...
   at his best, his explanations
     A. are essentially a retelling of events
     B. only then form the basis of an organized discipline
     C. plausibly account for past occurrences
     D. are prophetic of future events
     E. are confirmed principles forming part of the
        political scientist's theory
2. With *which* of the following would the author probably   2. ...
   agree?
      I. Because of an abundance of reasonable explanations
         for past conduct, there is the possibility of contend-
         ing schools within the field of political science
         developing.
     II. Political science is largely devoid of predictive power.
    III. Political science has very few verified axioms.
   The *CORRECT* answer is:
     A. III only   B. I and III   C. I and II
     D. I, II, and III E. I only
3. The passage *implies* that many sociological theories   3. ...
     A. are capable of being widely applied to various situations
     B. do not even appear to be superficially theoretical in
        appearance
     C. contrast with those of political science in that there
        are many more confirmed lawlike statements
     D. are derived from deep analysis and exhaustive research
     E. appear theoretical but are really very well proved

4. The author's thesis would be *UNSUPPORTABLE* if   4. ...
   A. the theories of the political scientist possessed predictive power
   B. political science did not consist of redescription
   C. political scientists were not restricted to "hard core sciences"
   D. political science consisted of a body of theories capable of application to any situation
   E. None of the above

5. The author believes that sociology   5. ...
   A. as a "hard core science," contains reliable and functional explanations
   B. is never more than a compilation of conceptual schema
   C. is in nearly every respect unlike political science
   D. is a discipline which allows for varied inferences to be drawn from its general propositions
   E. is a science indigenous to *prima facie* theoretical appearance, containing very little codification posing as theory

———

TEST 5

James's own prefaces to his works were devoted to structural composition and analytics and his approach in those prefaces has only recently begun to be understood. One of his contemporary critics, with the purest intention to blame, wrote what might be recognized today as sophisticated praise when he spoke of the later James as "an impassioned geometer" and remarked that "what interested him was not the figures but their relations, the relations which alone make pawns significant." James's explanations of his works often are so bereft of interpretation as to make some of our own austere defenses against interpretation seem almost embarrassingly rich with psychological meanings. They offer, with a kind of brazen unselfconsciousness, an astonishingly artificial, even mechanical view of novelistic invention. It's not merely that James asserts the importance of technique; more radically, he tends to discuss character and situation almost entirely as functions of technical ingenuities. The very elements in a Jamesian story which may strike us as requiring the most explanation are presented by James either as a *solution* to a problem of compositional harmony or else as the *donnee* about which it would be irrelevant to ask any questions at all.

James should constantly be referred to as a model of structuralist criticism. He consistently redirects our attention from the referential aspect of a work of art (its extensions into "reality") to its own structural coherence as the principal source of inspiration.

What is most interesting about James's structurally functional view of character is that a certain devaluation of what we ordinarily think of as psychological interest is perfectly consistent with an attempt to portray reality. It's as if he came to feel that a kind of autonomous geometric pattern, in which the parts appeal for their value to nothing but their contributive place in the essentially abstract pattern, is the artist's most successful representation of life. Thus he could perhaps even think that verisimilitude - a word he liked - has less to do with the probability of the events the

8

novelist describes than with those processes, deeply characteristic of life, by which he creates sense and coherence from *any* event. The only faithful picture of life in art is not in the choice of a significant subject (James always argues against the pseudorealistic prejudice), but rather in the illustration of sense-, of design-making processes. James proves the novel's connection with life by deprecating its derivation from life; and it's when he is most abstractly articulating the growth of a structure that James is almost most successfully defending the mimetic function of art (and of criticism). His deceptively banal position that only execution matters means most profoundly that verisimilitude, properly considered, is the grace and the truth of a formal unity.

1. The author suggests that James, in explanations of his own art,
    A. was not bound by formalistic strictures but concentrated on verisimilitude
    B. was deeply psychological and concentrated on personal insight
    C. felt that his art had a one-to-one connection with reality
    D. was basically mechanical and concentrated on geometrical form
    E. was event-and-character-oriented rather than technique-oriented

2. The passage indicates that James's method of approaching reality was
    A. that objective reality did not exist and was patterned only by the mind
    B. that formalism and pattern were excellent means of approaching reality
    C. not to concentrate on specific events but rather on character development
    D. that the only objective reality is the psychological processes of the mind
    E. that in reality events occur which are not structured but rather as random occurrences

3. The *MAIN* purpose of the paragraph is to
    A. indicate that James's own approach to his work is only now beginning to be understood
    B. deprecate the geometrical approach towards the novel
    C. question whether James's novels were related to reality
    D. indicate that James felt that society itself could be seen as a geometric structure
    E. discuss James's explanation of his works

4. In discussing his own works, James
    I. talks of people and events as a function of technique to the exclusion of all else
    II. is quick to emphasize the referential aspect of the work
    III. felt that verisimilitude could be derived not from character but rather from the ordering of events
    The *CORRECT* answer is:
    A. I *only*   B. II *only*   C. III *only*
    D. I and III   E. I and II

5. The author 5. ...
   A. *approves* of James's explanations of his own work but *disapproves* his lack of discussion into the psychological makings of his characters
   B. *disapproves* of James's explanation of his own work and his lack of discussion into the psychological makings of his characters
   C. *approves* of James's explanations of his works in terms of structure as being well related to life
   D. *disapproves* of James's explanation of his works in terms of structure as lacking verisimilitude
   E. *approves* of James's explanation of his works because of the significance of the subjects chosen
6. The *following* is *NOT* true of James's explanation of his 6. ...
   own works: He
   A. did not explain intriguing elements of a story except as part of a geometric whole
   B. felt the artist could represent life by its patterns rather than its events
   C. defended the imitative function of art by detailing the growth of a structure
   D. attempted to give the reader insight into the psychology of his characters by insuring that his explanation followed a strict geometrical pattern
   E. was able to devalue psychological interest and yet be consistent with an attempt to truly represent life
7. James believed it to be *essential* to 7. ...
   A. carefully choose a subject which would lend itself to processes by which sense and cohesion is achieved
   B. defend the mimetic function of art by emphasizing verisimilitude
   C. emphasize the manner in which different facets of a story could fit together
   D. explain character in order to achieve literary harmony
   E. be artificial and unconcerned with representing life

TEST 6

   The popular image of the city as it is now is a place of decay, crime, of fouled streets, and of people who are poor or foreign or odd. But what is the image of the city of the future? In the plans for the huge redevelopment projects to come, we are being shown a new image of the city. Gone are the dirt and the noise - and the variety and the excitement and the spirit. That it is an ideal makes it all the worse; these bleak new utopias are not bleak because they have to be; they are the concrete manifestation - and how literally - of a deep, and at times arrogant, misunderstanding of the function of the city.

   Being made up of human beings, the city is, of course, a wonderfully resilient institution. Already it has reasserted itself as an industrial and business center. Not so many years ago, there was much talk of decentralizing to campus-like offices, and a wholesale exodus of business to the countryside seemed imminent. But a business pastoral is something of a contradiction in terms, and for the simple reason that the city is the center of things because it is a center, the suburban heresy never came off. Many industrial campuses have been built, but the overwhelming proportion of new office building has been taking place in the big cities.

But the rebuilding of downtown is not enough; a city deserted at night by its leading citizens is only half a city. If it is to continue as the dominant cultural force in American life, the city must have a core of people to support its theatres and museums, its shops and its restaurants - even a Bohemia of sorts can be of help. For it is the people who like living in the city who make it an attraction to the visitors who don't. It is the city dwellers who support its style; without them there is nothing to come downtown to.

The cities have a magnificant opportunity. There are definite signs of a small but significant move back from suburbia. There is also evidence that many people who will be moving to suburbia would prefer to stay in the city - and it would not take too much more in amenities to make them stay.

But the cities seem on the verge of muffing their opportunity - and muffing it for generations to come. In a striking failure to apply marketing principles and an even more striking failure of aesthetics, the cities are freezing on a design for living ideally calculated to keep everybody in suburbia. These vast, barracks-like superblocks are not designed for people who *like* cities, but for people who have no other choice. A few imaginative architects and planners have shown that redeveloped blocks don't have to be repellent to make money, but so far their ideas have had little effect. The institutional approach is dominant, and,unless the assumptions embalmed in it are re-examined,the city is going to be turned into a gigantic bore.

1. The author would *NOT* be pleased with   1. ...
    A. a crowded, varied, stimulating city
    B. the dedication of new funds to the reconstruction of
       the cities
    C. a more detailed understanding of the poor
    D. the elimination of assumptions which do not reflect
       the function of the city
    E. the adoption of a laissez faire attitude by those in
       charge of redevelopment.
2. "The rebuilding of downtown" (1st sentence, 3d paragraph)   2. ...
   refers to
    A. huge redevelopment projects to come
    B. the application of marketing and aesthetic principles
       to rejuvenating the city
    C. keeping the city as the center of business
    D. attracting a core of people to support the city's
       functions
    E. the doing away with barracks-like structures
3. According to the author, the city, in order to better it-   3. ...
   self, *must*
    A. increase its downtown population
    B. attract an interested core of people to support its
       cultural institutions

    C. adhere to an institutional approach rather than be satisfied with the status quo
    D. erect campus-like business complexes
    E. establish an ideal for orderly future growth

4. The *MAIN* purpose of the passage is to   4. ...
    A. show that the present people inhabiting the city do not make the city viable
    B. discuss the types of construction which should and should not take place in the city's future
    C. indicate that imaginative architects and planners have shown that redeveloped areas don't have to be ugly to make money
    D. discuss the human element in the city
    E. point out the lack of understanding by many city planners of the city's functions

5. The author's thesis would be *LESS* supportable *if*   5. ...
    I. city planners presently understood that stereotyped reconstruction is doomed to ultimate failure
    II. the institutional approach referred to in the passage was based upon assumptions which took into account the function of the city
    III. there were signs that a shift back to the city from suburbia were occurring
  The *CORRECT* answer is:
    A. II *only*   B. II and III   C. I and II
    D. I *only*   E. III *only*

TEST 7

    In estimating the child's conceptions of the world, the first question is to decide whether external reality is as external and objective for the child as it is for adults. In other words, can the child distinguish the self from the external world? So long as the child supposes that everyone necessarily thinks like himself, he will not spontaneously seek to convince others, nor to accept common truths, nor, above all, to prove or test his opinions. If his logic lacks exactitude and objectivity it is because the social impulses of maturer years are counteracted by an innate egocentricity. In studying the child's thought, not in this case in relation to others but to things, one is faced at the outset with the analogous problem of the child's capacity to dissociate thought from self in order to form an objective conception of reality.

    The child, like the uncultured adult, appears exclusively concerned with things. He is indifferent to the life of thought and the originality of individual points of view escapes him. His earliest interests, his first games, his drawings are all concerned solely with the imitation of what is. In short, the child's thought has every appearance of being exclusively realistic.

    But realism is of two types, or, rather, objectivity must be distinguished from realism. Objectivity consists in so fully realizing the countless intrusions of the self in everyday thought and the countless illusions which result - illusions of sense, language, point of view, value, etc. - that the preliminary step to every judgment is the effort to exclude the intrusive self. Realism, on the contrary, consists in ignoring the existence of self and thence regarding one's own perspective as immediately objective and ab- solute. Realism is thus anthropocentric illusion, finality - in short, all those illusions which teem in the history of science. So long as thought has not become conscious of self, it is a prey to perpetual confusions between objective and subjective, between the real and the ostensible; it values the entire content of con- sciousness on a single plane in which ostensible realities and the unconscious interventions of the self are inextricably mixed. It is thus not futile, but, on the contrary, indispensable to establish clearly and before all else the boundary the child draws between the self and the external world.

1. The result of a child's not learning that others think   1. ...
   differently than he does is that
     A. the child will not be able to function as an adult
     B. when the child has matured, he will be innately
        egocentric
     C. when the child has matured, his reasoning will be poor
     D. upon maturity, the child will not be able to distinguish
        thought from objects
     E. upon maturity, the child will not be able to make non-
        ego-influenced value judgments
2. Objectivity is the ability to   2. ...
     A. distinguish ego from the external world
     B. dissociate oneself from others
     C. realize that others have a different point of view
     D. distinguish illusion from realism
     E. dissociate ego from thought
3. When thought is *not* conscious of self,   3. ...
     A. one is able to draw the correct conclusions from his
        perceptions
     B. the apparent may not be distinguishable from the actual
     C. conscious thought may not be distinguishable from the
        unconscious
     D. the ego may influence the actual
     E. ontogony recapitulates phylogony
4. The *MAIN* purpose of the passage is to   4. ...
     A. argue that the child should be made to realize that
        others may not think like he does
     B. estimate the child's conception of the world
     C. explain the importance of distinguishing the mind
        from external objects
     D. emphasize the importance of non-ego-influenced per-
        spective
     E. show how the child establishes the boundary between
        himself and the external world
5. The author *implies* that, if an adult is to think logically, 5. ...
     A. his reasoning, as he matures, must be tempered by
        other viewpoints
     B. he must be able to distinguish one physical object
        from another
     C. he must be exclusively concerned with thought in-
        stead of things

13

    D. he must be able to perceive reality without the
       intrusions of the self
    E. he must not value the content of consciousness
       on a single plain
6. Realism, according to the passage, is   6. ...
    A. the realization of the countless intrusions of the self
    B. final and complete objectivity
    C. a desire to be truly objective and absolute
    D. the ability to be perceptive and discerning
    E. none of the above
7. The child who is exclusively concerned with things   7. ...
    A. thinks only objectively
    B. is concerned with imitating the things he sees
    C. must learn to distinguish between realism and
       anthropomorphism
    D. has no innate ability
    E. will, through interaction with others, often prove his
       opinions

TEST 8

    Democracy is not logically antipathetic to most doctrines of
natural rights, fundamental or higher law, individual rights, or any
similar ideals - but merely asks citizens to take note of the fact
that the preservation of these rights rests with the majority, in
political processes, and does not depend upon a legal or constitutional Maginot line. Democracy may, then, be supported by believers
in individual rights providing they believe that rights - or any
transcendental ends - are likely to be better safeguarded under
such a system. Support for democracy on such instrumental grounds
may, of course, lead to the dilemma of loyalty to the system vs.
loyality to a natural right - but the same kind of dilemma may
arise for anyone, over any prized value, and in any political system,
and is insoluble in advance.

    There is unanimous agreement that - as a matter of fact and law,
not of conjecture - no single right can be realized, except at the
expense of other rights and claims. For that reason their absolute
status, in some philosophic sense, is of little political relevance.
Political policies involve much more than very general principles
or rights. The main error of the older natural rights school was
not that it had an absolute right, but that it had too many absolute
rights. There must be compromise, and, as any compromise destroys
the claim to absoluteness, the natural outcome of experience was the
repudiation of all of them. And now the name of "natural right" can
only creep into sight with the reassuring placard, "changing content
gurranteed." Nor is it at all easy to see how any doctrine of inalienable, natural, individual rights can be reconciled with a
political.doctrine of common consent - except in an anarchist society,
or one of saints. Every natural right ever put forward, and the lists
are elusive and capricious, is every day invaded by governments, in
the public interest and with widespread public approval.

    To talk of relatively attainable justice or rights in politics
is not to plump for a moral relativism - in the sense that all

values are equally good. But while values may be objective, the
specific value judgments and policies are inevitably relative to a
context, and it is only when a judgment divorces context from general
principle that it looks like moral relativism. Neither, of course,
does the fact of moral diversity invalidate all moral rules.

Any political system, then, deals only with relatively attainable
rights, as with relative justice and freedoms. Hence we may differ
in given instances on specific policies, despite agreement on broad
basic principles such as a right or a moral "ought"; and,per contra,
we may agree on specific policies while differing on fundamental
principles or long-range objectives or natural rights. Politics
and through politics, law and policies, give these rights - and
moral principles - their substance and limits. There is no getting
away from the political nature of this or any other prescriptive
ideal in a free society.

1. With *which* of the following would the author *agree*?   1. ...
   A. Natural and individual rights can exist at all only
      under a democracy.
   B. While natural rights may exist, they are only relative-
      ly attainable.
   C. Civil disobedience has no place in a democracy where
      natural rights have no philosophic relevance.
   D. Utilitarianism, which draws its criteria from the hap-
      piness and welfare of individuals, cannot logically be
      a goal of a democratic state.
   E. Some natural rights should never be compromised for
      the sake of political policy.
2. It can be *inferred* that a democratic form of government   2. ...
   A. can be supported by natural rightists as the best
      pragmatic method of achieving their aims
   B. is a form of government wherein fundamental or higher
      law is irrelevant
   C. will in time repudiate all inalienable rights
   D. forces a rejection of moral absolutism
   E. will soon exist in undeveloped areas of the world
3. The *MAIN* purpose of the passage is to   3. ...
   A. discuss natural rights doctrine
   B. compare and contrast democracy to individual rights
   C. discuss the reconciliation of a doctrine of inalien-
      able natural rights with a political system
   D. discuss the safegurrding of natural rights in a
      democratic society
   E. indicate that moral relativism is antipathetic to
      democracy
4. The author indicates that natural rights   4. ...
    I. are sometimes difficult to define
   II. are easily definable but at times unreconcilable with
      a system of government predicated upon majority rule
 III. form a basis for moral relativism
   The *CORRECT* answer is:
   A. I *only*   B. I *only*   C. I and II
   D. III *only*   E. II and III

5. The fact that any political system deals with relatively   5. ...
   attainable rights
   A. shows that all values are equally good or bad
   B. is cause for divorcing political reality from moral
      rules
   C. shows that the list of natural rights is elusive and
      capricious
   D. is inconsistent with the author's thesis
   E. does not necessarily mean that natural rights do not
      exist
6. The passage indicates that an important conflict which   6. ...
   can exist in a democracy is the
   A. rights of competing groups, i.e., labor versus manage-
      ment
   B. adherence to the democratic process versus non-democratic
      actions by government
   C. difficulty in choosing between two effective compromises
   D. adherence to the democratic process versus the desire
      to support a specific right
   E. difficulty in reconciling conflict by natural rights

KEYS (CORRECT ANSWERS)

TEST 1	TEST 2	TEST 3	TEST 4
1. D	1. D	1. E	1. C
2. A	2. C	2. C	2. D
3. B	3. A	3. C	3. A
4. E	4. D	4. B	4. A
	5. A	5. B	5. D
	6. B	6. A	
	7. D		

TEST 5	TEST 6	TEST 7	TEST 8
1. D	1. D	1. C	1. B
2. B	2. C	2. E	2. A
3. E	3. B	3. B	3. C
4. C	4. E	4. D	4. A
5. C	5. C	5. A	5. E
6. D		6. E	6. D
7. C		7. B	

16

READING COMPREHENSION
UNDERSTANDING AND INTERPRETING WRITTEN MATERIAL
EXAMINATION SECTION

DIRECTIONS: Each question or incomplete statement is followed by several suggested answers or completions. Select the one that BEST answers the question or completes the statement. *PRINT THE LETTER OF THE CORRECT ANSWER IN THE SPACE AT THE RIGHT.*

TEST 1

1. Most managers make the mistake of using *absolutes* as signals of trouble or its absence. A quality problem emerges - that means trouble; a test is passed - we have no problems. Outside of routine organizations, there are always going to be such signals of trouble or success, but they are not very meaningful. Many times everything looks good, but the roof is about to cave in because something no one thought about and for which there is no rule, procedure, or test has been neglected. The specifics of such problems cannot be predicted, but they are often signaled in advance by changes in the organizational system: Managers spend less time on the project; minor problems proliferate; friction in the relationships between adjacent work groups or departments increases; verbal progress reports become overly glib, or overly reticent; changes occur in the rate at which certain events happen, not in whetner or not they happen. And they are monitored by random probes into the organization - seeing how things are going.
According to the above paragraph,
  A. managers do not spend enough time managing
  B. managers have a tendency to become overly glib when writing reports
  C. managers should be aware that problems that exist in the organization may not exhibit predictable signals of trouble
  D. managers should attempt to alleviate friction in the relationship between adjacent work groups by monitoring random probes into the organization's problems

1.____

2. *Lack of challenge* and *excessive zeal* are opposite villains. 2.___
   You cannot do your best on a problem unless you are motivated. Professional problem solvers learn to be motivated
   somewhat by money and future work that may come their way
   if they succeed. However, challenge must be present for
   at least some of the time, or the process ceases to be
   rewarding. On the other hand, an excessive motivation to
   succeed, especially to succeed quickly, can inhibit the
   creative process. The tortoise-and-the-hare phenomenon
   is often apparent in problem solving. The person who
   thinks up the simple elegant solution, although he or she
   may take longer in doing so, often wins. As in the race,
   the tortoise depends upon an inconsistent performance from
   the rabbit. And if the rabbit spends so little time on
   conceptualization that the rabbit merely chooses the first
   answers that occur, such inconsistency is almost guaranteed.
   According to the above paragraph,
   A. excessive motivation to succeed can be harmful in
      problem solving
   B. it is best to spend a long time on solving problems
   C. motivation is the most important component in problem
      solving
   D. choosing the first solution that occurs is a valid
      method of problem solving

3. Virginia Woolf's approach to the question of women and   3.___
   fiction, about which she wrote extensively, polemically,
   and in a profoundly feminist way, was grounded in a
   general theory of literature. She argued that the writer
   was the product of her or his historical circumstances
   and that material conditions were of crucial importance.
   Secondly, she claimed that these material circumstances
   had a profound effect on the psychological aspects of
   writing, and that they could be seen to influence the
   nature of the creative work itself.
   According to this paragraph,
   A. the material conditions and historical circumstances
      in which male and female writers find themselves
      greatly influence their work
   B. a woman must have an independent income to succeed
      as a writer
   C. Virginia Woolf preferred the writings of female
      authors, as their experiences more clearly reflected
      hers
   D. male writers are less likely than women writers to
      be influenced by material circumstances

4. A young person's first manager is likely to be the most   4.___
   influential person in his or her career. If this manager
   is unable or unwilling to develop the skills the young
   employee needs to perform effectively, the latter will set
   lower personal standards than he or she is capable of
   achieving, that person's self-image will be impaired, and
   he or she will develop negative attitudes toward the job,
   the employer, and - in all probability - his or her career.

Since the chances of building a successful career with the
employer will decline rapidly, he or she will leave, if
that person has high aspirations, in hope of finding a
better opportunity. If, on the other hand, the manager
helps the employee to achieve maximum potential, he or
she will build a foundation for a successful career.
According to the above paragraph,
    A. if an employee has negative attitudes towards his or
       her job, the manager is to blame
    B. managers of young people often have a great influence
       upon their careers
    C. good employees will leave a job they like if they are
       not given a chance to develop their skills
    D. managers should develop the full potential of their
       young employees

5. The reason for these differences is not that the Greeks
   had a superior sense of form or an inferior imagination
   or joy in life, but that they thought differently. Perhaps
   an illustration will make this clear. With the historical
   plays of Shakespeare in mind, let the reader contemplate
   the only extant Greek play on a historical subject, the
   Persians of Aeschylus, a play written less than ten years
   after the event which it deals with, and performed before
   the Athenian people who had played so notable a part in
   the struggle - incidentally, immediately below the
   Acropolis which the Persians had sacked and defiled. Any
   Elizabethan dramatist would have given us a panorama of
   the whole war, its moments of despair, hope, and triumph;
   we should see on the stage the leaders who planned and some
   of the soldiers who won the victory. In the PERSIANS we
   see nothing of the sort. The scene is laid in the Persian
   capital, one action is seen only through Persian eyes, the
   course of the war is simplified so much that the naval
   battle of Artemisium is not mentioned, nor even the heroic
   defense of Thermopylae, and not a single Greek is mentioned
   by name. The contrast could hardly be more complete.
   Which sentence is BEST supported by the above paragraph?
     A. Greek plays are more interesting than Elizabethan plays.
     B. Elizabethan dramatists were more talented than Greek
        dramatists.
     C. If early Greek dramatists had the same historical
        material as Shakespeare had, the final form the Greek
        work would take would be very different from the
        Elizabethan work.
     D. Greeks were historically more inaccurate than
        Elizabethans.

6. The problem with present planning systems, public or
   private, is that accountability is weak. Private planning
   systems in the global corporations operate on a set of
   narrow incentives that frustrate sensible public policies
   such as full employment, environmental protection, and
   price stability. Public planning is Olympian and confused
   because there is neither a clear consensus on social values

5.___

6.___

3

nor political priorities. To accomplish anything, explicit
choices must be made, but these choices can be made effectively only with the active participation of the people
most directly involved. This, not nostalgia for small-town
times gone forever, is the reason that devolution of political power to local communities is a political necessity.
The power to plan locally is a precondition for sensible
integration of cities, regions, and countries into the
world economy.
According to the author,

   A. people most directly affected by issues should parti-
      cipate in deciding those issues
   B. private planning systems are preferable to public
      planning systems
   C. there is no good system of government
   D. county governments are more effective than state
      governments

Questions 7-11.

DIRECTIONS: Questions 7 through 11 are to be answered SOLELY on
               the basis of the following passage.

The ideal relationship for the interview is one of mutual confidence: To try to pretend, to put on a front of cordiality and friend-
ship is extremely unwise for the interviewer because he will certainly
convey, by subtle means, his real feelings. It is the interviewer's
responsibility to take the lead in establishing a relationship of
mutual confidence.

As the interviewer, you should help the interviewee to feel at
ease and ready to talk. One of the best ways to do this is to be at
ease yourself. If you are, it will probably be evident; if you are
not, it will almost certainly be apparent to the interviewee.

Begin the interview with topics for discussion which are easy to
talk about and non-menacing. This interchange can be like the con-
versation of people when they are waiting for a bus, at the ballgame,
or discussing the weather. However, do not prolong this warm-up too
long since the interviewee knows as well as you do that these are
not the things he came to discuss. Delaying too long in getting down
to business may suggest to him that you are reluctant to deal with
the topic.

Once you get onto the main topics, do all that you can to get the
interviewee to talk freely with as little prodding from you as possible. This will probably require that you give him some idea of
the area and of ways of looking at it. Avoid, however, prejudicing
or coloring his remarks by what you say; especially, do not in any
way indicate that there are certain things you want to hear, others
which you do not want to hear. It is essential that he feel free to
express his own ideas unhampered by your ideas, your values and
preconceptions.

Do not appear to dominate the interview, nor have even the
suggestion of a patronizing attitude. Ask some questions which will

enable the interviewee to take pride in his knowledge. Take the attitude that the interviewee sincerely wants the interview to achieve its purpose. This creates a warm, permissive atmosphere that is most important in all interviews.

7. Of the following, the BEST title for the above passage is   7.____
    A. PERMISSIVENESS IN INTERVIEWING
    B. INTERVIEWING TECHNIQUES
    C. THE FACTOR OF PRETENSE IN THE INTERVIEW
    D. THE CORDIAL INTERVIEW

8. Which of the following recommendations on the conduct of   8.____
    an interview is made by the above passage?
    A. Conduct the interview as if it were an interchange between people discussing the weather.
    B. The interview should be conducted in a highly impersonal manner.
    C. Allow enough time for the interview so that the interviewee does not feel rushed.
    D. Start the interview with topics which are not threatening to the interviewee.

9. The above passage indicates that the interviewer should   9.____
    A. feel free to express his opinions
    B. patronize the interviewee and display a permissive attitude
    C. permit the interviewee to give the needed information in his own fashion
    D. provide for privacy when conducting the interview

10. The meaning of the word *unhampered*, as it is used in the   10.____
    last sentence of the fourth paragraph of the above passage,
    is MOST NEARLY
    A. unheeded   B. unobstructed
    C. hindered   D. aided

11. It can be INFERRED from the above passage that   11.____
    A. interviewers, while generally mature, lack confidence
    B. certain methods in interviewing are more successful than others in obtaining information
    C. there is usually a reluctance on the part of interviewers to deal with unpleasant topics
    D. it is best for the interviewer not to waiver from the use of hard and fast rules when dealing with clients

Questions 12-19.

DIRECTIONS: Questions 12 through 19 are to be answered SOLELY on the basis of the following passage.

Disabled cars pose a great danger to bridge traffic at any time, but during rush hours it is especially important that such vehicles be promptly detected and removed. The term *disabled car* is an all-inclusive label referring to cars stalled due to a flat tire, mechanical failure, an accident, or locked bumpers. Flat tires are the most common reason why cars become disabled. The presence of disabled vehicles caused 68% of all traffic accidents last year. Of these, 75% were serious enough to require hospitalization of at least one of the vehicle's occupants.

The basic problem in the removal of disabled vehicles is detection of the car. Several methods have been proposed to aid detection. At a 1980 meeting of traffic experts and engineers, the idea of sinking electronic eyes into roadways was first suggested. Such *eyes* let officers know when traffic falls below normal speed and becomes congested. The basic argument against this approach is the high cost of installation of these *eyes*. One midwestern state has, since 1978, employed closed circuit television to detect the existence and locations of stalled vehicles. When stalled vehicles are seen on the closed circuit television screen, the information is immediately communicated by radio to units stationed along the roadway, thus enabling the prompt removal of these obstructions to traffic. However, many cities lack the necessary manpower and equipment to use this approach. For the past five years, several east-coast cities have used the method known as *safety chains*, consisting of mobile units which represent the links at the *safety chain*. These mobile units are stationed as posts one or two miles apart along roadways to detect disabled cars. Standard procedure is for the units in the *safety chain* to have roof blinker lights turned on to full rotation. The officer, upon spotting a disabled car, at once assumes a post that gives him the most control in directing traffic around the obstruction. Only after gaining such control does he investigate and decide what action should be taken.

12. From the above passage, the PERCENTAGE of accidents   12.___
caused by disabled cars in which hospitalization was required by at least one of the occupants of a vehicle last year was
    A. 17%   B. 51%   C. 68%   D. 75%

13. According to the above passage, vehicles are MOST frequent- 13.___
ly disabled because of
    A. flat tires   B. locked bumpers
    C. brake failure   D. overheated motors

14. According to the above passage, in the electronic eye   14.___
method of detection, the *eyes* are placed
    A. on lights along the roadway
    B. on patrol cars stationed along the roadway
    C. in booths spaced two miles apart
    D. into the roadway

15. According to the above passage, the factor COMMON to   15.___
both the *safety chain* method and the *closed circuit tele-vision* method of detecting disabled vehicles is that both
    A. require the use of electronic *eyes*
    B. may be used where there is a shortage of officers
    C. employ units that are stationed along the highway
    D. require the use of trucks to move the heavy equipment used

16. The one of the following which is NOT discussed in the 16.___
    above passage as a method that may be used to detect
    disabled vehicles is
    A. closed circuit television   B. radar
    C. electronic *eyes*   D. safety chains

17. One DRAWBACK mentioned by the above passage to the use of 17.___
    the closed circuit television method for detection of
    disabled cars is that this technique
    A. cannot be used during bad weather
    B. does not provide for actual removal of the cars
    C. must be operated by a highly skilled staff of traffic
       engineers
    D. requires a large amount of manpower and equipment

18. The NEWEST of the methods discussed in the above passage 18.___
    for detection of disabled vehicles is
    A. electronic *eyes*   B. the mobile unit
    C. the safety chain   D. closed circuit television

19. When the *safety chain* method is being used, an officer 19.___
    who spots a disabled vehicle should FIRST
    A. turn off his roof blinker lights
    B. direct traffic around the disabled vehicle
    C. send a radio message to the nearest mobile unit
    D. conduct an investigation

20. The universe is 15 billion years old, and the geological 20.___
    underpinnings of the earth were formed long before the
    first sea creature slithered out of the slime. But it is
    only in the last 6,000 years or so that men have descended
    into mines to chop and scratch at the earth's crust. Human
    history is, as Carl Sagan has put it, the equivalent of a
    few seconds in the 15 billion year life of the earth. What
    alarms those who keep track of the earth's crust is that
    since 1950 human beings have managed to consume more
    minerals than were mined in all previous history, a splurge
    of a millisecond in geologic time that cannot be long
    repeated without using up the finite riches of the earth.
    Of the following, the MAIN idea of this paragraph is:
    A. There is true cause for concern at the escalating
       consumption of the earth's minerals in recent years
    B. Human history is the equivalent of a few seconds in
       the 15 billion year life of the earth
    C. The earth will soon run out of vital mineral resources
    D. The extraction of minerals from the earth's crust only
       began 6,000 years ago

21. The authors of the Economic Report of the President are 21.___
    collectively aware, despite their vision of the asset-rich
    household, of the real economy in which millions of
    Americans live. There are glimpses, throughout the Report,
    of the underworld in which *about 23 million people do not
    have public or private health insurance; in which the number
    of people receiving unemployment compensation was 41 percent
    of the total unemployed*, in which the average dole for the

compensated unemployed *is about one-half of take-home pay.*
The authors understand, for example, that *a worker may
become physically disabled* and that *individuals generally
do not like the risk of losing their ability to earn income.*
But such realities justify no more than the most limited
interference in the (imperfect) market for disability
insurance. There is only, as far as I can tell, one moment
of genuine emotion in the entire Report when the authors'
passions are stirred beyond market principles. They are
discussing the leasing provisions of the 1981 Tax Act
(conditions which so reduce tax revenues that they are
apparently opposed in their present form by the Business
Roundtable, the American Business Conference, and the
National Association of Manufacturers).
In the dark days before the 1981 Act, according to the
Report, *firms with temporary tax losses (a condition especially characteristic of new enterprises) were often unable
to take advantage of investment tax incentives. The reason
was that temporarily unprofitable companies had no taxable
income against which to apply the investment tax deduction.*
It was a piteous contingency for the truly needy entrepreneur.
But all was made right with the Tax Act. Social security for
the disabled incompetent corporation: the compassionate
soul of Reagan's new economy.
According to the above passage,
  A. the National Association of Manufacturers and those
     companies that are temporarily unprofitable oppose
     the leasing provisions of the 1981 Tax Act
  B. the authors of the Report are willing to ignore market
     principles in order to assist corporations unable to
     take advantage of tax incentives
  C. the authors of the Report feel the National Association
     of Manufacturers and the Business Roundtable are wrong
     in opposing the leasing provisions of the 1981 Tax Act
  D. the authors of the Report have more compassion for
     incompetent corporations than for disabled workers

22. Much of the lore of management in the West regards   22. ___
    ambiguity as a symptom of a variety of organizational
    ills whose cure is larger doses of rationality, specificity,
    and decisiveness. But is ambiguity sometimes desirable?
    Ambiguity may be thought of as a shroud of the unknown
    surrounding certain events. The Japanese have a word for
    it, ma, for which there is no English translation. The word
    is valuable because it gives an explicit place to the
    unknowable aspect of things. In English, we may refer to
    an empty space between the chair and the table; the Japanese
    don't say the space is empty but *full of nothing.* However
    amusing the illustration, it goes to the core of the issue.
    Westerners speak of what is unknown primarily in reference
    to what is known (like the space between the chair and the
    table), while most Eastern languages give honor to the
    unknown in its own right.
    Of course, there are many situations that a manager finds
    himself in where being explicit and decisive is not only
    helpful but necessary. There is considerable advantage,

however, in having a dual frame of reference-recognizing the value of both the clear and the ambiguous. The point to bear in mind is that in certain situations, ambiguity may serve better than absolute clarity.
Which sentence is BEST supported by the above passage?
    A. We should cultivate the art of being ambiguous.
    B. Ambiguity may sometimes be an effective managerial tool.
    C. Westerners do not have a dual frame of reference.
    D. It is important to recognize the ambiguous aspects of all situations.

23. Everyone ought to accustom himself to grasp in his thought   23.____
at the same time facts that are at once so few and so simple, that he shall never believe that he has knowledge of anything which he does not mentally behold with a distinctiveness equal to that of the objects which he knows most distinctly of all. It is true that some people are born with a much greater aptitude for such discernment than others, but the mind can be made much more expert at such work by art and exercise. But there is one fact which I should here emphasize above all others; and that is everyone should firmly persuade himself that none of the sciences, however abstruse, is to be deduced from lofty and obscure matters, but that they all proceed only from what is easy and more readily understood.
According to the author,
    A. people should concentrate primarily on simple facts
    B. intellectually gifted people have a great advantage over others
    C. even difficult material and theories proceed from what is readily understood
    D. if a scientist cannot grasp a simple theory, he or she is destined to fail

24. Goethe's casual observations about language contain a   24.____
profound truth. Every word in every language is a part of a system of thinking unlike any other. Speakers of different languages live in different worlds; or rather, they live in the same world but can't help looking at it in different ways. Words stand for patterns of experience. As one generation hands its language down to the next, it also hands down a fixed pattern of thinking, seeing, and feeling. When we go from one language to another, nothing stays put; different peoples carry different nerve patterns in their brains, and there's no point where they fully match.
According to the above passage,
    A. language differences and their ramifications are a major cause of tensions between nations
    B. it is not a good use of one's time to read novels that have been translated from another language because of the tremendous differences in interpretation

C. differences in languages reflect the different experiences of people the world over
D. language students should be especially careful to retain awareness of the subtleties of their native language

Questions 25-27.

DIRECTIONS: Questions 25 through 27 are to be answered SOLELY on the basis of the following passage.

The context of all education is twofold - individual and social. Its business is to make us more and more ourselves, to cultivate in each of us our own distinctive genius, however modest it may be, while showing us how this genius may be reconciled with the needs and claims of the society of which we are a part. Thought it is not education's aim to cultivate eccentrics, that society is richest, most flexible, and most humane that best uses and most tolerates eccentricity. Conformity beyond a point breeds sterile minds and, therefore, a sterile society.

The function of secondary - and still more of higher education is to affect the environment. Teachers are not, and should not be, social reformers. But they should be the catalytic agents by means of which young minds are influenced to desire and execute reform. To aspire to better things is a logical and desirable part of mental and spiritual growth.

25. Of the following, the MOST suitable title for the above   25.___
    passage is
      A. EDUCATION'S FUNCTION IN CREATING INDIVIDUAL DIFFERENCES
      B. THE NEED FOR EDUCATION TO ACQUAINT US WITH OUR SOCIAL ENVIRONMENT
      C. THE RESPONSIBILITY OF EDUCATION TOWARD THE INDIVIDUAL AND SOCIETY
      D. THE ROLE OF EDUCATION IN EXPLAINING THE NEEDS OF SOCIETY

26. On the basis of the above passage, it may be inferred   26.___
    that
      A. conformity is one of the forerunners of totalitarianism
      B. education should be designed to create at least a modest amount of genius in everyone
      C. tolerance of individual differences tends to give society opportunities for improvement
      D. reforms are usually initiated by people who are somewhat eccentric

27. On the basis of the above passage, it may be inferred that   27.___
      A. genius is likely to be accompanied by a desire for social reform
      B. nonconformity is an indication of the inquiring mind
      C. people who are not high school or college graduates are not able to affect the environment
      D. teachers may or may not be social reformers

Questions 28-30.

DIRECTIONS: Questions 28 through 30 are to be answered SOLELY on
the basis of the following passage.

Disregard for odds and complete confidence in one's self have
produced many of our great successes. But every young man who wants
to go into business for himself should appraise himself as a candidate for the one percent to survive. What has he to offer that is
new or better? Has he special talents, special know-how, a new
invention or service, or more capital than the average competitor?
Has he the most important qualification of all, a willingness to
work harder than anyone else? A man who is working for himself without limitation of hours or personal sacrifice can run circles around
any operation that relies on paid help. But he must forget the
eight-hour day, the forty-hour week, and the annual vacation. When
he stops work, his income stops unless he hires a substitute. Most
small operations have their busiest day on Saturday, and the owner
uses Sunday to catch up on his correspondence, bookkeeping, inven-
torying, and maintenance chores. The successful self-employed man
invariably works harder and worries more than the man on a salary.
His wife and children make corresponding sacrifices of family unity
and continuity; they never know whether their man will be home or in
a mood to enjoy family activities.

28.   The title that BEST expresses the ideas of the above   28.____
passage is
A. OVERCOMING OBSTACLES
B. RUNNING ONE'S OWN BUSINESS
C. HOW TO BECOME A SUCCESS
D. WHY SMALL BUSINESSES FAIL

29.   The above passage suggests that   29.____
A. small businesses are the ones that last
B. salaried workers are untrustworthy
C. a willingness to work will overcome loss of income
D. working for one's self may lead to success

30.   The author of the above passage would MOST likely believe   30.____
in
A. individual initiative
B. socialism
C. corporations
D. government aid to small business

KEY (CORRECT ANSWERS)

1.	C	11.	B	21.	D
2.	A	12.	B	22.	B
3.	A	13.	A	23.	C
4.	B	14.	D	24.	C
5.	C	15.	C	25.	C
6.	A	16.	B	26.	C
7.	B	17.	D	27.	D
8.	D	18.	A	28.	B
9.	C	19.	B	29.	D
10.	B	20.	A	30.	A

———

READING COMPREHENSION
UNDERSTANDING AND INTERPRETING WRITTEN MATERIAL

EXAMINATION SECTION

DIRECTIONS: Each question or incomplete statement is followed by several suggested answers or completions. Select the one that BEST answers the question or completes the statement. *PRINT THE LETTER OF THE CORRECT ANSWER IN THE SPACE AT THE RIGHT.*

TEST 1

1. The question *Who shall now teach Hegel?* is shorthand for the question *Who is going to teach this genre - all the so-called Continental philosophers?* The obvious answer to this question is *Whoever cares to study them.* This is also the right answer, but we can only accept it whole-heartedly if we clear away a set of factitious questions. One such question is *Are these Continental philosophers really philosophers?* Analytic philosophers, because they identify philosophical ability with argumentative skill and notice that there is nothing they would consider an argument in the bulk of Heidegger or Foucault, suggest that these must be people who tried to be philosophers and failed--incompetent philosophers. This is as silly as saying that Plato was an incompetent sophist, or that a hedgehog is an incompetent fox. Hegel knew what he thought about philosophers who imitated the method and style of mathematics. He thought they were incompetent. These reciprocal charges of incompetence do nobody any good. We should just drop the questions of what philosophy really is or who really counts as a philosopher.
Which sentence is BEST supported by the above paragraph?
   A. The study of Hegel's philosophy is less popular now than in the past.
   B. Philosophers must stop questioning the competence of other philosophers.
   C. Philosophers should try to be as tolerant as Foucault and Heidegger.
   D. Analytic philosophers tend to be more argumentative than other philosophers.

1.___

2. It is an interesting question: the ease with which organizations of different kinds at different stages in their history can continue to function with ineffectual leadership at the top, or even function without a clear system of authority. Certainly, the success of some experiments in worker self-management shows that *bosses* are not always necessary, as some contemporary Marxists argue. Indeed, sometimes the function of those at the top is merely to symbolize organizational accountability, especially in dealing with outside authorities, but not to guide the actions of those within the organization. A vice president of a large insurance company remarked to us that *Presidents are powerless; no one needs them. They should all be sent*

2.___

off to do public relations for the company. While this is clearly a self-serving statement from someone next in line to command, it does give meaning to the expression *being kicked upstairs.*

According to the author,

    A. organizations function very smoothly without bosses

    B. the function of those at the top is sometimes only to symbolize organizational accountability

    C. company presidents are often inept at guiding the actions of those within the organization

    D. presidents of companies have less power than one might assume they have

3. The goal of a problem is a terminal expression one wishes to cause to exist in the world of the problem. There are two types of goals: specified goal expressions in proof problems and incompletely specified goal expressions in find problems. For example, consider the problem of finding the value of X, given the expression 4X + 5 = 17. In this problem, one can regard the goal expression as being of the form X = ___, the goal expression. The goal expression in a find problem of this type is incompletely specified. If the goal expression were specified completely - for example, X = 3 - then the problem would be a proof problem, with only the sequence of operations to be determined in order to solve the problem. Of course, if one were not guaranteed that the goal expression X = 3 was true, then the terminal goal expression should really be considered to be incompletely specified - something like the statement *X = 3 is (true or false).*

3.___

According to the preceding paragraph,

    A. the goal of the equation 4X + 5 = 17 is true, not false

    B. if the goal expression was specified as being equal to 3, the problem 4X + 5 = 17 would be a proof problem

    C. if the sequence of operations of the problem given in the paragraph is predetermined, the goal of the problem becomes one of terminal expression, or the number 17

    D. X cannot be found unless X is converted into a proof problem

4. We have human psychology and animal psychology, but no plant psychology. Why? Because we believe that plants have no perceptions or intentions. Some plants exhibit *behavior* and have been credited with *habits.* If you stroke the midrib of the compound leaf of a sensitive plant, the leaflets close. The sunflower changes with the diurnal changes in the source of light. The lowest animals have not much more complicated forms of behavior. The sea anemone traps and digests the small creatures that the water brings to it; the pitcher plant does the same thing and even more, for it presents a cup of liquid that attracts insects, instead of letting the surrounding medium drift them into its trap. Here as everywhere in nature where the great, general classes of living things diverge, the lines between them are not perfectly clear. A sponge is an animal; the pitcher plant is a flowering plant, but it comes nearer to

4.___

feeding itself than the animal. Yet the fact is that we credit all animals, and only the animals, with some degree of feeling.

Of the following, the MAIN idea expressed in the above paragraph is:

A. The classification of plants has been based on beliefs about their capacity to perceive and feel
B. Many plants are more evolved than species considered animals
C. The lines that divide the classes of living things are never clear
D. The abilities and qualities of plants are undervalued

5. Quantitative indexes are not necessarily adequate measures of true economic significance or influence. But even the raw quantitative data speak loudly of the importance of the new transnationalized economy. The United Nations estimates value added in this new sector of the world economy at $500 billion in 1971, amounting to one-fifth of total GNP of the non-socialist world and exceeding the GNP of any one other country except the United States. Furthermore, all observers agree that the share of this sector in the world economy is growing rapidly. At least since 1950, its annual rate of growth has been high and remarkably steady at 10 percent compared to 4 percent for noninternationalized output in the Western developed countries. One spokesman for the new system frankly envisages that within a generation some 400 to 500 multinational corporations will own close to two-thirds of the world's fixed assets.

According to the author, all of the following are true EXCEPT:

A. Quantitative indexes are not necessarily adequate measures of actual economic influence
B. The transnational sector of the world economy is growing rapidly
C. Since 1950, the rate of growth of transnationals has been 10% compared to 4% for internationalized output in the Western developed countries
D. Continued growth for multinational corporations is likely

5.___

6. A bill may be sent to the Governor when it has passed both houses. During the session, he is given ten days to act on bills that reach his desk. Bills sent to him within ten days of the end of the session must be acted on within 30 days after the last day of the session. If the Governor takes no action on a ten day bill, it auto-matically becomes a law. If he disapproves or vetoes a ten day bill, it can become law only if it is re-passed by two-thirds vote in each house. If he fails to act on a 30 day bill, the bill is said to have received a *pocket veto*. It is customary for the Governor to act, however, on all bills submitted to him, and give his reason in writing for approving or disapproving important legislation.

6.___

3

According to the above paragraph, all of the following are true EXCEPT:
- A. Bills sent to the Governor in the last ten days of the session must be acted on within thirty days after the last day of the session
- B. If the Governor takes no action on a 10 day bill, it is said to have received a *pocket veto*
- C. It is customary for the Governor to act on all bills submitted to him
- D. If the Governor vetoes a ten day bill, it can become law only if passed by a two-thirds vote of the Legislature

7. It is particularly when I see a child going through the mechanical process of manipulating numbers without any intuitive sense of what it is all about that I recall the lines of Lewis Carroll: *Reeling and Writhing, of course, to begin with...and then the different branches of Arithmetic- Ambition, Distraction, Uglification, and Derision.* Or, as Max Beberman has put it, much more gently: *Somewhat related to the notion of discovery in teaching is our insistence that the student become aware of a concept before a name has been assigned to the concept.* I am quite aware that the issue of intuitive understanding is a very live one among teachers of mathematics, and even a casual reading of the YEARBOOK of the National Council of Teachers of Mathematics makes it clear that they are also very mindful of the gap that exists between proclaiming the importance of such understanding and actually producing it in the classroom.
The MAIN idea expressed in the above paragraph is:
- A. Math teachers are concerned about the difficulties inherent in producing an understanding of mathematics in their students
- B. It is important that an intuitive sense in approaching math problems be developed, rather than relying on rote, mechanical learning
- C. Mathematics, by its very nature, encourages rote, mechanical learning
- D. Lewis Carroll was absolutely correct in his assessment of the true nature of mathematics

7. ___

8. Heisenberg's Principle of Uncertainty, which states that events at the atomic level cannot be observed with certainty, can be compared to this: in the world of everyday experience, we can observe any phenomenon and measure its properties without influencing the phenomenon in question to any significant extent. To be sure, if we try to measure the temperature of a demitasse with a bathtub thermometer, the instrument will absorb so much heat from the coffee that it will change the coffee's temperature substantially. But with a small chemical thermometer, we may get a sufficiently accurate reading. We can measure the temperature of a living cell with a miniature thermo- meter, which has almost negligible heat capacity.
But in the atomic world, we can never overlook the dis- turbance caused by the introduction of the measuring apparatus.

8. ___

Which sentence is BEST supported by the above paragraph?
- A. There is little we do not alter by the mere act of observation.
- B. It is always a good idea to use the smallest measuring device possible.
- C. Chemical thermometers are more accurate than bathtub thermometers.
- D. It is not possible to observe events at the atomic level and be sure that the same events would occur if we were not observing them.

9. It is a myth that American workers are pricing themselves out of the market, relative to workers in other industrialized countries of the world. The wages of American manufacturing workers increased at a slower rate in the 1970's than those of workers in other major western countries. In terms of American dollars, between 1970 and 1980, hourly compensation increased 489 percent in Japan and 464 percent in Germany, compared to 128 percent in the United States. Even though these countries experienced faster productivity growth, their unit labor costs still rose faster than in the United States, according to the Bureau of Labor Statistics. During the 1970's, unit labor costs rose 192 percent in Japan, 252 percent in Germany, and only 78 percent in the United States.
According to the above passage,
- A. unit labor costs in the 1970's were higher in Japan than they were in Germany or the United States
- B. the wages of American workers need to be increased to be consistent with other countries
- C. American workers are more productive than Japanese or German workers
- D. the wages of American workers in manufacturing increased at a slower rate in the 1970's than the wages of workers in Japan or Germany

9.____

10. No people have invented more ways to enjoy life than the Chinese, perhaps to balance floods, famines, warlords, and other ills of fate. The clang of gongs, clashing cymbals, and beating of drums sound through their long history. No month is without fairs and theatricals when streets are hung with fantasies of painted lanterns and crowded with *carriages that flow like water, horses like roaming dragons.* Night skies are illumined by firecrackers - a Chinese invention - bursting in the form of flowerpots, peonies, fiery devils. The ways of pleasure are myriad. Music plays in the air through bamboo whistles of different pitch tied to the wings of circling pigeons. To skim a frozen lake in an ice sleigh with a group of friends on a day when the sun is warm is rapture, like *moving in a cup of jade.* What more delightful than the ancient festival called *Half an Immortal,* when everyone from palace officials to the common man took a ride on a swing? When high in the air, one felt like an Immortal, when back to earth once again human - no more than to be for an instant a god.

10.____

5

According to the above passage,
  A. if the Chinese hadn't had so many misfortunes, they wouldn't have created so many pleasurable pasttimes
  B. the Chinese invented flowerpots
  C. every month the Chinese have fairs and theatricals
  D. pigeons are required to play the game *Half an Immortal*

11. In our century, instead, poor Diphilus is lost in the crowd of his peers. We flood one another. No one recognizes him as he loads his basket in the supermarket. What grevious fits of melancholy have I not suffered in one of our larger urban bookstores, gazing at the hundreds, thousands, tens of thousands of books on shelves and tables? And what are they to the hundreds of thousands, the millions that stand in our research libraries? More books than Noah saw raindrops. How many readers will read a given one of them - mine, yours - in their lifetimes? And how will it be in the distant future? Incomprehensible masses of books, Pelion upon Ossa, hordes of books, each piteously calling for attention, respect, love, in competition with the vast disgorgements of the past and with one another in the present. Neither is it at all helpful that books can even now be reduced to the size of a postage stamp. Avanti! Place the Bible on a pinhead! Crowding more books into small spaces does not cram more books into our heads. Here I come to the sticking point that unnerves the modern Diphilus. The number of books a person can read in a given time is, roughly speaking, a historical constant. It does not change significantly even when the number of books available for reading does. Constants are pitted against variables to confound both writer and reader.
Of the following, the MAIN idea in this passage is:
  A. It is difficult to attain immortality because so many books are being published
  B. Too many books are being published, so fewer people are reading them
  C. Because so many books are being published, the quality of the writing is poorer
  D. Because so many books are available, but only a fixed amount of time to read them, frustration results for both the reader and the writer

12. Until recently, consciousness of sexual harassment has been low. But workers have become aware of it as more women have arrived at levels of authority in the workplace, feminist groups have focused attention on rape and other violence against women, and students have felt freer to report perceived abuse by professors. In the last 5 years, studies have shown that sexual misconduct at the workplace is a big problem. For example, in a recently published survey of federal employees, 42% of 694,000 women and 15% of 1,168,000 men said they had experienced some form of harassment.
According to the author,
  A. the awareness of sexual harassment at the workplace is increasing

11.___

12.___

B. the incidence of harassment is higher in universities than workplaces
C. sexual harassment is much more commonly experienced by women than men
D. it is rare for men to experience sexual harassment

Questions 13-17.

DIRECTIONS: Questions 13 through 17 are to be answered SOLELY on the basis of the following paragraph.

Since discounts are in common use in the commercial world and apply to purchases made by government agencies as well as business firms, it is essential that individuals in both public and private employment who prepare bills, check invoices, prepare payment vouchers, or write checks to pay bills have an understanding of the terms used. These include cash or time discount, trade discount, and discount series. A cash or time discount offers a reduction in price to the buyer for the prompt payment of the bill and is usually expressed as a percentage with a time requirement, stated in days, within which the bill must be paid in order to earn the discount. An example would be 3/10, meaning a 3% discount may be applied to the bill if the payment is forwarded to the vendor within ten days. On an invoice, the cash discount terms are usually followed by the net terms, which is the time in days allowed for ordinary payment of the bill. Thus, 3/10, Net 30 means that full payment is expected in thirty days if the cash discount of 3% is not taken for having paid the bill within ten days. When the expression Terms Net Cash is listed on a bill, it means that no deduction for early payment is allowed. A trade discount is normally applied to list prices by a manufacturer to show the actual price to retailers so that they may know their cost and determine markups that will allow them to operate competitively and at a profit. A trade discount is applied by the seller to the list price and is independent of a cash or time discount. Discounts may also be used by manufacturers to adjust prices charged to retailers without changing list prices. This is usually done by series discounting and is expressed as a series of percentages. To compute a series discount, such as 40%, 20%, 10%, first apply the 40% discount to the list price, then apply the 20% discount to the remainder, and finally apply the 10% discount to the second remainder.

13. According to the above paragraph, trade discounts are   13.___
    A. applied by the buyer
    B. independent of cash discounts
    C. restricted to cash sales
    D. used to secure rapid payment of bills

14. According to the above paragraph, if the sales terms   14.___
    5/10, Net 60 appear on a bill in the amount of $100
    dated December 5, 1984 and the buyer submits his payment
    on December 15, 1984, his PROPER payment should be
       A. $60   B. $90   C. $95   D. $100

15. According to the above paragraph, if a manufacturer gives   15.___
a trade discount of 40% for an item with a list price of
$250 and the terms are Net Cash, the price a retail mer-
chant is required to pay for this item is
   A. $250   B. $210   C. $150 .   D. $100

16. According to the above paragraph, a series discount of   16.___
25%, 20%, 10% applied to a list price of $200 results
in an ACTUAL price to the buyer of
   A. $88   B. $90   C. $108   D. $110

17. According to the above paragraph, if a manufacturer gives   17.___
a trade discount of 50% and the terms are 6/10, Net 30,
the cost to a retail merchant of an item with a list price
of $500 and for which he takes the time discount, is
   A. $220   B. $235   C. $240   D. $250

Questions 18-22.

DIRECTIONS: Questions 18 through 22 are to be answered SOLELY on
the basis of the following paragraph.

The city may issue its own bonds or it may purchase bonds as an
investment. Bonds may be issued in various denominations, and the
face value of the bond is its par value. Before purchasing a bond,
the investor desires to know the rate of income that the investment
will yield. In computing the yield on a bond, it is assumed that the
investor will keep the bond until the date of maturity, except for
callable bonds which are not considered in this passage. To compute
exact yield is a complicated mathematical problem, and scientifically
prepared tables are generally used to avoid such computation. However, the approximate yield can be computed much more easily. In
computing approximate yield, the accrued interest on the date of
purchase should be ignored, because the buyer who pays accrued
interest to the seller receives it again at the next interest date.
Bonds bought at a premium (which cost more) yield a lower rate of
income than the same bonds bought at par (face value), and bonds
bought at a discount (which cost less) yield a higher rate of income
than the same bonds bought at par.

18. An investor bought a $10,000 city bond paying 6% interest.   18.___
Which of the following purchase prices would indicate that
the bond was bought at a PREMIUM?
   A. $9,000   B. $9,400   C. $10,000   D. $10,600

19. During 1974, a particular $10,000 bond paying $7\frac{1}{2}$% sold   19.___
at fluctuating prices.
Which of the following prices would indicate that the
bond was bought at a DISCOUNT?
   A. $9,800   B. $10,000   C. $10,200   D. $10,750

20. A certain group of bonds was sold in denominations of   20.___
$5,000, $10,000, $20,000, and $50,000.
In the following list of four purchase prices, which
one is MOST likely to represent a bond sold at par value?
   A. $10,500   B. $20,000   C. $22,000   D. $49,000

8

21. When computing the approximate yield on a bond, it is   21.____
    DESIRABLE to
      A. assume the bond was purchased at par
      B. consult scientifically prepared tables
      C. ignore accrued interest on the date of purchase
      D. wait until the bond reaches maturity

22. Which of the following is MOST likely to be an exception   22.____
    to the information provided in the above paragraph?
    Bonds
      A. purchased at a premium   B. sold at par
      C. sold before maturity   D. which are callable

Questions 23-25.

DIRECTIONS: Questions 23 through 25 are to be answered SOLELY on
              the basis of the following passage.

There is one bad habit of drivers that often causes chain col-
lisions at traffic lights. It is the habit of keeping one foot poised
over the accelerator pedal, ready to step on the gas the instant the
light turns green. A driver who is watching the light, instead of
watching the cars in front of him, may *jump the gun* and bump the car
in front of him, and this car in turn may bump the next car. If a
driver is resting his foot on the accelerator, his foot will be
slammed down when he bumps into the car ahead. This makes the colli-
sion worse and makes it very likely that cars further ahead in the
line are going to get involved in a series of violent bumps.

23. Which of the following conclusions can MOST reasonably be   23.____
    drawn from the information given in the above passage?
      A. American drivers have a great many bad driving habits.
      B. Drivers should step on the gas as soon as the light
         turns green.
      C. A driver with poor driving habits should be arrested
         and fined.
      D. A driver should not rest his foot on the accelerator
         when the car is stopped for a traffic light.

24. From the information given in the above passage, a reader   24.____
    should be able to tell that a chain collision may be
    defined as a collision
      A. caused by bad driving habits at traffic lights
      B. in which one car hits another car, this second car
         hits a third car, and so on
      C. caused by drivers who fail to use their accelerators
      D. that takes place at an intersection where there is
         a traffic light

25. The above passage states that a driver who watches the   25.____
    light instead of paying attention to traffic may
      A. be involved in an accident
      B. end up in jail
      C. lose his license
      D. develop bad driving habits

9

TEST 2

Questions 1-4.

DIRECTIONS: Each of the statements in this section is followed by
several labeled choices. In the space at the right,
write the letter of the sentence which means MOST
NEARLY what is stated or implied in the passage.

1. It may be said that the problem in adult education seems to   1.___
    be not the piling up of facts but practice in thinking.
    This statement means MOST NEARLY that
        A. educational methods for adults and young people should
           differ
        B. adults seem to think more than young people
        C. a well-educated adult is one who thinks but does not
           have a store of information
        D. adult education should stress ability to think

2. Last year approximately 19,000 fatal accidents were sus-   2.___
    tained in industry. There were approximately 130 non-fatal
    injuries to each fatal injury.
    According to the above statement, the number of non-fatal
    accidents was
        A. 146,000   B. 190,000   C. 1,150,000 D. 2,500,000

3. No employer expects his stenographer to be a walking   3.___
    encyclopedia, but it is not unreasonable for him to expect
    her to know where to look for necessary information on a
    variety of topics.
    The above statement means MOST NEARLY that the stenographer
    should
        A. be a college graduate
        B. be familiar with standard office reference books
        C. keep a scrapbook of all interesting happenings
        D. go to the library regularly

4. For the United States, Canada has become the most important   4.___
    country in the world, yet there are few countries about
    which Americans know less. Canada is the third largest
    country in the world; only Russia and China are larger.
    The area of Canada is more than a quarter of the whole
    British Empire.
    According to the above statement, the
        A. British Empire is smaller than Russia or China
        B. territory of China is greater than that of Canada
        C. Americans know more about Canada than they do about
           China or Russia
        D. Canadian population is more than one-quarter the
           population of the British Empire

Questions 5-8.

DIRECTIONS: Questions 5 through 8 are to be answered SOLELY on the
basis of the following paragraph.

A few people who live in old tenements have the bad habit of
throwing garbage out of their windows, especially if there is an
empty lot near their building. Sometimes the garbage is food;
sometimes the garbage is half-empty soda cans. Sometimes the garbage
is a little bit of both mixed together. These people just don't
care about keeping the lot clean.

5. The above paragraph states that throwing garbage out of   5.____
windows is a
    A. bad habit   B. dangerous thing to do
    C. good thing to do   D. good way to feed rats

6. According to the above paragraph, an empty lot next to an   6.____
old tenement is sometimes used as a place to
    A. hold local gang meetings B. play ball
    C. throw garbage   D. walk dogs

7. According to the above paragraph, which of the following   7.____
throw garbage out of their windows?
    A. Nobody   B. Everybody
    C. Most people   D. Some people

8. According to the above paragraph, the kinds of garbage   8.____
thrown out of windows are
    A. candy and cigarette butts
    B. food and half-empty soda cans
    C. fruit and vegetables
    D. rice and bread

Questions 9-12.

DIRECTIONS: Questions 9 through 12 are to be answered SOLELY on the
basis of the following paragraph.

The game that is recognized all over the world as an all-American
game is the game of baseball. As a matter of fact, baseball heroes
like Joe DiMaggio, Willie Mays, and Babe Ruth were as famous in their
day as movie stars Robert Redford, Paul Newman, and Clint Eastwood
are now. All these men have had the experience of being mobbed by
fans whenever they put in an appearance anywhere in the world. Such
unusual popularity makes it possible for stars like these to earn
at least as much money off the job as on the job. It didn't take
manufacturers and advertising men long to discover that their sales
of shaving lotion, for instance, increased when they got famous stars
to advertise their product for them on radio and television.

9. According to the above paragraph, baseball is known every-   9.____
where as a(n) _____ game.
    A. all-American   B. fast
    C. unusual   D. tough

11

10. According to the above paragraph, being so well known   10.___
    means that it is possible for people like Willie Mays
    and Babe Ruth to
       A. ask for anything and get it
       B. make as much money off the job as on it
       C. travel anywhere free of charge
       D. watch any game free of charge

11. According to the above paragraph, which of the following   11.___
    are known all over the world?
       A. Baseball heroes   B. Advertising men
       C. Manufacturers   D. Basketball heroes

12. According to the above paragraph, it is possible to sell   12.___
    much more shaving lotion on television and radio if
       A. the commercials are in color instead of black and white
       B. you can get a prize with each bottle of shaving lotion
       C. the shaving lotion makes you smell nicer than usual
       D. the shaving lotion is advertisied by famous stars

Questions 13-15.

DIRECTIONS: Questions 13 through 15 are to be answered SOLELY on
             the basis of the following passage.

That music gives pleasure is axiomatic. Because this is so, the
pleasures of music may seem a rather elementary subject for discussion.
Yet the source of that pleasure, our musical instinct, is not at all
elementary. It is, in fact, one of the prime puzzles of consciousness. Why is it that we are able to make sense out of these nerve
signals so that we emerge from engulfment in the orderly presentation
of sound stimuli as if we had lived through an image of life?

If music has impact for the mere listener, it follows that it
will have much greater impact for those who sing it or play it themselves with proficiency. Any educated person in Elizabethan times
was expected to read musical notation and take part in a madrigal-
sing. Passive listeners, numbered in the millions, are a comparatively recent innovation.

Everyone is aware that so-called serious music has made great
strides in general public acceptance in recent years, but the term
itself still connotes something forbidding and hermetic to the mass
audience. They attribute to the professional musician a kind of
initiation into secrets that are forever hidden from the outsider.
Nothing could be more misleading. We all listen to music, profes-
sionals, and non-professionals alike in the same sort of way, in a
dumb sort of way, really, because simple or sophisticated music
attracts all of us in the first instance, on the primordial level
of sheer rhythmic and sonic appeal. Musicians are flattered, no
doubt, by the deferential attitude of the layman in regard to what
he imagines to be our secret understanding of music. But in all
honesty, we musicians know that in the main we listen basically as
others do, because music hits us with an immediacy that we recognize
in the reactions of the most simple minded of music listeners.

13. A suitable title for the above passage would be 13.___
    A. HOW TO LISTEN TO MUSIC
    B. LEARNING MUSIC APPRECIATION
    C. THE PLEASURES OF MUSIC
    D. THE WORLD OF THE MUSICIAN

14. The author implies that the passive listener is one who 14.___
    A. cannot read or play music
    B. does not appreciate serious music
    C. does not keep time to the music by hand or toe tapping
    D. will not attend a concert if he has to pay for the
       privilege

15. The author of the above passage is apparently inconsistent 15.___
    when he discusses
    A. the distinction between the listener who pays for the
       privilege and the one who does not
    B. the historical development of musical forms
    C. the pleasures derived from music by the musician
    D. why it is that we listen to music

Questions 16-18.

DIRECTIONS: Questions 16 through 18 are to be answered SOLELY on
              the basis of the following passage.

Who are the clerisy? They are people who like to read books.
The use of a word so unusual, so out of fashion, can only be excused
on the ground that it has no familiar synonym. The word is little
known because what it describes has disappeared, though I do not
believe it is gone forever. The clerisy are those who read for
pleasure, but not for idleness; who read for pasttime, but not to
kill time; who love books, but do not live by books.

Let us consider the actual business of reading -- the interpre-
tative act of getting the words off the page and into your head in
the most effective way. The most effective way is not the quickest
way of reading; and for those who think that speed is the greatest
good, there are plenty of manuals on how to read a book which profess
to tell how to strip off the husk and guzzle the milk, like a chimp
attacking a coconut. Who among today's readers would whisk through
a poem, eyes aflicker, and say that he had read it? The answer to
that last question must unfortunately be: far too many. For reading
is not respected for the art it is.

Doubtless there are philosophical terms for the attitude of mind
of which hasty reading is one manifestation, but here let us call it
end-gaining, for its victims put ends before means; they value not
reading, but having read. In this, the end-gainers make mischief
and spoil all they do; end-gaining is one of the curses of our
nervously tense, intellectually flabby civilization. In reading,
as in all arts, it is the means, and not the end, which gives delight
and brings the true reward. Not straining forward toward the completion, but the pleasure of every page as it comes, is the secret
of reading. We must desire to read a book, rather than to have read

it. This change in attitude, so simple to describe, is by no means simple to achieve, if one has lived the life of an end-gainer.

16. A suitable title for the above passage would be   16.___
      A. READING FOR ENLIGHTENMENT
      B. THE ART OF RAPID READING
      C. THE WELL-EDUCATED READER
      D. VALUES IN READING

17. The author does NOT believe that most people read because   17.___
    they
      A. are bored
      B. have nothing better to do
      C. love books
      D. wish to say that they have read certain books

18. The *change in attitude* to which the author refers in the   18.___
    last sentence of the above passage implies a change from
      A. dawdling while reading so that the reader can read a
         greater number of books
      B. reading light fiction to reading serious fiction and
         non-fiction
      C. reading works which do not amuse the reader
      D. skimming through a book to reading it with care

Questions 19-22.

DIRECTIONS: Questions 19 through 22 are to be answered SOLELY on
             the basis of the following passage.

     Violence is not new to literature. The writings of Shakespeare
and Cervantes are full of it. But those classic writers did not
condone violence. They viewed it as a just retribution for sins
against the divine order or as a sacrifice sanctioned by heroism.
What is peculiar to the modern literature is violence for the sake of
violence. Perhaps our reverence for life has been dulled by mass
slaughter, though mass slaughter has not been exceptional in the
history of mankind. What is exceptional is the boredom that now
alternates with war. The basic emotion in peacetime has become a
horror of emptiness: a fear of being alone, of having nothing to
do, a neurosis whose symptoms are restlessness, an unmotivated and
undirected rage, sinking at times into vapid listlessness. This
neurotic syndrome is intensified by the prevailing sense of insecurity.
The threat of atomic war has corrupted our faith in life itself.

     This universal neurosis has developed with the progress of tech-
nology. It is the neurosis of men whose chief expenditure of energy
is to pull a lever or push a button, of men who have ceased to make
things with their hands. Such inactivity applies not only to muscles
and nerves but to the creative processes that once engaged the mind.
If one could contrast visually, by time-and-motion studies, the daily
actions of an eighteenth-century carpenter with a twentieth-century
machinist, the latter would appear as a confined, repetitive clot,
the former as a free and even fantastic pattern. But the most
significant contrast could not be visualized - the contrast between

a mind suspended aimlessly above an autonomous movement and a mind consciously bent on the shaping of a material substance according to the persistent evidence of the senses.

19. A suitable title for the above passage would be   19.___
    A. INCREASING PRODUCTION BY MEANS OF SYSTEMATIZATION
    B. LACK OF A SENSE OF CREATIVENESS AND ITS CONSEQUENCE
    C. TECHNOLOGICAL ACHIEVEMENT IN MODERN SOCIETY
    D. WHAT CAN BE DONE ABOUT SENSELESS VIOLENCE

20. According to the author, Shakespeare treated violence as a   20.___
    A. basically sinful act not in keeping with religious thinking
    B. just punishment of transgressors against moral law
    C. means of achieving dramatic excitement
    D. solution to a problem provided no other solution was available

21. According to the author, boredom may lead to   21.___
    A. a greater interest in leisure-time activities
    B. chronic fatigue
    C. senseless anger
    D. the acceptance of a job which does not provide a sense of creativity

22. The underlined phrase refers to the   22.___
    A. hand movements made by the carpenter
    B. hand movements made by the machinist
    C. relative ignorance of the carpenter
    D. relative ignorance of the machinist

23. The concentration of women and female-headed families in   23.___
    the city is both cause and consequence of the city's fiscal woes. Women live in cities because it is easier and cheaper for them to do so, but because fewer women are employed, and those that are receive lower pay than men, they do not make the same contribution to the tax base that an equivalent population of men would. Concomitantly, they are more dependent on public resources, such as transportation and housing. For these reasons alone, urban finances would be improved by increasing women's employment opportunities and pay. Yet nothing in our current urban policy is specifically geared to improving women's financial resources. There are some proposed incentives to business to create more jobs, but not necessarily ones that would utilize the skills women currently have. The most innovative proposal was a tax credit for new hires from certain groups with particularly high unemployment rates. None of the seven targeted groups were women.
    Which sentence is BEST supported by the above paragraph?
    A. Innovative programs are rapidly improving conditions for seven targeted groups with traditionally high unemployment rates.

15

    B. The contribution of women to a city's tax base reflects
       their superior economic position.
    C. Improving the economic position of women who live in
       cities would help the financial conditions of the
       cities themselves.
    D. Most women in this country live in large cities.

24. None of this would be worth saying if Descartes had been   24.____
right in positing a one-to-one correspondence between
stimuli and sensations. But we know that nothing of the
sort exists. The perception of a given color can be evoked
by an infinite number of differently combined wavelengths.
Conversely, a given stimulus can evoke a variety of sensations, the image of a duck in one recipient, the image of
a rabbit in another. Nor are responses like these entirely
innate. One can learn to discriminate colors or patterns
which were indistinguishable prior to training. To an
extent still unknown, the production of data from stimuli
is a learned procedure. After the learning process, the
same stimulus evokes a different datum. I conclude that,
though data are the minimal elements of our individual
experience, they need be shared responses to a given stimulus only within the membership of a relatively homogeneous
community: educational, scientific, or linguistic.
Which sentence is BEST supported by the above paragraph?
    A. One stimulus can give rise to a number of different
       sensations.
    B. There is a one-to-one correspondence between stimuli
       and sensations.
    C. It is not possible to produce data from stimuli by
       using a learned procedure.
    D. It is not necessary for a group to be relatively
       homogeneous in order to share responses to stimuli.

25. Workers who want to move in the direction of participative   25.____
structures will need to confront the issues of power and
control. The process of change needs to be mutually shared
by all involved, or the outcome will not be a really participative model. The demand for a structural redistribution
of power is not sufficient to address the problem of change
toward a humanistic, as against a technological, workplace.
If we are to change our institutional arrangements from
hierarchy to participation, particularly in our workplaces,
we will need to look to transformations in ourselves as
well. As long as we are imbued with the legitimacy of
hierarchical authority, with the sovereignty of the status
quo, we will never be able to generate the new and original
participative forms that we week. This means if we are
to be equal to the task of reorganizing our workplaces, we
need to think about how we can reeducate ourselves and
become aware of our own assumptions about the nature of
our social life together. Unless the issue is approached
in terms of these complexities, I fear that all the
worker participation and quality of work life efforts will
fail.

According to the above paragraph, which of the following is NOT true?
  A. Self-education concerning social roles must go hand in hand with workplace reorganization.
  B. The structural changing of the workplace, alone, will not bring about the necessary changes in the quality of work life.
  C. Individuals can easily overcome their attitudes towards hierarchical authority.
  D. Changing the quality of work life will require the participation of all involved.

KEY (CORRECT ANSWERS)

TEST 1	TEST 2
1. B	1. D
2. B	2. D
3. B	3. B
4. A	4. B
5. C	5. A
6. B	6. C
7. B	7. D
8. D	8. B
9. D	9. A
10. C	10. B
11. D	11. A
12. A	12. D
13. B	13. C
14. C	14. A
15. C	15. C
16. C	16. D
17. B	17. C
18. D	18. D
19. A	19. B
20. B	20. B
21. C	21. C
22. D	22. B
23. D	23. C
24. B	24. A
25. A	25. C

PSAT/SAT MATH INTRODUCTION

One way of testing your basic ability is through mathematics. The P.S.A.T./S.A.T. does not attempt to test how much math you have studied; this is tested on the Achievement Tests. In fact, several important formulas are given to you right in the directions on each S.A.T. I.

The math on the P.S.A.T./S.A.T. I is divided very roughly as follows: 30 percent arithmetic, 30 percent algebra, 30 percent geometry, 10 percent miscellaneous. There are no math questions on any topics beyond geometry. The P.S.A.T./S.A.T. I math questions test how quickly and precisely you work, how accurately you read the questions, and how well you grasp some of the most basic mathematical concepts.

A study guide cannot attempt to review all of the mathematics you have learned in your life. This would be impossible and also not useful in improving your S.A.T. I math score. We focus specifically on improving your ability to answer the kinds of math questions asked on the P.S.A.T./S.A.T. I.

We study the three types of math questions asked on the P.S.A.T./S.A.T. I: standard multiple choice questions, quantitative comparison questions, and student produced response questions. We study questions arranged by topics: fractions, algebra, percents, geometry, as well as complete exams, so that you will be thoroughly familiar with the test strategy needed to improve your score.

Recent research proves conclusively that practice can improve your score, often substantially. It is our experience that your score will almost definitely improve if you take full advantage of this passbook.

STRATEGIES IN PROBLEM-SOLVING

Remember that each question is worth the same number of points. Don't waste time on questions that you find very hard, but spend your time on questions that you know you can answer. Come back to the difficult questions later if you have time. Remember that the questions generally tend to get more difficult toward the end of a question type, so the regular mathematics questions at the end of the first mathematics section are more difficult, and most students get fewer of these correct. This doesn't mean that you won't be able to answer questions toward the end of the section, but if you find that you can't do several in a row, read through the rest of the questions quickly, looking for any you can answer and then return to the earlier questions that you omitted and try them again.

You might find that you can come up with a way to solve them. Later you may want to eliminate unreasonable answer choices in those questions you have been unable to solve and then guess from among the remaining choices.

Be flexible in solving the problem. It may not be what it seems. The following points may help you come up with an approach to the problem.

A. Orient yourself to the problem - get into it. Read it carefully, and note key words that tell you what the problem calls for. Underline these key words in your test book. Consider all the information given, and avoid making quick assumptions. Check the answer choices to see what kind of an answer is expected; otherwise, you may waste time putting the answer in a form that is not given and then need to make another calculation to put it in the given form.

B. Determine whether you must (1) compute the answer and then select the answer choice, or (2) look at the answers before you compute. For example, look at the following problems where the key word is underlined.

Example: The greatest integer x such that $9x + 5 < 100$ is
A. 7 B. 8 C. 9 D. 10 E. 11

To solve this problem, you would first subtract 5 from both sides. This gives $9x < 95$. Nine times 11 is 99, so 11 is too large. Nine times 10 is 90, so D is the answer. To solve this problem, you could also use your calculator on the expression $9x < 95$ by dividing by 9 to get $x < 10.555$. The greatest integer value of x is, therefore, 10.

Example: If n is an odd integer, which of the following is even?
A. 2n+1 B. n(n+2) C. n+(n-1) D. (n-2)(n+2)
E. 2(n+1)

To solve this problem, you must look at the answer choices. If you look at all of them before beginning to plug in numbers and compute results, you will see E. 2(n+1) must always be even because the number resulting from n+1 is multiplied by 2.

C. Think about the steps required to translate the information in the problem into an equation. Ask yourself if it is a one-step (or more) problem, and then don't forget to do all the steps. If the problem seems too difficult, think of an easier one like it that you can solve, figure out how you did it, and then solve the harder one the same way. Or try to restate it by substituting smaller numbers for the ones given. This may clarify the problem so that selecting the operation needed to solve it is easier.

Example: 9 = _____ percent of 12.

If you cannot work this problem, perhaps you can substitute simpler numbers. Six is half of 12; half of 12 is 50 percent. How do you get 50 percent from 1/2? By dividing the top of the fraction by the bottom. So, by going back to the harder problem, and dividing the top of the fraction by the bottom (9/12 or 3/4), you figure out the correct answer (75 percent).

Even if the problem seems simple to you, take time to understand exactly what it calls for and then go over in your mind the steps by which you'll reach the solution. Many people who are good in math have trouble with tests because they jump to conclusions about solving problems before they understand what is required.

D. Look to see what units the answer calls for. This will help to set up the calculation.

Example: It took Chris 200 seconds to solve a puzzle. If it took Kim 160 seconds to solve the same puzzle, by what fraction of a _minute_ was Chris's time longer than Kim's?

A. $\frac{1}{5}$ B. $\frac{1}{4}$ C. $\frac{2}{5}$ D. $\frac{1}{2}$ E. $\frac{2}{3}$

The key words here are *what fraction of a minute*. Don't waste time setting up a complicated ratio or equation. Chris took 40 seconds longer than Kim. 40 seconds is 2/3 of a minute, so E is the answer.

E. If you can't figure out how to do problems requiring a creative solution in a minute or so, try to eliminate some of the answers, guess among the remaining responses, mark the question in your test book, and go on to the next problem. If you have time later, return to the question and try again.

Avoid careless errors. Compute carefully. You may write calculations in your test book. Watch out for the position of decimal points, and be sure you haven't omitted zeros.

After you compute the answer, recheck what the question calls for, and be sure you haven't forgotten a step or figured the answer in the wrong units.

REVIEW THE TEST QUESTIONS

You should go over each question, particularly those you got wrong, to try to figure out the correct answer and why you missed it. Although it is highly unlikely that you will encounter that exact question again, you can learn from your mistake. Don't be satisfied with just knowing what the correct answer is - be sure you understand the processes involved in finding the right answer.

Check to see whether your mistake was in computing the answer, in applying the wrong concept or formula to a situation, or in interpreting the choices - like choosing a *3* when you wanted a *-3*, or not seeing a *0.25* because you were looking for a *1/4*.

Consider the following question:

A set of P purple blocks was divided into g groups of b blocks each and there were 2 blocks left over. Which of the following equations describes this situation?

A. $P = gb + 2$ B. $P = gb - 2$ C. $\frac{P}{b} = g + 2$

D. $\frac{P}{b} = g - 2$ E. $\frac{P}{g} = b + 2$

Your first impulse might be to divide P by g to obtain the size of the group b. Since 2 blocks were left over, you may have been tempted by choice E, which appears to satisfy the condition. However, E is equivalent to $P = gb + 2g$ and, therefore, does not show *2 blocks left over*.

The answer can be found by thinking of the first sentence as *P blocks = g groups of b blocks plus 2*. Written in an equation, this is $P = gb + 2$, or choice A. The division approach will also work provided the remainder is properly represented as a fraction of g. This result leads to the equations:

$$\frac{P}{g} = b + \frac{2}{g} \quad \text{or} \quad P = gb + 2$$

This question is quite difficult. When it was used on an actual PSAT/NMSQT, it appeared near the end of the section along with other difficult questions.

Although you may be interested primarily in reviewing the questions you answered wrong or omitted, it would also be helpful to spend a little time looking at questions you answered right. You may not have been sure about the answer, but instead may have made an educated guess, or you may have guessed randomly and been lucky. Ask your teacher to help you solve the problem correctly, and next time you'll be more confident of your answer.

Try to learn the meaning of any new mathematical concepts that you encountered on the practice test, but don't memorize questions and answers. It's highly unlikely that you will ever see them again.

REVIEW YOUR TEST-TAKING STRATEGIES

Pacing

Not finishing one or both sections of the test may indicate that you have a problem with pacing. Leaving difficult questions unanswered doesn't necessarily mean you didn't pace yourself properly, but if you didn't reach a number of questions at the end of a section you might have spent too much time on a particular question or you might have worked too slowly throughout the test section.

There are some algebra forms to look for.

$$(x+y)^2 = x^2 + 2xy + y^2 \qquad x^2 - y^2 = (x+y)(x-y)$$

$$\frac{(x-y)}{(y-x)} = -1 \text{ if } x \neq y$$

Definitions of Symbols

= is equal to	≤ is less than or equal to
≠ is unequal to	≥ is greater than or equal to
< is less than	‖ is parallel to
> is greater than	⊥ is perpendicular to

Circles

1. The area of a circle is πr^2 or $\dfrac{\pi d^2}{4}$.

2. The circumference of a circle is $2\pi r$ or πd.

3. The number of degrees of arc in a circle is 360.

4. In a circle, equal arcs have equal central angles and vice versa.

5. A diameter of a circle is the longest line segment that can be drawn between two points on the circle.

6. A central angle is equal in degree measure to its intercepted arc.

7. In a circle, if arcs are equal, then chords are equal and vice versa.

8. The area of a sector of a circle is related to the area of the circle in the same way as the central angle of the sector is related to 360.

9. In a circle, the greater of two chords is nearer the center.

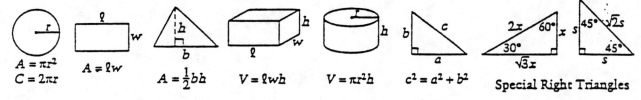

$A = \pi r^2$
$C = 2\pi r$
$A = \ell w$
$A = \frac{1}{2}bh$
$V = \ell wh$
$V = \pi r^2 h$
$c^2 = a^2 + b^2$
Special Right Triangles

Polygons

1. The opposite sides of a parallelogram are parallel and equal.

2. The angles of a rectangle are right angles.

3. The area of a rectangle is A = bh.

4. The area of a square is A = s^2.

5. The diagonal of a square is d = s$\sqrt{2}$.

6. The area of a parallelogram is A = bh.

7. The consecutive angles of a parallelogram are supplementary.

Decimal Equivalents of Common Fractions

1/2	= .5	= 50%	1/6	= .16 2/3	= 16 2/3%
			5/6	= .83 1/3	= 83 1/3%
1/3	= .33 1/3	= 33 1/3%			
2/3	= .66 2/3	= 66 2/3%	1/7	= .14 2/7	= 14 2/7%
1/4	= .25	= 25%	1/8	= .12½	= 12½%
3/4	= .75	= 75%	3/8	= .37½	= 37½%
			5/8	= .62½	= 62½%
1/5	= .2	= 20%	7/8	= .87½	= 87½%
2/5	= .4	= 40%			
3/5	= .6	= 60%	1/9	= .111...	= 11.1%
4/5	= .8	= 80%	2/9	= .222...	= 22.2%
			Etc.		
100/100 = 1.0		= 100%			
200/100 = 2		= 200%			

Pythagorean Triples

3, 4, 5	5, 12, 13	8, 15, 17	7, 24, 25
6, 8, 10	10, 24, 26	16, 30, 34	14, 48, 50
9, 12, 15			
12, 16, 20	1, 1, 2 (45°, 45°, 90° triangles)		
15, 20, 25	1, 2, 3 (30°, 60°, 90° triangles)		

Powers and Roots

Powers

$$a^m \cdot a^n = a^{m+n}$$

$$\left(\frac{a}{b}\right)^m = \frac{a^m}{b^m} \quad (b \neq 0)$$

$$(a^m)^n = a^{mn}$$

$$(\sqrt{a})^m = \sqrt{a^m} \quad (a \geqslant 0)$$

Examples

$$2^2 \cdot 2^3 = 2^{(2+3)} = 2^5 = 32$$

$$\left(\frac{2}{3}\right)^2 = \frac{2^2}{3^2} = \frac{4}{9}$$

$$(2^2)^3 = 2^{(2 \cdot 3)} = 2^6 = 64$$

$$(\sqrt{2})^2 = \sqrt{2^2} = \sqrt{4} = 2$$

Roots	Examples
If $a > 0$, $\sqrt{a}$ is the positive square root of a	$\sqrt{9} = 3$
$\sqrt{ab} = \sqrt{a}\sqrt{b}$ where a and b are >0	$\sqrt{(9)(4)} = \sqrt{9}\sqrt{4} = 3 \cdot 2 = 6$

If a fraction is greater than zero and less than 1, its square is smaller than the fraction

$0 < 5/7 < 1 \qquad 5/7 > (5/7) \qquad 5/7 > 25/49$

Strategies for Regular Math Questions

A. Memorize the rules for operations with zero, estimates of π, the square root of 2, the square root of 3, and the first 10 prime numbers.

B. When using squares and other powers, remember the effect of negative numbers.

C. When working with negative numbers, remember -8 is less than -4 and -1 is less than -1/2.

D. When working with fractions, remember that 1/8 is less than 1/4.

E. When working with decimals, rewrite the problem in vertical form with the decimals lined up before you add or subtract.

F. Use the sum or product in the ones column to help you eliminate answer choices.

G. Don't think you have to do all the calculations in your head. Use the test book for scratch work. DO NOT USE THE ANSWER SHEET FOR SCRATCH WORK.

SOME PSAT/SAT TIPS

1. Do not spend 3 or 4 minutes on a problem. You get just as much credit on an easy problem as you get on a hard problem. Time is not a luxury you have on this test.

2. Be aware of *must* versus *could* in a problem.

3. If, in a quantitative comparison, you can solve for a variable by setting Column A = Column B, then any other value of x will make the answer D. Be aware of any conditions placed upon the variable.

4. Try the choices. When doing this, it might be helpful to start with choice C when the magnitude of the answer is important. Based on whether choice C is high or low, or is the correct answer, will determine whether you should head towards choice A or E.

5. Know shortcuts. Examples of these are common pythagorean triples (and their multiples): 3-4-5; 5-12-13; 8-15-17; 7-24-25; as well as the characteristics of the special 30°,60°,90° and 45°,45°,90° right triangles.

6. It is not always necessary to solve for x and y individually in order to solve for x+y, x-y, xy, etc. In fact, there are times when it is impossible to solve for the individual variables.

7. It is often helpful to redraw figures that are *not drawn to scale*. In this way, you might visually arrive at the correct answer.

8. On diagrams, if it does NOT say *Figure not drawn to scale.* you can believe what you see with your eyes, with two exceptions. For instance, if an angle clearly looks obtuse, assume it is. However, you cannot assume the following: (1) RIGHT ANGLES - You must see or read something that clearly implies this: *right angle, perpendicular, 90*.   (2) PARALLEL LINES

EXAMINATION SECTION
TEST 1

DIRECTIONS: Each question or incomplete statement is followed by several suggested answers or completions. Select the one that BEST answers the question or completes the statement. *PRINT THE LETTER OF THE CORRECT ANSWER IN THE SPACE AT THE RIGHT.*

1. If $5(n+3) = 30$, which of the following is TRUE?   1.___
   - A. $n + 3 = 25$
   - B. $n + 15 = 30$
   - C. $5n + 3 = 30$
   - D. $5n + 15 = 30$
   - E. $5n + 15 = 150$

2. According to the graph shown at the right, approximately how many years did it take Maine's population to double from what it was in 1840?   2.___
   - A. 25
   - B. 40
   - C. 70
   - D. 115
   - E. 130

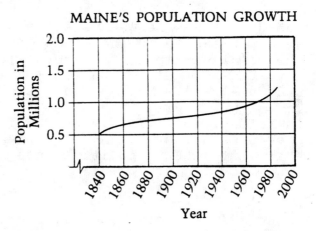

MAINE'S POPULATION GROWTH

Population in Millions — Year

3. $-1, 0, 1, -1, 0, 1,...$ 3.___
   The numbers $-1, 0$ and 1 repeat in a sequence, as shown above.
   If this pattern continues, what will be the sum of the 12th and 16th numbers in the sequence?
   - A. -2 B. -1 C. 0 D. 1 E. 2

4. In the figure shown at the right, the polygon with center O is equilateral and equiangular.   4.___
   The combined areas of the shaded regions represent what fraction of the total area of the polygon?

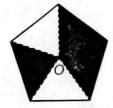

   - A. $\frac{2}{5}$
   - B. $\frac{1}{2}$
   - C. $\frac{3}{5}$
   - D. $\frac{2}{3}$
   - E. $\frac{3}{4}$

5. If x – 8 = 8 – x, then x =   5.___
   A. –16   B. –8   C. 0   D. 8   E. 16

6. Tickets numbered from 1 to 40, inclusive, are placed in   6.___
   a bowl and one ticket is to be selected at random.
   What is the probability that the ticket selected will
   have a single-digit number on it?

   A. $\frac{1}{40}$ B. $\frac{9}{40}$ C. $\frac{1}{4}$ D. $\frac{1}{2}$ E. $\frac{3}{4}$

7. Four straight lines that lie in the same plane intersect   7.___
   each other at point P.
   Which of the following is the sum of the measures of the
   non-overlapping angles formed?
   A. 60°   B. 90°   C. 180°   D. 320°   E. 360°

8. The difference between 2 times a number n and 7 is 81.   8.___
   Which of the following equations could be used to express
   the relationship in the above statement?
   A. 2n – 7 = 81   B. 2n + 7 = 81   C. 2(n–7) = 81
   D. n – 2(7) = 81   E. n – 2 + 7 = 81

9. An integer is divisible by 20, is a multiple of 30, and   9.___
   has 40 as a factor.
   What is the LEAST positive integer that satisfies these
   conditions?
   A. 10   B. 60   C. 120   D. 240   E. 360

10. If ab = 15, what is the value of the ratio of a to b?   10.___
    A. 1 to 15
    B. 3 to 5
    C. 5 to 3
    D. 15 to 1
    E. It cannot be determined from the information given

11. If a + 2a + 3a = 8, what is the value of 3a + 4a + 5a?   11.___
    A. 10   B. 12   C. 16   D. 20   E. 24

12. In the figure shown at the right, if   12.___
    BC is extended to the left to point A
    (not shown) so that B is the midpoint
    of AC, and if the length of AC is 2x,
    what is the length of CD in terms of
    x?
    A. $\sqrt{2x}$
    B. $\sqrt{3x}$
    C. $\sqrt{5x}$
    D. 1.5x
    E. 2x

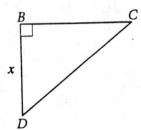

Note: Figure
not drawn to
scale.

13. For which of the following pairs of numbers is the   13.___
    second number 5 more than twice the first number?
       A. 5 and 30   B. 5 and 35   C. 10 and 40
       D. 20 and 50   E. 25 and 55

14. The line that passes through (-3,5) and (0,4) also   14.___
    passes through which of the following points?
       A. (1,7)   B. (3,3)   C. (3,5)   D. (5,3)   E. (7,1)

15. The average (arithmetic mean) of 5 test scores is 81.   15.___
    If 3 of the scores are 92, 83, and 78, which of the
    following could NOT be the other 2 scores?
       A. 73 and 79   B. 72 and 80   C. 69 and 83
       D. 64 and 86   E. 59 and 93

16.   2G   16.___
       H7
       4H
      +38
      ────
      164

    If the sum of the four two-digit numbers shown above
    equals 164, what is digit G?
       A. 8   B. 7   C. 6   D. 5   E. 4

17. Each face of the solid cube shown   17.___
    at the right is to be completely
    covered with 2-inch-wide strips
    of tape that do not overlap.
    What is the TOTAL length of the
    tape that is needed to cover the
    cube?
       A. 300 in.
       B. 450 in.
       C. 600 in.
       D. 900 in.
       E. 1,000 in.

18. If $r = x + y + z$, $x = 2y$ and $2z = 3y$, what is the value   18.___
    of r in terms of y?
       A. $\frac{7}{2}y$ B. $\frac{9}{2}y$ C. $5y$ D. $\frac{11}{2}y$ E. $6y$

19. In the figure shown at the right, if the area of △OPT equals the area of △TRS, what are the coordinates of P?

A. (0,2)

B. $(0, \frac{5}{2})$

C. (0,3)
D. (0,4)
E. (0,5)

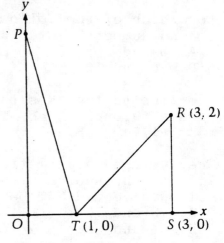

Note: Figure not drawn to scale.

19.___

20. If n>1, which of the following numbers will always be greater than 1?

I. $\dfrac{n}{n + 1}$ 　　II. $(n-1)^2$ 　　III. $\dfrac{2n - 1}{n}$

The CORRECT answer is:
A. None of the above 　　B. II *only*
C. III *only* 　　D. I and III
E. II and III

20.___

21. A square is inscribed in a circle of radius 10 centimeters, as shown in the figure at the right. What is the area, in square centimeters, of the square?

A. 225
B. 200
C. $125\sqrt{2}$
D. 169
E. 100

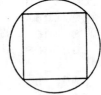

21.___

22. All tickets to a certain concert are equally priced. A survey showed that increasing the price of these concert tickets by 5 percent would decrease the number of tickets sold by 20 percent.
By what percent would this decrease the amount of money received from the sale of concert tickets?
A. 84% 　　B. 80% 　　C. 20% 　　D. 16% 　　E. 15%

22.___

23. $4^x + 4^x + 4^x + 4^x =$

A. 4^{x+1} 　　B. 4^{x+2} 　　C. 4^{x+4} 　　D. 4^{4x} 　　E. 4^{x^4}

23.___

24. The numbers on the meter shown at the right are spaced at equal intervals along its circumference.
If the hand is turned clockwise from its present position for 3,466 intervals and then turned counter-clockwise for 7,934 intervals, at which number will the hand then be pointing?

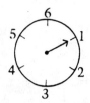

24.___

    A. 2
    B. 3
    C. 4
    D. 5
    E. 6

25. During 100 minutes of playing time, each of 5 teams plays each of the other 4 teams exactly once. Only 2 teams play at any given time.
If the total playing time for each team is the same, what is the TOTAL number of minutes that each team plays?

25.___

    A. 50   B. 40   C. 36   D. 30   E. 20

KEY (CORRECT ANSWERS)

1. D		11. C	
2. E		12. A	
3. C		13. E	
4. C		14. B	
5. D		15. D	
6. B		16. E	
7. E		17. A	
8. A		18. B	
9. C		19. D	
10. E		20. C	

21. B
22. D
23. A
24. B
25. B

ANSWERS GRIDDED

TEST 2

DIRECTIONS: Each question or incomplete statement is followed by several suggested answers or completions. Select the one that BEST answers the question or completes the statement. *PRINT THE LETTER OF THE CORRECT ANSWER IN THE SPACE AT THE RIGHT.*

Questions 1-15.

DIRECTIONS: Questions 1 through 15 each consist of two quantities in boxes, one in Column A and one in Column B. You are to compare the two quantities and mark your answer:
    A, if the quantity in Column A is greater;
    B, if the quantity in Column B is greater;
    C, if the two quantities are equal;
    D, if the relationship cannot be determined from the information given.

Notes:
1. In some questions, information is given about one or both of the quantities to be compared. In such cases, the given information is centered above the two columns and is not boxed.
2. In a given question, a symbol that appears in both columns represents the same thing in Column A as it does in Column B.
3. Letters such as x, n, and k stand for real numbers.

Examples:

Column A	Column B	
E1 $.5^2$	20	CORRECT: A

E2

$150°$ $x°$

| x | 30 | CORRECT: C |

COLUMN A	COLUMN B	
1.	1 gallon = 4 quarts 1 quart = 4 cups	1.___
2 gallons	8 cups	

COLUMN A   COLUMN B

2.

$x°$ triangle with sides 2, 2, 2

| x |

$y°$ triangle with sides 4, 4, 4

| y |

2.___

3.

| The number of positive integers less than 10 |

| The number of negative integers greater than -10 |

3.___

4.   x and y are positive integers   4.___

| 2^x |

| 4^y |

5.

| Louise's average speed, in miles per hour, if she drove 110 miles in 2 hours |

| Theresa's average speed, in miles per hour, if she drove 220 miles in 4 hours |

5.___

6.   S and T are two points on a
            circle of radius 6   6.___

| The length of line segment ST |

| 13 |

7.   The month of April always has
            30 days   7.___

| The number of Mondays in April in year Y |

| The number of Fridays in April in year Y |

COLUMN A   COLUMN B

8.   8.___

$$y$$

$$O \qquad x$$

$$\bullet (t, u)$$

$$\boxed{t} \qquad\qquad\qquad\qquad \boxed{u}$$

9. $2n = -3q$ 9.___

$$\boxed{n} \qquad\qquad\qquad\qquad \boxed{q}$$

10.   The lengths of the sides of   10.___
           a triangle are 5, 5, and t

$$\boxed{5} \qquad\qquad\qquad\qquad \boxed{t}$$

11. $3x > 15$ 11.___
                       $4 - y > 5$

$$\boxed{x} \qquad\qquad\qquad\qquad \boxed{y}$$

12.   Lines l and m lies in a plane   12.___
           and are neither parallel nor
           perpendicular to each other.

$$\boxed{\begin{array}{l} \text{The degree measure} \\ \text{of the smaller angle} \\ \text{formed by } l \text{ and } m \end{array}} \qquad \boxed{90}$$

13. For all integers x and y,
     let x∎y be defined as
     $x \blacksquare y = xy^2$.

     13.___

     (3∎2)-(2∎3)

     0

14. $x + 3 = y$
     $x + y = 10$

     14.___

     2x + 3

     10

15. r and s are two different
     positive integers.

     $\frac{r}{s}$ is an integer.

     15.___

     The number of integers
     that divide r with
     remainder zero

     The number of integers
     that divide s with
     remainder zero

Questions 16-25.

Directions for Student-Produced Response Questions

Each of the remaining 10 questions requires you to solve the problem and enter your answer by marking the ovals in the special grid, as shown in the examples below.

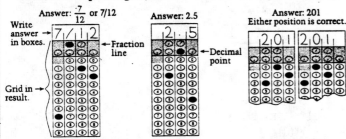

Note: You may start your answers in any column, space permitting. Columns not needed should be left blank.

- Mark no more than one oval in any column.
- Because the answer sheet will be machine-scored, **you will receive credit only if the ovals are filled in correctly.**
- Although not required, it is suggested that you write your answer in the boxes at the top of the columns to help you fill in the ovals accurately.

- Some problems may have more than one correct answer. In such cases, grid only one answer.
- No question has a negative answer.
- **Mixed numbers** such as $2\frac{1}{2}$ must be gridded as 2.5 or 5/2. (If [2 1/2] is gridded, it will be interpreted as $\frac{21}{2}$, not $2\frac{1}{2}$.)
- **Decimal Accuracy:** If you obtain a decimal answer, **enter the most accurate value that the grid will accommodate.** For example, if you obtain an answer such as 0.6666..., you should record the result as .666 or .667. **Less accurate values such as .66 or .67 are not acceptable.**

Acceptable ways to grid $\frac{2}{3}$ = .6666 . . .

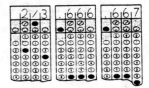

16. If $\frac{k}{10} + \frac{k}{10} + \frac{k}{10} = 3$, what is the value of k?　　　　16.___

17. Set S consists of all multiples of 3 between 10 and 25.　　17.___
Set T consists of all multiples of 4 between 10 and 25.
What is one possible number that is in set S but NOT in
set T?

18. -980, -76, -54, 0, 1, 2, 3, 54, 76, 980　　　　　18.___
What is the average (arithmetic mean) of the 10 numbers
in the list above?

19. If $(3x+1)(4x+3) = ax^2 + bx + c$ for all values of x,　　19.___
what is the value of b?

20. What is the perimeter of the　　　　　　　　　　20.___
eight-sided figure shown at
the right?

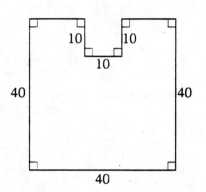

21. If 3s + 7t = 22 and s and t are positive integers, what　21.___
is the value of s?

22. A cubic foot of a certain material weighs 4 pounds.　　22.___
How much will 216 cubic inches of this material weigh,
in pounds?　(1 cubic foot = 1,728 cubic inches)

23. In a certain factory, 0.2 percent of a batch of micro-　23.___
chips are defective.
If this batch contains 4 defective microchips, how many
microchips are in the batch?

24. If $\frac{3}{y^3} = 81$, what is the value of y?　　　　　24.___

25. Points P, Q, R, and S are the centers　　　　　25.___
of four of the faces of the cube shown
in the figure at the right.
What is the area of quadrilateral
PQRS?

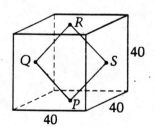

KEY (CORRECT ANSWERS)

1. A		11. A	
2. C		12. B	
3. C		13. B	
4. D		14. C	
5. C		15. A	
6. B		16. 10	
7. D		17. 15, 18, or 21	
8. A		18. .6 or 3/5	
9. D		19. 13	
10. D		20. 180	

21. 5
22. 1/2 or .5
23. 2000
24. 1/3 or .333
25. 800

ANSWERS GRIDDED

1. (A) (B) (C) (D)
2. (A) (B) (C) (D)
3. (A) (B) (C) (D)
4. (A) (B) (C) (D)
5. (A) (B) (C) (D)
6. (A) (B) (C) (D)
7. (A) (B) (C) (D)
8. (A) (B) (C) (D)
9. (A) (B) (C) (D)
10. (A) (B) (C) (D)

11. (A) (B) (C) (D)
12. (A) (B) (C) (D)
13. (A) (B) (C) (D)
14. (A) (B) (C) (D)
15. (A) (B) (C) (D)

16. 110
17. 115
18. 1.6
19. 113
20. 180

21. 5
22. 1.5
23. 2000
24. .333
25. 800

EXAMINATION SECTION
TEST 1

DIRECTIONS: Each question or incomplete statement is followed by several suggested answers or completions. Select the one that BEST answers the question or completes the statement. *PRINT THE LETTER OF THE CORRECT ANSWER IN THE SPACE AT THE RIGHT.*

1. Which of the following fractions is the GREATEST?   1.___

   A. $\frac{16}{17}$ B. $\frac{8}{9}$ C. $\frac{14}{15}$ D. $\frac{9}{10}$ E. $\frac{11}{12}$

2. Sue ate 1/3 of a sandwich at noon and then 1/2 of the   2.___
   remainder at supper.
   What part of the sandwich remained uneaten?

   A. $\frac{1}{6}$ B. $\frac{1}{5}$ C. $\frac{1}{3}$ D. $\frac{1}{2}$ E. $\frac{2}{3}$

3. In a certain class of 30 students, 18 are girls.   3.___
   If 2/3 of the girls are 16 years old or younger, what
   fractional part of the class is girls over 16?

   A. $\frac{2}{15}$ B. $\frac{1}{5}$ C. $\frac{1}{3}$ D. $\frac{2}{5}$ E. $\frac{1}{2}$

4. In a certain factory, 3/4 of the workers are married and   4.___
   3/4 of these married workers have children.
   What fraction of the workers in the factory are married
   without children?

   A. $\frac{1}{16}$ B. $\frac{3}{16}$ C. $\frac{1}{4}$ D. $\frac{1}{2}$ E. $\frac{9}{16}$

5. Every student who studies art in a certain school receives   5.___
   exactly one of the grades A, B, C, or D.
   If 1/5 of the students receive A's, 1/4 receive B's,
   1/2 receive C's, and 10 students receive D's, how many
   students in the school study art?
   A. 50   B. 60   C. 90   D. 100   E. 200

6. The gauge of a gas tank shows 1/8 full. After 12 gallons   6.___
   are added, the tank is 7/8 full.
   What is the capacity, in gallons, of the tank?
   A. 14   B. 15   C. 16   D. 17   E. 18

7. If x ranges in value from 0.0001 to 0.01 and y ranges   7.___
   in value from 0.001 to 0.1, what is the MAXIMUM value
   of x/y?
   A. 0.001   B. 0.1   C. 1   D. 10   E. 1,000

8. Sally used 1/4 of her inheritance to pay her tuition
   and 2/3 of the remainder to buy a new car.
   How much money was left from her original inheritance
   of $60,000?   8.___
       A. 12,000   B. 15,000   C. 18,000   D. 20,000   E. 24,000

Questions 9-10.

DIRECTIONS: Questions 9 and 10 consist of two quantities, one in
              Column A and one in Column B. You are to compare the
              two quantities and in the space at the right write]
                A if the quantity in Column A is greater;
                B if the quantity in Column B is greater;
                C if the two quantities are equal;
                D if the relationship cannot be determined from
                  the information given
              AN E RESPONSE WILL NOT BE SCORED

	Column A	Column B	

9. $x = \{0.98, 0.098, 0.09\}$ 9.___
       $y = \{0.089, 0.89, 0.9\}$

   The greatest number in   The greatest number in
   set x.   set y.

10. $\dfrac{\frac{2}{3}}{\frac{3}{2}}$ 1   10.___

Questions 11-16.

DIRECTIONS: Questions 11 through 16 are problems involving percents.

11. In a senior class, there are 200 boys and 300 girls.   11.___
     If 40 percent of the senior boys and 50 percent of the
     senior girls bought class rings, how many seniors bought
     class rings?
         A. 200   B. 225   C. 230   D. 250   E. 275

12. If 10 is 5 percent of N, then N =   12.___
         A. 2   B. 5   C. 20   D. 50   E. 200

13. In a basket of 120 apples, exactly 6 were rotten.   13.___
     What percent of the apples were rotten?
         A. 5%   B. 6%   C. 10%   D. 20%   E. 25%

14. In the rectangle shown at the   14.___
     right, PQ = x and QR = 2x.
     What percent of the perimeter of
     the rectangle is the sum PQ + QR
     + RS?
         A. 50%
         B. 66 2/3%
         C. 75%
         D. 80%
         E. 83 2/3%

15. If the length and width of rectangle A are 10 percent   15.____
    less and 30 percent less, respectively, than the length
    and width of rectangle B, the area of A is equal to
    what percent of the area of B?
       A. 63%   B. 60%   C. 40%   D. 6%   E. 3%

16. The population of Norson, the largest city in Transitania,   16.____
    is 50 percent of the rest of the population of Transi-
    tania.
    The population of Norson is what percent of the entire
    population of Transitania?
       A. 20%   B. 25%   C. 30%   D. 33 1/3% E. 50%

Questions 17-20.

DIRECTIONS: Questions 17 through 20 each consist of two quantities,
                one in Column A and one in Column B. You are to
                compare the two quantities and mark your answer]
                  A if the quantity in Column A is greater;
                  B if the quantity in Column B is greater;
                  C if the two quantities are equal;
                  D if the relationship cannot be determined from
                    the information given
                AN E RESPONSE WILL NOT BE SCORED

Column A	Column B

17. A coat that was priced at $36.50 is sold at 30 percent   17.____
    discount.

    Price of coat after $25.55
    discount

18. On a certain day, 80 percent of the girls and 75 percent   18.____
    of the boys were present in a mathematics class.

    The number of girls   The number of boys absent
    absent

19.   x is 10% of y.   19.____

    The percent that y   100%
    is of x

20.   x percent of y is z.   20.____

    100                $\dfrac{xy}{z}$

21. A grocer has 100 apples, 100 oranges, and 100 pears.   21.____
    If he packs 1 apple, 2 oranges, and 1 pear in a bag,
    then the MAXIMUM number of bags he can fill in this
    manner is
       A. 20   B. 25   C. 50   D. 75   E. 100

22. Which of the following conditions will make x - y a positive number?

    A. 0<y   B. y<x   C. x<o   D. x<y   E. x=y

22.___

23. If xy is positive, which of the following CANNOT be true about x and y?

    A. x<y<o   B. y<x<o   C. x<o<y   D. o<x<y   E. o<y<x

23.___

24. The area of a living room is 465 square feet. If this area were increased by 25 square feet, the enlarged area would be twice the area of the adjoining dining room. What is the area, in square feet, of the dining room?

    A. 245   B. 240   C. 235   D. 230   E. 220

24.___

25. If the two middle digits of 4,579 are interchanged, the resulting number is

    A. 18 less than 4,579   B. 180 less than 4,579
    C. equal to 4,579   D. 18 more than 4,579
    E. 180 more than 4,579

25.___

KEY (CORRECT ANSWERS)

1. A		11. C	
2. C		12. E	
3. B		13. A	
4. B		14. B	
5. E		15. A	
6. C		16. D	
7. D		17. C	
8. B		18. D	
9. A		19. A	
10. B		20. C	

21. C
22. B
23. C
24. A
25. E

ANSWERS GRIDDED

	A	B	C	D	E
1.	●				
2.					
3.		●			
4.					
5.					●
6.					
7.				●	
8.		●			
9.	●				
10.		●			

	A	B	C	D	E
11.			●		
12.				●	
13.		●			
14.		●			
15.	●				
16.				●	
17.			●		
18.				●	
19.	●				
20.			●		

	A	B	C	D	E
21.			●		
22.		●			
23.			●		
24.	●				
25.					●

TEST 2

DIRECTIONS: Each question or incomplete statement is followed by several suggested answers or completions. Select the one that BEST answers the question or completes the statement. *PRINT THE LETTER OF THE CORRECT ANSWER IN THE SPACE AT THE RIGHT.*

1. What is the difference between the greatest and least of all three-digit positive integers, each of whose digits is a different non-zero multiple of 3?
   A. 324   B. 540   C. 567   D. 594   E. 604   1.___

2. A two-digit number has a tens' digit x and a units' digit y.
   What is the product of this number and the number 5, in terms of x and y?
   A. 5x + y   B. 5x + 5y   C. 5x + 50y   2.___
   D. 50x + 50y   E. 50x + 5y

3. An arithmetic progression is a sequence of numbers for which each new number is found by adding a given number n to the previous number. In the arithmetic progression below, only two numbers are known: 3.___
   __, __, 3, __, __, __, 19, __, X, Y
   What is the sum of x and y?
   A. 52   B. 54   C. 55   D. 56   E. 58

4. Jack begins reading at the top of page N and finishes at the bottom of page R.   4.___
   If the pages are numbered and read consecutively and if there are no blank pages, how many pages has he read?
   A. R - N + 1   B. N - R + 1   C. N - R - 1
   D. R - N   E. N - R

5. If a, b, c, d, and e are whole numbers, the expression a(b(c+d)+e) will be an even number whenever which of the   5.___
   following is even?
   A. a   B. b   C. c   D. d   E. e

Questions 6-11.

DIRECTIONS: Questions 6 through 11 are student-produced response questions. Grid your answers.

6. A chemist has 80 pints of a 20% iodine solution.   6.___
   How many pints of iodine must be added to produce a solution that is 33 1/3% iodine?
   A. 15   B. 16   C. 20   D. 32

7. A model for a certain battery-driven car will provide
30 hours of driving time at 50 miles per hour without
recharging the batteries.
The present distance that the car can travel at 50 miles
per hour is how many miles less than the design goal of
2,000 miles?
    A. 500   B. 600   C. 750   D. 1500

7.___

8. What is the sum of 5 consecutive integers if the middle
one is 70?
    A. 300   B. 350   C. 450   D. 500

8.___

9. If 45 cards can be copied in 30 minutes, how many hours
will it take to copy 540 such cards at the same rate?
    A. 6   B. 9   C. 12   D. 15

9.___

10. If 3 persons who work at the same rate can do a job
together in 5 days, what fractional part of that job
can one of these persons do in 1 day?

    A. $\frac{1}{9}$ B. $\frac{1}{12}$ C. $\frac{1}{14}$ D. $\frac{1}{15}$

10.___

11. If $m^2 = 16$ and $n^2 = 36$, then the difference between the
greatest possible value of $m - n$ and the least possible
value of $m - n$ is
    A. 20   B. 24   C. 26   D. 30

11.___

12. For which of the following pairs of numbers is the square
of one of the numbers the reciprocal of the other number?
    I. 0.25, 2   II. 1, 1   III. 0.5, 4

The CORRECT answer is:
    A. I *only*   B. II *only*   C. III *only*
    D. I and II *only*   E. I, II, III

12.___

Questions 13-15.

DIRECTIONS: Questions 13 through 15 each consist of two quantities,
one in Column A and one in Column B. You are to
compare the two quantities and mark your answer:
    A if the quantity in Column A is greater;
    B if the quantity in Column B is greater;
    C if the two quantities are equal;
    D if the relationship cannot be determined from
      the information given
AN E RESPONSE WILL NOT BE SCORED

    Column A   Column B

13. $-1 < x < 1$
                     $x \neq 0$
    $1/x$ x

13.___

Column A	Column B	

14. x and y are points
on the number line

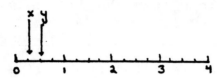

    x . y . 2 . 3 . 4   4   14.___

15. Remainder when 731^{500} 1   15.___
is divided by 10

Questions: 16-25 - Grid your answers.

16. If 6.363 = 63k, what does k equal?   16.___
    A. .001   B. .002   C. .101   D. .103

17. In a certain country, a Q-type coin is equivalent to   17.___
25 cents and a D-type coin is equivalent to 10 cents.
How many D-type coins have a total value equal to the
value of 30 Q-type coins?
    A. 15   B. 25   C. 35   D. 75

18. Square ABCD shown at the right is   18.___
divided into 16 equal squares.
The total area of the shaded
regions is what fraction of the
area of ABCD?

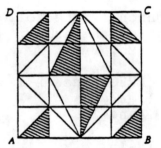

    A. $\frac{1}{5}$ or .2

    B. $\frac{1}{4}$ or .25

    C. $\frac{1}{3}$ or .33

    D. $\frac{1}{2}$ or .5

19. If x = 2, what is the value of $\frac{2(x-2)^2}{x+2}$?   19.___
    A. -2   B. -1   C. 0   D. 2

20. In the last step of a series of computations, a student   20.___
divided by 2 when he should have multiplied by 2.
If his incorrect answer was 0.25 and he made no other
errors, what was the correct answer?
    A. 0   B. 1   C. 2   D. 4

21. In the triangle shown at the right, what is the value of 4x?
    A. 45
    B. 66
    C. 70
    D. 72

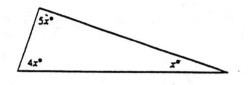

21.___

22. Four cake pans are graduated in size so that the capacity of each pan is twice that of the next smaller one. If the capacity of the smallest pan is 1/3 cup, what is the capacity, in cups, of the largest pan?

    A. $\frac{8}{3}$ or 2.67   B. 3

    C. $\frac{10}{3}$ or 3.33   D. 4

22.___

23. Set S contains all integers from 100 to 200, inclusive. If x is a number in S that is an integer multiple of both 6 and 10, what is one possible value of x?
    A. 100   B. 150   C. 160   D. 170

23.___

24. In the figure shown at the right, if PQ is a diameter of the circle with center 0, and OR and RQ are of equal length, what is the value of y/3?
    A. 20
    B. 30
    C. 35
    D. 40

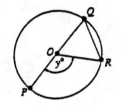

24.___

25. A discount store offers a calculator listed at $60 for $48.
What would be the selling price, in dollars, of a model listed at $150 if it were discounted at 1½ times the percent discount on the $60 model? (Disregard the $ sign when gridding your answer.)
    A. 65   B. 75   C. 100   D. 105

25.___

KEY (CORRECT ANSWERS)

1. D	6. B	11. A	16. C	21. D
2. E	7. A	12. E	17. D	22. A
3. E	8. B	13. D	18. B	23. B
4. A	9. A	14. B	19. C	24. D
5. A	10. D	15. C	20. B	25. D

ANSWERS GRIDDED

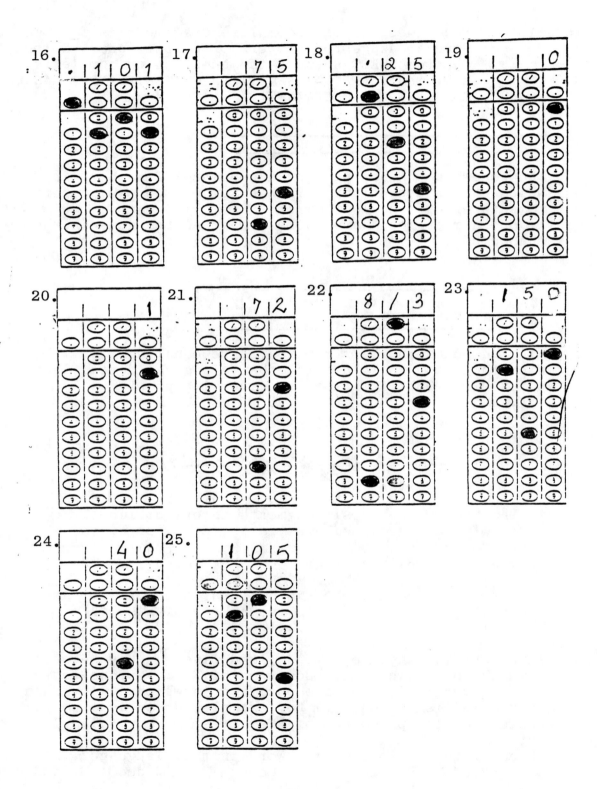

TEST 3

DIRECTIONS: Each question or incomplete statement is followed by several suggested answers or completions. Select the one that BEST answers the question or completes the statement. *PRINT THE LETTER OF THE CORRECT ANSWER IN THE SPACE AT THE RIGHT.*

1. 1.___

   The boxes above show part of a sequence of numbers in which each number after 3 is the sum of the two numbers immediately to the left of it.
   If one number goes in each box, what number goes in the shaded box?
   A. 13   B. 21   C. 31   D. 34   E. 65

2. 2.___

   All the boxes in the strip above are equal size.
   When the strip is folded together along the dotted line, point P is MOST likely to coincide with point
   A. A   B. B   C. C   D. D   E. E

3. 3.___

   In the figure above, six segments intersect line l.
   Which of the degree measures, a, b, c, d, or e, is equal to x?
   A. a   B. b   C. c   D. d   E. e

4. If the *center* of a number is defined to be 1/2 of the number, then what number is the *center* of itself?   4.___
   A. -1   B. 0   C. 1   D. 2   E. 10

5. In a certain language, a *word* is defined as any 5-letter combination in which the position of at least one letter in the *word* is in the same position in which it is found in the English alphabet. For example, *dbacc* is a word, because of the placement of the letter b, but *bdaac* is not.   5.___
   Which of the following is a word in this language?
   A. cddcd   B. cdddc   C. ccdcc   D. dcdcc   E. dddcd

6. For any sentence J, the expression N (J) is defined to   6.___
mean the number of times the letter *t* appears in J.
If J is the sentence *All cats are good luck*, then N (J) =
   A. 0   B. 1   C. 2   D. 3   E. 4

7. After Jane gave Bill $4, she then had $12 more than Bill.   7.___
How much more money than Bill did Jane have originally?
   A. $4   B. $8   C. $12   D. $16   E. $20

8.   8.___

2	x	14	y
x	14	y	2
14	y	2	x
y	2	x	14

In the figure above, the sums of the numbers in each row,
column, and main diagonals are the same.
What is the value of x?
   A. 2   B. 8   C. 12   D. 14   E. 16

9.   9.___

	Event I	Event II	Event III
First Place 5 pt.	School A	School B	
Second Place 3 pt.		School C	
Third Place 1 pt.			

Shown above is a partially completed score card for an
athletic contest among schools A, B, and C.
If each school entered one contestant in each of these
events and there were no ties, what is the LEAST possible
total score that any one of these schools could achieve
for all three events?
   A. 3   B. 4   C. 5   D. 6   E. 7

10. If the odometer of an automobile registers 62,222 miles,   10.___
what is the FEWEST number of miles that the automobile
must travel before the odometer again shows four of the
five digits the same?
   A. 99   B. 444   C. 555   D. 999   E. 1,111

11. If half the people in a room leave at the end of every   11.___
five-minute interval and at the end of twenty minutes the
next to the last person leaves, how many people were in
the room to start with? (Assume that no one enters the
room once the process begins.)
   A. 32   B. 28   C. 16   D. 12   E. 8

12. In the correctly computed multiplication problem shown at the right, if △ and □ are different digits, then △ =
    A.
    A. 1   B. 5   C. 6   D. 7   E. 8

$$\begin{array}{r} 5\ \triangle\ 2 \\ \times\ \ \ \ 9 \\ \hline 5,\ 2\square 8 \end{array}$$

12.____

13. In the addition problem shown at the right, □ represents the same digit in each number. What must □ represent in order to make the answer correct?
    A. 8
    B. 6
    C. 5
    D. 4
    E. 2

$$\begin{array}{r} \square 4 \\ 3\square \\ \square 3 \\ 5\square \\ \square 1 \\ \hline 15\square \end{array}$$

13.____

14. If the road distances between any two points are as indicated on the map shown at the right, what is the SHORTEST road distance from P to R?
    A. 27
    B. 28
    C. 29
    D. 30
    E. 33

14.____

15. In the figure shown at the right, the pattern is repeated every 15 symbols. Which of the following, when placed below the arrows in the design, will continue the pattern of the design?
    A. □□
    B. ●●
    C. ▲▲
    D. ☆△
    E. △☆

15.____

16. A machine began knitting a row of 100 stitches by making 3 knit stitches and 2 purl stitches and repeated the same pattern thereafter.
    What is the order in which it knitted the 77th, 78th, 79th, and 80th stitches in the row?
    A. 2 knit, 2 purl   B. 1 knit, 2 purl, 1 knit
    C. 3 knit, 1 purl   D. 2 purl, 2 knit
    E. 1 purl, 2 knit, 1 purl

16.____

17. If it is now 4:00 P.M. Saturday, in 253 hours from now what time and day will it be? (Assume no daylight saving time changes in the period.)
    A. 5:00 A.M. Saturday   B. 1:00 A.M. Sunday
    C. 5:00 P.M. Tuesday   D. 1:00 A.M. Wednesday
    E. 5:00 A.M. Wednesday

17.____

18. If the figure at the right is the
mirror image of an accurate clock, what
time will it be 15 minutes after the
time shown?
    A. 1:50
    B. 1:40
    C. 1:10
    D. 10:40
    E. 10:05

18.____

19. The twelve-hour digital clock shown
at the right shows one example of a
time at which the number representing
the hour is equal to the number
representing the minutes.
What is the LEAST possible number of
minutes from the instant one such
double reading appears to the instant
the next appears?
    A. 11   B. 30   C. 49   D. 60   E. 61

19.____

20. Each jar shown at the right
contains 6 marbles.
What is the LEAST number of
marbles that must be transferred to make the ratio:
marbles in X : marbles in Y :
marbles in Z = 3 : 2 : 1?
    A. 6   B. 5   C. 4   D. 3   E. 2

20.____

Questions 21-25.

DIRECTIONS: Questions 21 through 25 consist of two quantities, one
in Column A and one in Column B. You are to compare
the two quantities and in the space at the right mark
your answer:
    A if the quantity in Column A is greater;
    B if the quantity in Column B is greater;
    C if the two quantities are equal;
    D if the relationship cannot be determined from
       the information given
AN E RESPONSE WILL NOT BE SCORED

Column A   Column B

21. Ann has 6 more marbles than Nancy, Nancy has 3 more
marbles than Joe, and Joe has 4 more marbles than Pete.

    The least number of marbles   8
    that must change hands if
    each is to have an equal
    number of marbles

21.____

	Column A	Column B	
22.	Area of a circle with radius 1	Area of a square with side 1	22.___
23.	$2x + 3 = y$		23.___
	$20x + 20$	$10y$	
24.	25% of $x = 60$		24.___
	50% of x	120	
25.	$x < y < z$		25.___
	xy	yz	

KEY (CORRECT ANSWERS)

1. D		11. C	
2. B		12. E	
3. E		13. E	
4. B		14. B	
5. B		15. A	
6. B		16. A	
7. E		17. E	
8. B		18. A	
9. C		19. C	
10. B		20. D	

21. C
22. A
23. A
24. C
25. B

ANSWERS GRIDDED

```
         A  B  C  D  E
 1.      ⊙  ⊙  ⊙  ●  ⊙
 2.      ⊙  ●  ⊙  ⊙  ⊙
 3.      ⊙  ⊙  ⊙  ⊙  ●
 4.      ⊙  ⊙  ⊙  ⊙  ⊙
 5.      ⊙  ●  ⊙  ⊙  ⊙
 6.      ⊙  ⊙  ⊙  ⊙  ⊙
 7.      ⊙  ⊙  ⊙  ⊙  ●
 8.      ⊙  ⊙  ⊙  ⊙  ⊙
 9.      ⊙  ⊙  ●  ⊙  ⊙
10.      ⊙  ●  ⊙  ⊙  ⊙
```

```
11.      ⊙  ⊙  ●  ⊙  ⊙
12.      ⊙  ⊙  ⊙  ⊙  ●
13.      ⊙  ⊙  ⊙  ⊙  ●
14.      ⊙  ●  ⊙  ⊙  ⊙
15.      ●  ⊙  ⊙  ⊙  ⊙
16.      ●  ⊙  ⊙  ⊙  ⊙
17.      ⊙  ⊙  ⊙  ⊙  ●
18.      ●  ⊙  ⊙  ⊙  ⊙
19.      ⊙  ⊙  ●  ⊙  ⊙
20.      ⊙  ⊙  ⊙  ●  ⊙
```

```
21.      ⊙  ⊙  ●  ⊙  ⊙
22.      ●  ⊙  ⊙  ⊙  ⊙
23.      ●  ⊙  ⊙  ⊙  ⊙
24.      ⊙  ⊙  ●  ⊙  ⊙
25.      ⊙  ●  ⊙  ⊙  ⊙
```

———————

EXAMINATION SECTION
TEST 1

DIRECTIONS: Each question or incomplete statement is followed by
                several suggested answers or completions. Select the
                one that BEST answers the question or completes the
                statement. *PRINT THE LETTER OF THE CORRECT ANSWER IN
                THE SPACE AT THE RIGHT.*

1. Three dogs weigh 6, 10, and 12 kilograms, respectively.   1.___
    The weight of the lightest dog is how much less than the
    average (arithmetic mean) weight of the three dogs?
    _____ kg
        A. 6   B. 4   C. 3 2/3   D. 3 1/3   E. 2 2/3

2. What is the average of 1/5 and 1/7?   2.___

        A. $\frac{1}{12}$ B. $\frac{1}{6}$ C. $\frac{6}{35}$ D. $\frac{12}{35}$ E. $\frac{36}{35}$

3. If the average (arithmetic mean) of –5 and x is –5, then   3.___
    x =
        A. 10   B. 5   C. 0   D. –5   E. –10

4. A class took a math test that resulted in the following   4.___
    scores: 40,50,65,65,70,85,85,85,95.
    By how many points did the mode differ from the median?
        A. 0   B. 5   C. 10   D. 15   E. 20

5. A teacher gave a test to 30 students and the average   5.___
    score was x. Scores on the test ranged from 0 to 90,
    inclusive.
    If the average score for the first 10 papers graded was
    60, what is the difference between the greatest and
    least POSSIBLE values of x?
        A. 20   B. 30   C. 40   D. 50   E. 60

Questions 6-10.

DIRECTIONS: Questions 6 through 10 each consist of two quantities,
                one in Column A and one in Column B. You are to
                compare the two quantities and mark your answer:
                    A if the quantity in Column A is greater;
                    B if the quantity in Column B is greater;
                    C if the two quantities are equal;
                    D if the relationship cannot be determined from
                      the information given
                AN E RESPONSE WILL NOT BE SCORED

Column A   Column B

6. On a certain test, the average score for the juniors was   6.___
87 and the average score for the sophomores was 81.

The average score for   84
the total group

7. $$x + y = 10$$ 7.___

The average (arithmetic   5
mean) of x and y

8. $$y = x + 1$$ 8.___

The average (arithmetic   The average (arithmetic
mean) of 7, 9, and x   mean) of 2, 13, and y

9. In a school with 6 classrooms, there are more than 1 and   9.___
less than 20 students in 1 classroom and exactly 20
students in each of the other 5 classrooms.

Average (arithmetic mean)   20
of students per classroom

10. The average (arithmetic mean) of 18, 30, x, and y equals   10.___
12.

$$x > 0$$

y   0

11. The following scores were reported: 7, 9, 7, 4, 8, 3, 4,   11.___
7, 5.
Which of the following is/are TRUE?
  I. The mean of the scores is not equal to any of the
     individual scores.
 II. The median of the scores is equal to the mode, and
     both are greater than the mean.
III. If a score of 6 is added to the existing scores, none
     of the mean, median, or mode will change.

The CORRECT answer is:
  A. II *only*   B. I, II   C. I, III
  D. II, III   E. I, II, III

12. If for all numbers n, #n = n(n+1)(n+2), then $\frac{\#8}{\#4}$ =   12.___

  A. #1   B. #2   C. #3   D. #4   E. #6

Questions 13-14.

DIRECTIONS: Questions 13 and 14 each consist of two quantities, one in Column A and one in Column B. You are to compare the two quantities and mark your answer:
A if the quantity in Column A is greater;
B if the quantity in Column B is greater;
C if the two quantities are equal;
D if the relationship cannot be determined from the information given
AN E RESPONSE WILL NOT BE SCORED

These questions refer to the following definition of x where x is any real number:

$$\boxed{x} = (x-1)^4 + (x-1)^2 + 1$$

Column A	Column B	
13. $\boxed{1}$	1	13.___
14. $\boxed{10}$	$\boxed{-10}$	14.___

Questions 15-16.

DIRECTIONS: Questions 15 and 16 refer to the following definition:

A	B
C	D

A block sum is a figure, like the one above, that has the following properties:

1. A, B, C, and D are digits from 1 to 9, inclusive.
2. A + B = 10C + D

For example,

5	8
1	3

is a block sum because 1, 3, 5, and 8 satisfy property 1 and 5 + 8 = 13 satisfies property 2.

15. If the figure at the right is a block sum, what is the value of A + B?   15.___

A	B
1	2

A. 12
B. 3
C. 2
D. 1
E. It cannot be determined from the information given

16. If the figure at the right is a block sum, what digit does D represent?   16.___

9	7
C	D

A. 1
B. 3
C. 6
D. 16
E. It cannot be determined from the information given

17.

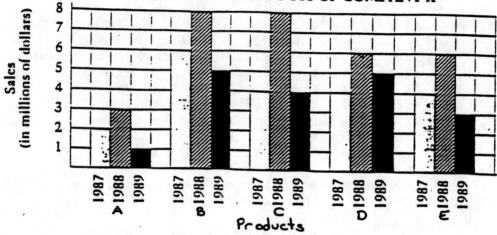

SALES OF FIVE PRODUCTS OF COMPANY X

For which of the five products - A, B, C, D, and E - shown in the above graph was the percent increase in sales from 1987 to 1988 the same as the percent decrease from 1988 to 1989?

A. A   B. B   C. C   D. D   E. E

Questions 18-19.

DIRECTIONS: Questions 18 and 19 are to be answered on the basis of the following graph.

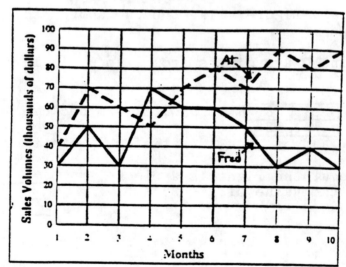

VOLUMES OF SALES FOR A 10-MONTH PERIOD FOR TWO SALESPEOPLE

18.   Consider Al's sales record from month 4 to month 5. What was the percent increase?

    A. 25%   B. 33 1/3%   C. 40%
    D. 133 1/3%   E. 175%

19. How much greater (in thousands of dollars) were the   19.___
    sales for Fred's best month than Al's worst month?
         A. 10   B. 20   C. 30   D. 40   E. 70

20. If $a \neq 0$, then $\dfrac{(-2a)^3}{-2a^3} =$ 20.___

         A. -4   B. -1   C. 1   D. 3   E. 4

21. If $6+x+y = 20$ and if $x+y = k$, then $20-k$ is equal to   21.___
         A. 14   B. 9   C. 6
         D. 3 2/3   E. none of the above

22. If $x + y = k$ and $x - y = \dfrac{1}{k}$, then when $k \neq 0$, $x^2 - y^2 =$ 22.___

         A. $\dfrac{1}{k}$ B. k   C. k^2 D. 2   E. 1

23. If $x^2 = 1$, then x^3 is equal to   23.___
         A. -3   B. -1 *only*   C. 1 *only*
         D. 3   E. -1 or 1

24. If $x = 2a$ and $y = \dfrac{1}{4a + 2}$, what is y in terms of x?   24.___

         A. $\dfrac{1}{2x + 2}$ B. $\dfrac{1}{2x + 4}$ C. $\dfrac{2}{x + 4}$

         D. $\dfrac{1}{8x + 2}$ E. $\dfrac{1}{8x + 4}$

25. On a certain typing assignment, Bob types 2 times as   25.___
    many pages per hour as Sam, and he makes 3 times as
    many errors per page as Sam.
    If Sam averages 1 error every 15 minutes, how many errors
    does Bob average in an hour?
         A. 2   B. 3   C. 6   D. 12   E. 24

26. At a sale, the original price of an item was discounted   26.___
    by 20 percent, and the discounted price was reduced by
    an additional 5 percent for paying cash.
    If the original price was x dollars, which of the follow-
    ing represents the amount paid in dollars for a cash
    purchase of this item at the sale?
         A. 0.75x   B. 0.76x   C. 0.79x   D. 0.80x   E. 0.85x

Questions 27-33.

DIRECTIONS: Questions 27 through 33 each consist of two quantities,
              one in Column A and one in Column B. You are to compare
              the two quantities and mark your answer:
                A if the quantity in Column A is greater;
                B if the quantity in Column B is greater;
                C if the two quantities are equal;
                D if the relationship cannot be determined from
                  the information given
              AN E RESPONSE WILL NOT BE SCORED

Column A	Column B

27.
$$1 \text{ skedallion} = 4.6 \text{ skippers}$$
$$2 \text{ phantoms} = 9.3 \text{ skippers}$$

Value of one skedallion | Value of one phantom | 27.___

28. $x > 1$

$\dfrac{x + x + x}{x \cdot x}$ | $\dfrac{3}{x^2}$ | 28.___

29. $x \neq \pm 2$

$\dfrac{x^2 + 4x + 4}{x + 2}$ | $\dfrac{x^2 - 4}{x - 2}$ | 29.___

30. $x^2 + 8x + 15 = 0$

$x^2 + 8x$ | 15 | 30.___

31.
$$x + 2y = 10$$
$$2x - 2y = 5$$

x | y | 31.___

32. $2x + 2 < 1$

x | 0 | 32.___

33.
$$xy = 6$$
$$x^2 + y^2 = 13$$

$(x+y)^2$ | 18 | 33.___

34. $(45)^2 + 2(45)(55) + (55)^2 =$ 34.___
   A. 5,050   B. 9,100   C. 9,900   D. 10,000 E. 14,950

35. From which of the following statements must it follow   35.___
that $x > y$?
   A. $x = 2y$ B. $2x = y$ C. $x + 2 = y$
   D. $x - 2 = y$ E. None of the above

36. Ms. Smith is S years old and is 3 years older than Ms.   36.___
Lopez.
In terms of S, how many years old was Ms. Lopez 2 years
ago?
   A. $S - 5$ B. $S - 3$ C. $S - 2$ D. $S - 1$ E. $S + 1$

37. If k is a positive integer such that $\frac{k}{3}$ is an even integer   37.___

    and $\frac{k}{2}$ is an odd integer, which of the following statements

    must be TRUE?

    I. k is even   II. $(\frac{k}{2})^2$ is even   III. $\frac{k}{2} - \frac{k}{3}$ is odd

    The CORRECT answer is:
    A. I *only*   B. II *only*   C. III *only*
    D. I, II   E. I, III

38. If a car travels x kilometers in t hours and 20 minutes,   38.___
    what is its average speed in kilometers per hour?

    A. $\frac{x}{t + 20}$ B. $\frac{t + 20}{x}$ C. x(t + 1/3)

    D. $\frac{t + 1/3}{x}$ E. $\frac{x}{t + 1/3}$

39. A 20-centimeter wire is cut into exactly three pieces.   39.___
    If the first piece is 3 centimeters shorter than the
    second piece and the third piece is 4 centimeters
    shorter than the second piece, what is the length, in
    centimeters, of the SHORTEST piece?
    A. 1   B. 3   C. 4   D. 5

40. Carol has twice as many books as Beverly has. After   40.___
    Carol gives Beverly 5 books, she still has 10 more books
    than Beverly has.
    How many books did Carol have originally?
    A. 15   B. 20   C. 30   D. 40

KEY (CORRECT ANSWERS)

1. D	11. B	21. C	31. A
2. C	12. A	22. E	32. B
3. D	13. C	23. E	33. A
4. D	14. B	24. A	34. D
5. E	15. A	25. E	35. D
6. D	16. C	26. B	36. A
7. C	17. E	27. B	37. E
8. C	18. C	28. A	38. E
9. B	19. C	29. C	39. D
10. B	20. E	30. B	40. D

ANSWERS GRIDDED

	A	B	C	D	E
1.				●	
2.			●		
3.				●	
4.				●	
5.					●
6.				●	
7.			●		
8.			●		
9.		●			
10.		●			
11.		●			
12.	●				
13.			●		
14.		●			
15.		●			
16.			●		
17.					●
18.			●		
19.			●		
20.					●
21.			●		
22.					●
23.					●
24.	●				
25.					●
26.		●			
27.		●			
28.	●				
29.			●		
30.		●			
31.	●				
32.		●			
33.	●				
34.				●	
35.					●
36.	●				
37.				●	
38.					●
39.				●	
40.				●	

TEST 2

DIRECTIONS: Each question or incomplete statement is followed by
several suggested answers or completions. Select the
one that BEST answers the question or completes the
statement. *PRINT THE LETTER OF THE CORRECT ANSWER IN
THE SPACE AT THE RIGHT.*

1. In the figure shown
    at the right, if AB
    is parallel to DE,
    then x =
    A. 105
    B. 90
    C. 80
    D. 75
    E. 65

1.___

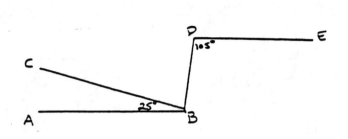

2. In the figure shown at the right,
    $\ell \parallel m$.
    Which of the following pairs of
    angles must be equal?
    A. 1 and 3
    B. 2 and 3
    C. 3 and 5
    D. 4 and 6
    E. 5 and 7

2.___

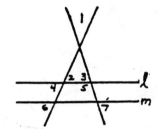

3. In the figure shown at
    the right, ACD is a line
    segment.
    What is the value of x?
    A. 30
    B. 33
    C. 36
    D. 40
    E. 45

3.___

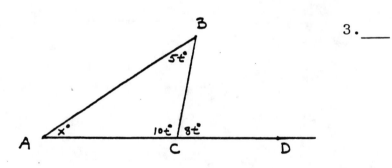

4. If ℓ_1, ℓ_2, and ℓ_3 inter-
    sect as shown at the
    right, then x =
    A. 30
    B. 50
    C. 60
    D. 90
    E. 100

4.___

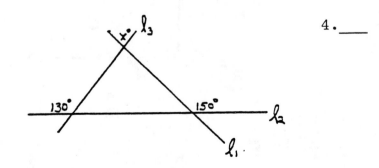

Questions 5-8.

DIRECTIONS: Questions 5 through 8 each consist of two quantities,
              one in Column A and one in Column B. You are to
              compare the two quantities and mark your answer:
              A if the quantity in Column A is greater;
              B if the quantity in Column B is greater;
              C if the two quantities are equal;
              D if the relationship cannot be determined from
                the information given
              AN E RESPONSE WILL NOT BE SCORED

<u>Column A</u>   <u>Column B</u>

5.   5.___

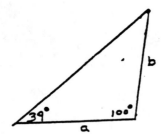

      a   b

6.   6.___

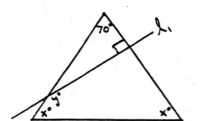

     2x   y

7.   7.___

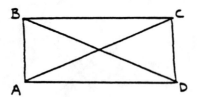

             Note: Figure not drawn to scale.
             In parallelogram ABCD, ∠ABC ≠ ∠BAD.

      Length of AC   Length of BD

Column A   Column B

8.   8.___

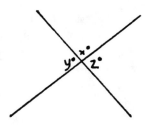

$$x + y + z = 4x$$

$\frac{3}{2}x$ y

9. In the figure shown at the   9.___
    right, line r intersects line s
    at p.
    If another line m is drawn through
    p with angles formed as indicated
    in the figure, then what is the
    value of y in terms of x?
        A. 60
        B. x
        C. 2x
        D. 180 - x
        E. 180 - 2x

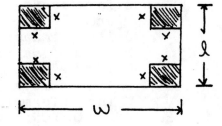

10. In the figure shown at the   10.___
    right, the 4 shaded areas are
    squares.
    The area of the unshaded region
    of the rectangle is
        A. $lw - 4x^2$
        B. $(l-2x)(w-2x)$
        C. $(l-x)(w-x)$
        D. $lx + wx$
        E. $(l-4x)(w-4x)$

11. In the figure shown at the right, if one   11.___
    circle has radius r and the other has
    diameter r, what is the area of the
    shaded region?

        A. $\frac{\pi}{2}$

        B. $\frac{3\pi r}{4}$

        C. $\frac{\pi r}{2}$

        D. $\frac{\pi r^2}{2}$

        E. $\frac{3\pi r^2}{4}$

12. The figure shown at the right is a
    square.
    What is its area?
    A. 9
    B. 4
    C. 1
    D. 1/4
    E. It cannot be determined from
       the information given

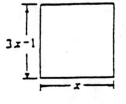

12.___

13. In the figure shown at the right,
    the two axes divide the enclosed
    region into four regions that
    have the same size and shape.
    Of the following, which is CLOSEST
    to the area of the entire enclosed
    region?
    A. 7
    B. 10
    C. 19
    D. 22
    E. 29

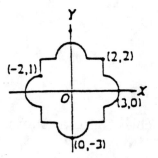

13.___

14. If the perimeter of square A is double that of square B,
    then the area of A is how many times the area of B?
    A. 1/2   B. 1   C. 2   D. 3   E. 4

14.___

Questions 15-16.

DIRECTIONS: Questions 15 through 16 each consist of two quantities,
             one in Column A and one in Column B. You are to
             compare the two quantities and mark your answer:
                 A if the quantity in Column A is greater;
                 B if the quantity in Column B is greater;
                 C if the two quantities are equal;
                 D if the relationship cannot be determined from
                   the information given
             AN E RESPONSE WILL NOT BE SCORED

       Column A   Column B

15.   15.___

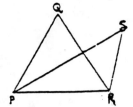

        Perimeter of $\triangle$PQR = Perimeter of $\triangle$PSR

      PQ + QR   PS + SR

COLUMN A   COLUMN B

16.

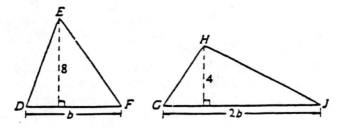

16.___

Note: Figures not drawn to scale.

Area of ΔDEF   Area of ΔGHJ

17. What is the circumference of the circle shown at the right?
    A. 5Π
    B. 10Π

    C. $\frac{25}{2}$ Π

    D. 20Π
    E. 25Π

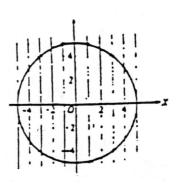

17.___

18. What is the diameter of a circle with circumference 1?
    A. Π   B. 1   C. 1/2   D. 1/Π   E. −Π + 1

18.___

19. A circular track 400 meters in diameter is shown in the figure at the right. A runner starts at P, directly south of the center of the track, and runs counter-clockwise. At the end of exactly how many meters of travel will the runner be at the point where he is traveling directly north?
    A. 25Π   B. 100Π   C. 400Π   D. 800Π   E. 1,000Π

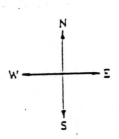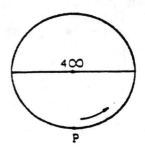

19.___

20. In the figure shown at the right, inscribed ABC is equilateral. If the radius of the circle is r, then the length of arc AXB is

    A. $\frac{2\Pi r}{3}$

    B. $\frac{4\Pi r}{3}$

    C. $\frac{3\Pi r}{2}$

    D. $\frac{\Pi r^2}{3}$

    E. $\frac{2\Pi r^2}{3}$

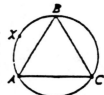

20.___

Questions 21-24.

DIRECTIONS: Questions 21 through 24 each consist of two quantities,
one in Column A and one in Column B. You are to
compare the two quantities and mark your answer:
   A if the quantity in Column A is greater;
   B if the quantity in Column B is greater;
   C if the two quantities are equal;
   D if the relationship cannot be determined from
      the information given
AN E RESPONSE WILL NOT BE SCORED

    Column A   Column B

21.

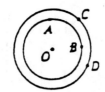

21.___

    Note: Figure not drawn to scale.
Minor arcs AB and CD have equal length and each lies on
a different circle with center O.

Degree measure of   Degree measure of
minor arc AB   minor arc CD

22. The length of the   The length of the   22.___
hypotenuse of a right   hypotenuse of a right
triangle with legs of   triangle with legs of
lengths 8 and 6   lengths of 12 and 5

23.   23.___

    Note: Figure not drawn to scale.
      180 > x > y + z

c^2 $a^2 + b^2$

24.   24.___

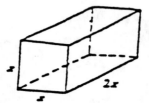

Total surface area of $10x^2$
the rectangle solid shown

25. A 25-foot ladder is placed against a vertical wall of a
    building, with the bottom of the ladder standing on
    concrete 7 feet from the base of the building.
    If the top of the ladder slips down 4 feet, then the
    bottom of the ladder will slide out ____ feet.
    A. 4   B. 5   C. 6   D. 7   E. 8

25.___

26. In the figure shown at the right, if an
    edge of each small cube has length 2,
    what is the volume of the entire
    rectangle solid?
    A. 192
    B. 144
    C. 72
    D. 52
    E. 48

26.___

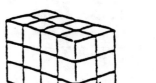

27. What is the volume of a cube with surface area $54x^2$?
    A. $9x^2$ B. $27x^3$ C. $81x^2$ D. $81x^3$ E. $729x^3$

27.___

28.

28.___

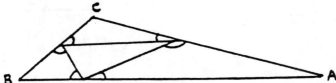

    In the figure above, if ABC is a triangle, what is the
    sum of the degree measures of the marked angles?
    A. 90   B. 180   C. 270   D. 360

29. What is the sum of the degree
    measures of all the exterior
    angles indicated by arrows
    in the figure shown at the
    right?
    A. 360
    B. 920
    C. 1440
    D. 2880

29.___

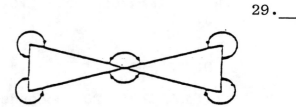

30. In the figure shown at the right,
    what is the average (arithmetic
    mean) degree measure of the 8
    marked angles?
    A. 75
    B. 90
    C. 135
    D. 240

30.___

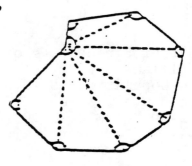

31. If $\frac{x+y}{x} = \frac{3}{2}$, then $\frac{y}{x} =$ 31.___

    A. $\frac{1}{5}$ B. $\frac{1}{4}$ C. $\frac{1}{3}$ D. $\frac{1}{2}$

32. Last year, Sue attended half the number of movies that Jim did and Pam attended 1/3 the number of movies that Jim did. 32.___
If Pam attended 6 movies, how many movies did Sue attend?
    A. 3   B. 9   C. 13   D. 15

33. $1 - \frac{1}{2} - \frac{1}{4} - \frac{1}{8} - \frac{1}{16} =$ 33.___

    A. $\frac{1}{16}$ B. $\frac{1}{13}$ C. $\frac{1}{10}$ D. $\frac{1}{8}$

34. In the figure shown at the right, what is the value of x? 34.___
    A. 22.5
    B. 23.5
    C. 30.5
    D. 32.5

35. If $42(66+x) = 4200$, then $x =$ 35.___
    A. 25   B. 30   C. 34   D. 45

36. In the figure shown at the right, if points P and Q have coordinates as shown, what is the combined area of the two shaded rectangles? 36.___
    A. 28
    B. 36
    C. 54
    D. 75

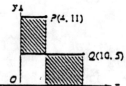

37. It took Chris 200 seconds to solve a puzzle. 37.___
If it took Kim 160 seconds to solve the same puzzle, by what fraction of a <u>minute</u> was Chris' time longer than Kim's?

    A. $\frac{2}{3}$ B. $\frac{3}{4}$ C. $\frac{5}{6}$ D. $\frac{11}{12}$

38. One out of 5 residents of Central Village was born in that village. 38.___
If its population is 12,000, what is the TOTAL number of residents who were NOT born in Central Village?
    A. 2400   B. 3800   C. 5400   D. 9600

39. In the figure shown at the right, what is the value of x + y + z?
     A. 1200
     B. 3600
     C. 4800
     D. 5400

39.____

40.

     PP
    +QQ
    ‾‾‾‾
     RR

40.____

If P, Q, and R are digits in the correctly worked addition problem above and P = 2Q, what is one possible value of R?
     A. 2   B. 4   C. 6   D. 8

———

KEY (CORRECT ANSWERS)

1. C	11. E	21. A	31. D
2. D	12. D	22. B	32. B
3. A	13. D	23. A	33. A
4. E	14. E	24. C	34. A
5. A	15. C	25. E	35. C
6. B	16. C	26. A	36. C
7. D	17. B	27. B	37. A
8. C	18. D	28. D	38. D
9. E	19. B	29. C	39. B
10. A	20. A	30. C	40. C

———

ANSWERS GRIDDED

MATHEMATICS
EXAMINATION SECTION
TEST 1

DIRECTIONS:
Each question or incomplete statement is followed by several suggested answers or completions. Select the one that *BEST* answers the question or completes the statement. *PRINT THE LETTER OF THE CORRECT ANSWER IN THE SPACE AT THE RIGHT.*

1. x is what percent of 10?   1. ...
   A. 10x   B. $\frac{x}{10}$ C. 100x   D. 50x
   E. $\frac{10}{x}$

2. Write $\frac{1}{4}$ percent as a fraction.   2. ...
   A. 25/100   B. 1/400   C. 25/1000   D. 1/4
   E. 1/40

3. The number of students in a school increased from 100 to   3. ...
   300. What is the percent increase?
   A. 150   B. 200   C. 250   D. 300
   E. 450

4. $\sqrt{.005}$ is what percent of $\sqrt{2}$?   4. ...
   A. 5   B. 10   C. 15   D. 20
   E. 25

5. What is 2/5 percent as a decimal?   5. ...
   A. .4   B. .04   C. .004   D. .0004
   E. .00004

6. One worker picks 25 percent as many bushels as all the   6. ...
   other workers combined. This worker picks 20 bushels.
   How many bushels were picked by all the workers?
   A. 100   B. 90   C. 80   D. 75   E. 70

7. A man bought a suit for $45 during a 10-percent-discount   7. ...
   sale. How much money did he save?
   A. $14   B. $3.50   C. $5   D. $4.50   E. $7

8. A factory turns out 400 cars each month. This is an   8. ...
   increase of 25 percent over the previous months. How
   many cars were turned out the previous months?
   A. 300   B. 320   C. 330   D. 350
   E. 400

9. 2/5 of 14 is what percent of 7?   9. ...
   A. 5 3/5   B. 125   C. 80   D. $87\frac{1}{2}$
   E. 90

10. What is $\frac{1}{2}$ percent written as a decimal?   10. ...
   A. .5   B. .05   C. .005   D. .0005   E. .50

11. In triangle ABC, angle A is 150 percent as large as   11. ...
   angle B, and angle B is 50 percent of angle C. How
   many degrees are there in angle C?
   A. 30   B. 40   C. 60   D. 80   E. 160

12. If each side of a square is increased by 50 percent,   12. ...
   by what percent is the area increased?
   A. 50   B. 100   C. 125   D. 150   E. 200

13. 1/3 is what percent of 3?   13. ...
   A. 33 1/3   B. 66 2/3   C. 11 1/9   D. 12 1/2
   E. 16 2/3

14. In one class 30 percent are boys and in another class,   14. ...
    $\frac{1}{2}$ as large, 40 percent are boys. Find the percentage
    of boys in both classes combined.
        A. $12\frac{1}{2}$ B. 15   C. 25   D. 33 1/3   E. 50

15. $\frac{x}{250}$ = 2.4 percent. Find x.   15. ...
        A. 3   B. 5   C. 6   D. 104 1/6   E. 600

___

KEY (CORRECT ANSWERS)

1. A
2. B
3. B
4. A
5. C

6. A
7. C
8. B
9. C
10. C

11. D
12. C
13. C
14. D
15. C

___

SOLUTIONS TO PROBLEMS

1. Let P = required percent. Then, $\frac{x}{10} = \frac{P}{100}$. Solving, P = 10x.

2. $\frac{1}{4}\% = \frac{1}{4} \div 100 = \frac{1}{400}$

3. Actual increase is 200. The percent increase = $(\frac{200}{100})(100) = 200$

4. Let x = required percent. $\sqrt{.005}/\sqrt{2} = x/100$. Then,
   $x = 100\sqrt{.0025} = 5$

5. $\frac{2}{5}\% = \frac{2}{5} \div 100 = .004$

6. Let x = number of bushels picked by all the other workers.
   Then, 20 = .25x, so x = 80. Now the number of bushels picked
   by all workers is 80 + 20 = 100.

7. Let x = original price. Then, $45 = .90x, so x = $50.
   The amount saved is $50 - $45 = $5.

8. Let x = number of cars produced in previous months.
   Then, 400 = 1.25x, so x = 320.

9. $(\frac{2}{5})(14) = 5.6$. Let x = required percent. Then, 5.6/7 = x/100.
   Solving, x = 80.

10. $\frac{1}{2}\% = \frac{1}{2} \div 100 = \frac{1}{200} = .005$

11. Let x = $\angle$B, 2x = $\angle$C, 1.5x = $\angle$A. Then, x + 2x + 1.5x = 180°.
    Solving, x = 40°. So, $\angle$C = 2x = 80°.

12. Let x = original side of the square, so that 1.5x = enlarged
    side of the square. Then, x^2 = original area and $2.25x^2$ =
    enlarged area. The increase is $1.25x^2$, which is 125%.

13. Let x = required percent. $\frac{1}{3}/3 = x/100$, so $x = \frac{100}{9} = 11\frac{1}{9}$

14. Let 2x = size of 1st class, x = size of 2nd class. The number
     of boys in the 1st class is (.30)(2x) = .60x, whereas the
     number of boys in the 2nd class is .40x. The ratio of boys to
     the total enrollment in both classes combined is x/3x, which
     is $33\frac{1}{3}\%$.

15. x/250 = 2.4% = .024. Then, x = (250)(.024) = 6

TEST 2

DIRECTIONS:
Each question or incomplete statement is followed by several suggested answers or completions. Select the one that *BEST* answers the question or completes the statement. *PRINT THE LETTER OF THE CORRECT ANSWER IN THE SPACE AT THE RIGHT.*

1. If 3 men can do a job in 6 days, how long will it take   1. ...
   9 men to do the same job?
      A. 2 days   B. 54 days   C. 8 days   D. 27 days   E. 6 days

2. It takes one minute to fill a tank 3/5 full. How much   2. ...
   longer will it take to fill up the tank?
      A. 5 seconds   B. 10 seconds   C. 20 seconds
      D. 30 seconds   E. 40 seconds

3. The ratio of the legs of a right triangle is 1 : 3. If   3. ...
   the area is 6, what is the length of the hypotenuse?
      A. 8   B. $\sqrt{40}$ C. $\sqrt{12}$ D. 30
      E. None of these

4. If 3 pencils cost x cents, how many pencils can be bought   4. ...
   for 30 cents
      A. $\dfrac{90}{x}$ B. $\dfrac{x}{90}$ C. $\dfrac{30}{x}$ D. $\dfrac{x}{30}$ E. 90x

5. If one kilometer equals 5/8 of a mile, how many kilometers   5. ...
   are there in 40 miles?
      A. 25   B. 30   C. 35   D. 40   E. 64

6. If it takes 3 minutes to fill a pool 4/5 full, how much   6. ...
   longer (in seconds) will it take to fill up the tank?
      A. 12   B. 15   C. 30   D. 45   E. 50

7. If one inch equals 2.54 centimeters, then 8 centimeters   7. ...
   equals approximately how many inches?
      A. 2.7   B. 2.9   C. 3.1   D. 3.3   E. 3.5

8. A 100-yard dash is run in 10 seconds. What is the ap-   8. ...
   proximate speed in miles per hour?
      A. 7   B. 9   C. 20   D. 25   E. 30

9. 8 men can complete a job in 24 days. How long will it   9. ...
   take 12 men working at the same rate to do the job?
      A. 10 days   B. 12 days   C. 14 days
      D. 16 days   **E. 20 days**

10. If a map is drawn to the scale of 1 inch to 75 miles,   10. ...
    what is the distance between 2 cities that are 4 3/4
    inches apart on the map?
       A. 340 1/3   B. 357 2/3   C. 370
       D. 344   E. 356 1/4

11. If *a* apples cost *b* cents, find the cost of *c* apples.   11. ...
       A. $\dfrac{bc}{a}$ B. $\dfrac{ac}{b}$ C. $\dfrac{ab}{c}$ D. $\dfrac{b}{ac}$ E. $\dfrac{c}{ab}$

12. Find the ratio of a yard to a foot.   12. ...
       A. 1:3   B. 3:1   C. 1:1   D. 12:1
       E. 2:1

13. Two girls buy a radio for $15, contributing amounts in   13. ...
    the ratio of 5:4. How much was the smaller amount?
       A. 1 2/3   B. 4   C. 5   D. 6 2/3   E 12

14. A gear with 48 teeth, rotating at 360 revolutions per   14. ...
    minute, meshes with a gear of 72 teeth. How many re-
    volutions per minute does the second gear make?
       A. 180   B. 240   C. 277   D. 530   E. 432
15. A troop of 75 men have enough rations to last 4 days.   15. ...
    if the troop is increased by 25 men, then how long
    will the same rations last?
       A. $\frac{4}{3}$ days   B. $\frac{3}{4}$ days   C. 12 days
       D. 3 days   E. 2 days

KEY (CORRECT ANSWERS)

1. A
2. E
3. B
4. A
5. E

6. D
7. C
8. C
9. D
10. E

11. A
12. B
13. D
14. B
15. D

SOLUTIONS TO PROBLEMS

1. The number of men is inversely proportional to the number of days. Let x = required number of days. Then, $3/9 = x/6$. Solving, x = 2

2. 1 min./$\frac{3}{5}$ = x min./$\frac{2}{5}$. Solving, x = $\frac{2}{3}$ min. = 40 seconds.

3. Let x, 3x = lengths of the two. $(\frac{1}{2})(x)(3x) = 6$, so $3x^2 = 12$ and x = 2. The two legs are 2 and 6. Thus, the hypotenuse = $\sqrt{2^2 + 6^2} = \sqrt{40}$

4. Let p = number of pencils. $3/x = p/30$, px = 90, so p = $\frac{90}{x}$

5. 40 miles = 40 ÷ $\frac{5}{8}$ = 64 kilometers

6. 3 min./$\frac{4}{5}$ = x min./$\frac{1}{5}$. Solving, x = $\frac{3}{4}$ min. = 45 seconds

7. 8 centimeters = 8 ÷ 2.54 ≈ 3.1 inches

8. 100 yards in 10 seconds means 36,000 yards per hour. Then, 36,000 yards = 36,000/1760 ≈ 20 miles. Thus, the speed is 20 mi/hr.

9. The number of men is inversely proportional to the number of days. Let x = required number of days. Then, $8/12 = x/24$. Solving, x = 16.

10. $4\frac{3}{4}$ inches corresponds to $(75)(4\frac{3}{4})$ = $356\frac{1}{4}$ miles

11. Let p = cost of c apples. $a/b = c/p$. Solving, p = $\frac{bc}{a}$

12. 1 yard : 1 foot = 3 feet : 1 foot = 3:1

13. Let 5x, 4x represent their respective contributions. Then, 5x + 4x = $15. Solving, x = $$1\frac{2}{3}$. The smaller amount is $(\$1\frac{2}{3})(4)$ = $$6\frac{2}{3}$

14. The number of teeth is inversely proportional to the number of revolutions per minute. Let x = required revolutions per minute. 48/72 = x/360. Solving, x = 240

15. The number of men is inversely proportional to the number of days. Let x = required number of days. 75/100 = x/4, so x = 3

———

TEST 3

DIRECTIONS:
Each question or incomplete statement is followed by several suggested answers or completions. Select the one that *BEST* answers the question or completes the statement. *PRINT THE LETTER OF THE CORRECT ANSWER IN THE SPACE AT THE RIGHT.*

1. A club goes on a boat ride for which the fare is 80 cents per adult and 60 cents per child. If there are 70 people on the ride, and the total cost is $47, *what* fractional part of the group is adults?
   A. 2/35   B. 5/14   E. 4/7   D. 9/14   E. 3/4   1. ...

2. A camping tent can be put up by 3 scout masters in 2 hours or by 5 boy scouts in 4 hours.
   How many hours will it take them to put up the tent if they all work together?
   A. 1   B. 1 1/3   C. 2 1/3   D. 3   E. 3½   2. ...

3. A grocer has 60 baskets of peaches of which y baskets are spoiled. If he sells 3/4 of the remainder, *how many* baskets does he have left of the good peaches?
   A. $\frac{15-y}{4}$ B. $15-y$ C. $15-\frac{y}{4}$ D. $\frac{y-15}{4}$ E. $\frac{y}{4} - 15$ 3. ...

4. A motorist drives 60 miles to his destination at 40 m.p.h. and returns at 30 m.p.h. Find his average speed in m.p.h. for the entire trip.
   A. 28   B. 32   C. 34 2/7   D. 36½   E. 43¼   4. ...

5. The afternoon classes in a school begin at 1 p.m. and end at 3:52 p.m. There are 4 class-periods with 4 minutes between classes.
   How many minutes are there in each period?
   A. 39   B. 40   C. 49   D. 59   E. 60   5. ...

6. If a man paid $60 for a suit after receiving a discount of 10%, *how much* did he save?
   A. $6   B. $6.50   C. $6.67   D. $6.75   E. $10   6. ...

7. A high school football squad consists of 40 players. They arrange to play a 60-minute practice game with another team.
   If only 11 out of the 40 players participate at one time, and each is to play the same length of time, *how many* minutes would each play?
   A. 12   B. 16½   C. 18   D. 20 3/4   E. 22   7. ...

8. If the base of a rectangle is increased by 30%, and the altitude decreased by 20%, by *what* percent is the area increased?
   A. 4   B. 5   C. 10   D. 25   E. 50   8. ...

9. If a flexible wire 220-feet long goes around a circle 5 times, approximately how many times will the same wire go around the square in which the circle is inscribed? (Use π = 22/7)
   A. 2 3/4   B. 3½   C. 4   D. 5½   E. 6¼   9. ...

10. A passenger ship traveling b miles an hour passes a
    freighter traveling c miles per hour. Fifteen minutes
    later the passenger ship reaches port.
    How many hours after this will the freighter reach port?

    A. $\dfrac{4(b-c)}{c}$ B. $\dfrac{4(b-c)}{b}$ C. $\dfrac{b-c}{4c}$ D. $\dfrac{b-c}{4b}$ E. $\dfrac{c}{4(b-c)}$

11. If a-b = 5 and a+c = 6, *what* is the value of b in terms
    of c?

    A. c-1   B. c+1   C. 1-c   D. c-11   E. 11 c

12. Twenty-five boys in a class have an average grade of 80.
    Fifteen girls in the same class have an average grade of
    72.
    What is the average grade for the entire class?

    A. 75   B. 76   C. 76.5   D. 77   E. 77.5

13. A line divides a square board into 2 equal triangles,
    each 200 square feet in area.
    How many feet are there in the length of the line?

    A. $10\sqrt{2}$ B. $10\sqrt{3}$ C. $20\sqrt{2}$ D. $20\sqrt{3}$ E. 100

14. A 20-ounce solution of salt and water contains 3 ounces
    of salt.
    If 5 ounces of water are evaporated, *what* is the percent
    of salt in the new solution?

    A. 12   B. 15   C. 20   D. 25   E. 33 1/3

15. If meat loses 20% of its weight when cooked, *how many*
    pounds of raw meat should be cooked to produce 2 lbs. of
    cooked meat?

    A. 2.25   B. 2.3   C. 2.5   D. 2.75   E. 3

16. *What* percent of 2 gallons is 6 pints?

    A. 30   B. 33 1/3   C. $37\frac{1}{2}$ D. $137\frac{1}{2}$ E. 300

17. *How many* inches are there in y yards?

    A. $\dfrac{y}{36}$ B. $\dfrac{y}{12}$ C. 3y   D. 12y   E. 36y

18. The missing number in the series: 2, 6, 12, 20, ?, 42,
    56, 72, is:

    A. 30   B. 32   C. 36   D. 38   E. 40

19. If a car travels at 50 miles per hour, *how long* does it
    take at this rate to travel 1 mile?

    A. 50 seconds   B. 70 seconds   C. 72 seconds
    D. 1 min. 15 sec.   E. 1 min. 20 sec.

20. If m-x = m, *what* does x equal?

    A. o   B. m   C. $\dfrac{m}{2}$ D. 2m   E. $\dfrac{2}{o}$

KEY (CORRECT ANSWERS)

1. B	6. C	11. C	16. C
2. B	7. B	12. D	17. E
3. C	8. A	13. C	18. A
4. C	9. C	14. C	19. C
5. B	10. C	15. C	20. A

SOLUTIONS TO PROBLEMS

1. Let x = number of adults, 30 - x = number of children.
    .80x = .60(30 - x) = $47. Solving, x = 25 adults, so there
    are 45 children. Now, 25/70 = $\frac{5}{14}$.

2. The rate for the scout masters is ½ of the work in 1 hour.
    For the scouts, their rate is ¼ of the work in 1 hour.
    Let x = number of hours required working together.
    ½x + ¼x = 1. Solving, x = 1 1/3

3. The grocer will sell $(\frac{3}{4})$(60 - y) = 45 - $\frac{3}{4}$y, where y = number
    of baskets with spoiled peaches. The number of baskets of
    good peaches left is 60 - y - (45 - $\frac{3}{4}$y) = 15 - $\frac{y}{4}$.

4. Average speed = total distance ÷ total time =
    (60 + 60)/($\frac{60}{40}$ + $\frac{60}{30}$) = 120/3½ = $34\frac{2}{7}$

5. With 4 class-periods, there are three 4-minute breaks between
    classes, which is 12 minutes. From 1 PM to 3:52 PM represents
    172 minutes. The actual number of minutes for each class
    period is (172 - 12)/4 = 40.

6. Let x = original price. Then, x - .10x = $60, so x = $66.67.
    The savings is $66.67 - $60 = $6.67.

7. Total player-minutes = (11)(60) = 660. Then, the number of
    minutes per player = 660 ÷ 40 = 16½.

8. Let x, y represent the original base and height, so that
    1.30x and .80y represent the new base and height. The
    original area = xy and the new area = (1.30)(.80)xy = 1.04xy.
    This is a 4% increase.

9. 220 ÷ 5 = 44 feet = circumference of circle. Then, the radius
    = 44 ÷ 2π = 7 feet. This implies that the side of the
    circumscribed square is 14 feet and its perimeter is 56 feet.
    Finally, 220 ÷ 56 ≈ 4.

10. In 15 minutes (= $\frac{1}{4}$ hour), the passenger ship travels $\frac{b}{4}$ miles to reach port. The freighter would need $\frac{b}{4} \div c = \frac{b}{4c}$ hours to travel $\frac{6}{4}$ miles. Thus, the extra time the freighter needs to reach port is $\frac{b}{4c} - \frac{1}{4} = \frac{b-c}{4c}$.

11. Subtracting a – b = 5 from a + c = 6 yields c + b = 1.
    Thus, b = 1 – c.

12. Average grade of entire class = [(25)(80) + (15)(72)]/(25 + 15)
    = 3080/40 = 77.

13. The area of the entire square is 400, and the line in question is a diagonal. Let x = length of this diagonal. Then, $\frac{1}{2}x^2$ = 400, so x = $\sqrt{800}$ = 20$\sqrt{2}$.

14. The original solution had 17 ounces of water. The new solution will have 12 ounces of water and (still) 3 ounces of salt. The percent of salt is (3/(3+12)(100) = 20.

15. Let x = number of pounds of raw meat.
    Then, x – .20x = 2. Solving, x = 2.5.

16. 2 gallons = (2)(8) = 16 pints. Then, $\frac{6}{16}$ = 37$\frac{1}{2}$%.

17. Since 1 yard = 36 inches, y yards = 36y inches.

18. The differences between consecutive terms are 4, 6, 8, –, –, 14, 16
    Then the difference between the 4th and 5th terms must be 10.
    Since the 4th term is 20, the 5th term must be 30. (Note: As
    a check, the difference between 30 and the 6th term should be
    12. The 6th term is 42.)

19. At 50 mi/hour, the car requires $\frac{1}{50}$ hour to travel 1 mile.
    Now, $\frac{1}{50}$ hour = 1$\frac{1}{5}$ minute = 72 seconds.

20. m – x = m. Then, x = m – m = 0

TEST 4

DIRECTIONS:

Each question or incomplete statement is followed by several suggested answers or completions. Select the one that *BEST* answers the question or completes the statement. *PRINT THE LETTER OF THE CORRECT ANSWER IN THE SPACE AT THE RIGHT.*

1. A part-time worker earns 3 times as much in September   1. ...
   as in each of the other months. *What* part of his entire
   year's earnings does he earn in September?
      A. 1/5   B. 3/14   C. 1/4   D. 3/11   E. 1/3

2. All the faces of a 4-inch cube have been painted. This   2. ...
   is now cut into 1-inch cubes. The *number* of cubes that
   will show *no* paint at all is
      A. 20   B. 8   C. 1   D. 4   E. 12

3. A 12-quart solution of alcohol and water is 10% alcohol.   3. ...
   If 4 quarts of water are added, the solution becomes
      A. 50%   B. 40%   C. 33-1/3%   D. 7.5%   E. 75%

4. It cost $3.60 for 2 adults and their child to attend the   4. ...
   circus. If a child's ticket is half the price of an
   adult's ticket, *what* is the price of an adult's ticket?
      A. $0.72   B. $0.90   C. $1.20   D. $1.44   E. $1.80

5. If the sides of a square are increased 100%, the increase 5. ...
   in area is
      A. 400%   B. 200%   C. 300%   D. 100%   E. 500%

6. A 100-yard dash run in 10 seconds is the *same* average   6. ...
   speed in miles per hour approximately as
      A. 5   B. 10   C. 20   D. 30   E. 40

7. A man bought 3 books for $1.50 and 2 books for $1.00   7. ...
   each. *What* was the average price per book?
      A. $1.00   B. $1.10   C. $1.20   D. $1.25   E. $1.30

8. The missing number in the series: 2, 5, 10,17, ?, 37, 50, 8. ...
   65 is:
      A. 22   B. 24   C. 26   D. 27   E. 29

9. If $y \sqrt{.04} = 1$, what is the value of y?   9. ...
      A. .05   B. .5   C. 5   D. 6.25   E. 50

10. The minimum temperatures for each day of one week were   10. ...
    as follows: 7, 13, 5, -4, -8, 0, 3.
    What was the *average minimum* temperature for the week?
       A. -2 2/3   B. -2 2/7   C. -2   D. 2 2/7   E. 2 2/3

11. A man sold a piece of land for $1500. If his profit was   11. ...
    200% of his cost, *how much* had the land cost him?
       A. $500   B. $750   C. $1000   D. $1200   E. $1250

12. *What* is the area in square feet of a rectangular garden 12. ...
    which is twice as long as it is wide if the fence around
    it is 240 feet long?
       A. 2400   B. 3200   C. 4800   D. 7200   E. 12,800

13. *Which* of these quantities is the smallest?   13. ...
       A. 7/9   B. 9/11   C. 4/5   D. 5/7   E. .74

14. A baseball team has won 50 games out of 75 played.   14. ...
    How many more games must the team win in succession to
    raise its record to 80%?
       A. 10   B. 20   C. 22   D. 25   E. 50

15. A tank contains 500 gallons of gasoline. If the gasoline 15. ...
    is withdrawn at the rate of x quarts a minute for 12 min-
    utes, *how many* gallons of gasoline will remain?
    A. 500-12x   B. 500-6x   C. 500-3x
    D. 12x   E. 125x

—

KEY (CORRECT ANSWERS)

1. B
2. B
3. D
4. D
5. C

6. C
7. E
8. C
9. C
10. D

11. A
12. B
13. D
14. E
15. C

—

SOLUTIONS TO PROBLEMS

1. Let 3x = earnings in September, x = earnings in each of the other 11 months. Then, 11x + 3x = 14x = earnings for 1 year. Ratio of September's earnings to entire year's earnings = 3x/14x = $\frac{3}{14}$.

2. There will be a total of 64 1-inch cubes of which the innermost 8 cubes will have no paint.

3. The amount of alcohol is still (.10)(12) = 1.2 quarts. Then, 1.2/16 = 7.5%.

4. Let x = price for each adult ticket, $\frac{1}{2}$x = price for each child's ticket. x + x + $\frac{1}{2}$x = $3.60. 2.5x = $3.60. Solving, x = $1.44.

5. Let x = original side and 2x = new side. Original area = x^2 and new area = $4x^2$. The increase is $3x^2$, which means 300%.

6. 100 yards in 10 seconds means 36,000 yards per hour. Then, 36,000 yards = 36,000/1760 ≈ 20 miles. Thus, the speed is 20 mi/hour.

7. The average price per book = [(3)($1.50) + (2)($1.00)]/(3 + 2) = $1.30.

8. The differences between consecutive terms are 3, 5, 7, _, _, 13, 15. The two blanks must be 9 and 11. Since the difference between the 4th and 5th terms is 9 and the 4th term is 17, the 5th term is 17 + 9 = 26.

9. y$\sqrt{.04}$ = 1. Then, .2y = 1, so y = 5.

10. (7 + 13 + 5 - 4 - 8 + 0 + 3)/7 = 16/7 = $2\frac{2}{7}$

11. Let x = cost. Profit = $1500 - x = 2x. Solving, x = $500

12. Let x = width, 2x = length. x + x + 2x + 2x = 240. Solving, x = 40 and 2x = 80. Area = (40)(80) = 3200 square feet.

13. Converting to decimals, answers A thru E appear as .$\overline{7}$, .$\overline{81}$, .8, .714, .74. Since .714 is the smallest, this corresponds to 5/7.

14. Let x = required number of wins. Then, (50 + x)/(75 + x) = .80. This leads to 50 + x = 60 + .80x. Solving, x = 50.

15. x quarts per minute means x gallons in 4 minutes. After 12 minutes, 3x gallons have been withdrawn from the tank. The number of gallons remaining is 500 - 3x.

TEST 5

DIRECTIONS:

Each question or incomplete statement is followed by several suggested answers or completions. Select the one that *BEST* answers the question or completes the statement. *PRINT THE LETTER OF THE CORRECT ANSWER IN THE SPACE AT THE RIGHT.*

1. A pool which holds 300 gallons of water can be filled by one pipe in 6 hours and emptied by another in 8 hours. *How many* hours will it take to fill it if *both* pipes are opened together?
   A. 4   B. 7   C. 12   D. 14   E. 24   1. ...

2. The floor of a kitchen 9 feet wide by 12 feet long is to be covered with linoleum which comes in a roll 27 inches wide. The *number* of yards of linoleum needed is:
   A. 16   B. 24   C. 36   D. 48   E. 54   2. ...

3. Four posts are set 15 feet apart along the edge of a field. How many feet is the first post from the last?
   A. 30   B. 35   C. 45   D. 55   E. 60   3. ...

4. During the second year of work a girl earned 5/4 as much as she did her first year. If she earned $3600 in the two years, *how much* did she earn the first year?
   A. $1440   B. $1600   C. $1800   D. $2000   E. $2880   4. ...

5. What fraction of 5 gallons is 3 quarts?
   A. 3/20   B. 1/4   C. 4/15   D. 5/12   E. 3/5   5. ...

6. A man gets 20 miles per gallon with grade X gasoline, which costs $1.00 per gallon; he gets 25 miles per gallon with grade Y, which costs $1.20 per gallon. *How much* does he save on a 1000-mile trip by using grade Y instead of grade X?
   A. $1.25   B. $1.50   C. $1.75   D. $2.00   E. $2.25   6. ...

7. How many twelfths are there in 83 1/3% of a pound?
   A. 5   B. 10   C. 12   D. 14   E. 16   7. ...

8. If there is 2.2 pounds in one kilogram and one kilogram equals 1000 grams, *how many* more grams are there in 8½ pounds than in 3 kilograms?
   A. 824   B. 864   C. 1648   D. 1728   E. 4502   8. ...

9. If, after receiving a discount of 12%, you pay $175 for a television set, the *original* price was:
   A. $187.50   B. $192.50   C. $198.86   D. $200   E. $225   9. ...

10. The 90 members of a certain organization contributed an average of 60 cents each toward a fund. If 2 of the members contributed $5.00 each, *how many* cents was the average contribution of the other 88 members?
    A. 50   B. 56   C. 60   D. 61   E. 70   10. ...

11. A person spent exactly one dollar in the purchase of 3-cent and 5-cent stamps. The number of 5-cent stamps he could *NOT* have bought is
    A. 7   B. 14   C. 11   D. 8   E. 5   11. ...

12. In the series 3, 7, 12, 18, 25, ..., the 10th term is
    A. 88   B. 75   C. 63   D. 50   E. 86   12. ...

13. 3/5 5/8 2/3 7/12. The fraction which is out of order is:
    A. 3/5   B/ 5/8   C. 2/3   D. 7/12   E. None of these   13. ...

14. At 3:20 p.m., *how many* degrees has the hour hand
    moved since noon?
      A. 200   B. 20   C. 10   D. 100   E. 120

15. (3/8) (1/8) = (?) (1/16)
      A. 1/8   B. 3/16   C. 3/8   D. 4/3   E. 3/4

14. ...

15. ...

———

KEY (CORRECT ANSWERS)

1. E
2. A
3. C
4. B
5. A

6. D
7. B
8. B
9. C
10. A

11. A
12. B
13. D
14. D
15. E

———

SOLUTIONS TO PROBLEMS

1. Let x = number of hours needed to fill the pool.
    x/6 - x/8 = 1. Then, 4x - 3x = 24, so x = 24.

2. 9 feet ÷ 27 inches = 108 inches ÷ 27 inches = 4. Thus, 4 rolls
    of linoleum will be needed, each of which must extend to
    12 feet = 4 yards. Total number of yards needed = (4)(4) = 16.

3. The distance from first post to last post is (15)(3) = 45 feet.

4. Let x and $\frac{5}{4}$x represent her earnings in each of the first 2 years.
    Then, x + $\frac{5}{4}$x = $3600. Solving, x = $1600

5. 3 quarts/5 gallons = 3 quarts/20 quarts = $\frac{3}{20}$

6. Using grade X, a trip of 1000 miles costs $(\frac{1000}{20})$($1.00) = $50.
    Using grade Y, this same trip costs $(\frac{1000}{25})$($1.20) = $48.
    The savings is $2.00.

7. $83\frac{1}{3}$% of a pound = $(\frac{5}{6})$(16) = $13\frac{1}{3}$ ounces. $\frac{1}{12}$ of a pound = $1\frac{1}{3}$ ounce
    Now, $13\frac{1}{3}$ ÷ $1\frac{1}{3}$ = 10.

8. 8.5 lbs. = 8.5 ÷ 2.2 = 3.8$\overline{63}$ kgms = 3863.$\overline{63}$ gms, whereas
    3 kgms = 3000 gms. The difference is about 864 gms.

9. Let x = original price. Then, x - .12x = $175.
    Solving, x = $198.86

10. (90)(.60) = $54.00. $54.00 - (2)($5) = $44.
    Finally, $44 ÷ 88 = $0.50

11. He could NOT have bought 7 5-cent stamps since $1.00 - (7)(.05)
    = .65 and .65 is not divisible by 3 cents.

12. The difference between successive terms increases by 1, with the
    difference between the first two terms being 4. Since the
    fifth term is 25, the 10th term will be 25 + 8 + 9 + 10 + 11
    + 12 = 75.

13. Since the first 3 fractions are in increasing order, $\frac{7}{12}$ is out
    of order because $\frac{7}{12}$ < $\frac{2}{3}$.

14. The hour hand has moved $3\frac{1}{3}$ numbers = $(3\frac{1}{3}/12)(360°)$ = $100°$

15. $(\frac{3}{8})(\frac{1}{8})$ = $\frac{3}{64}$. Then, $\frac{3}{64} \div \frac{1}{16}$ = $\frac{3}{4}$

TEST 6

DIRECTIONS:
    Each question or incomplete statement is followed by several suggested answers or completions. Select the one that *BEST* answers the question or completes the statement. *PRINT THE LETTER OF THE CORRECT ANSWER IN THE SPACE AT THE RIGHT.*

1. One end of a ladder 26 feet long is placed 10 feet from   1. ...
   the outer wall of a building. *How many* feet up the
   building will the ladder reach?
       A. 14   B. 20   C. 22   D. 23   E. 24
2. A quart of ice cream will serve 6 adults or 8 children.   2. ...
   If 39 adults have been served from a 10-quart container,
   how many children may then be served?
       A. 28   B. 50   C. 29   D. 41   E. 43
3. Fifty students had an average of 80%. Thirty other   3. ...
   students had an average of 86%. Find the average of *all*
   the students.
       A. 81   B. 81½   C. 82   D. 82¼   E. 83
4. A dealer paid 72¢ for a fountain pen listed at 90¢.   4. ...
   What rate of discount did he receive?
       A. 2%   B. 5%   C. 18%   D. 20%   E. 25%
5. A man makes a trip of 600 miles. He averages 40 m.p.h.   5. ...
   for the first 200 miles. At *what* rate, in m.p.h., must
   he complete the trip to average 45 m.p.h. for the entire
   trip?
       A. 47½   B. 50   C. 47   D. 48½   E. 48
6. The water which is 7" high in a fish tank 1¼ ft. by 8",   6. ...
   is poured into a tank 13" x 20". *What* height will it
   reach in the larger tank?
       A. .27"   B. .31"   C. 1.7"   D. 3.2"   E. 4.6"
7. .3% = ?   7. ...
       A. 3/1000   B. 3/100   C. 1/300   D. 3/10   E. 1/3
8. In one section of a test the first question is numbered   8. ...
   112 and the last 200. How many questions are there in
   this section of the test?
       A. 88   B. 89   C. 87   D. 86   E. None of these
9. A block of wood 8" x 4" x 12" is to be cut into cubes.   9. ...
   If the cubes are the largest that can be cut from this
   block, *how many* of them will there be?
       A. 2   B. 4   C. 6   D. 8   E. 12
10. A 5-quart solution of sulphuric acid and water is 60%   10. ...
    acid. If a gallon of water is added, *what* percent of
    the resulting solution is acid?
        A. 20   B. 33 1/3   C. 40   D. 48   E. 50
11. A baseball team has won 50 games out of 75 played. It   11. ...
    has 45 games still to play. *how many* of these must
    the team win to make its record for the season 60%.
        A. 20   B. 22   C. 25   D. 30   E. None of these
12. If in any two-digit numbers, the tens-digit is repre-   12. ...
    sented by x and the units-digit by y, the number is
    represented by
        A. x+y   B. xy   C. 10x + y   D. 10y + x   E. yx

13. *How many* pieces of cardboard 3" x 5" can be cut from a   13. ...
    sheet 17" x 22" with the *minimum* amount of waste?
    A. 20   B. 21   C. 24   D. 25   E. None of these

14. If p pencils cost c cents, n pencils at the same rate   14. ...
    will cost

    A. $\frac{pc}{n}$ cents   B. $\frac{cn}{p}$ cents   C. npc cents

    D. $\frac{np}{c}$ cents   E. $\frac{p}{nc}$ cents

15. If the population of a village was 300 before the war   15. ...
    and is now 1200, *what* is the percentage of increase in
    population?
    A. 25%   B. 75%   C. 300%   D. 400%   E. 3%

KEY (CORRECT ANSWERS)

1. E
2. A
3. D
4. D
5. E

6. D
7. A
8. B
9. C
10. B

11. B
12. C
13. B
14. B
15. C

SOLUTIONS TO PROBLEMS

1. Let x = number of feet up the wall. Then, $x^2 + 10^2 = 26^2$. Solving, x = 24.

2. 10 quarts will serve 60 adults. Since 39 adults have been served, 21 more adults could be still served. Realizing that for every 6 adults, 8 children could be served, the equivalent of 21 adults is $21 \div \frac{6}{8}$ = 28 children.

3. Average of all students = $[(50)(80) + (30)(86)]/(50 + 30) = 82\frac{1}{4}$

4. Discount = .90 - .72 = .18. Rate of discount = $\frac{.18}{.90}$ = 20%

5. Let x = rate for the remaining 400 miles. The time for this portion of the trip is 400/x hours. Then, 45 = average rate = $600/[\frac{200}{40} + \frac{400}{x}]$. Simplifying, $5 + \frac{400}{x} = 13\frac{1}{3}$. Solving, x = 48 mp

6. Volume in 1st tank = (7")(15")(8") = 840 cu.in. Let x = height in 2nd tank. Then, 840 = (13)(20)(x). Solving, x = 3.2

7. .3% = .3/100 = 3/1000

8. Number of questions = 200 - 111 = 89

9. (8)(4)(12) = 384 cubic inches. The largest possible side for each cube is 4 in. Each of these cubes has a volume of $(4)^3$ = 64 cu.in. Now, 384 ÷ 64 = 6

10. Amount of acid is (5)(.60) = 3 quarts. By adding a gallon of water, the new solution will contain 9 quarts. Finally, 3/9 = 33 1/3%.

11. Let x = number of additional games won. Then, (50 + x)/120 = .60 Solving, x = 22.

12. The number is represented as 10x + y. For example, 56 = (10)(5) + 6

13. 22 ÷ 3 = 7, with 1 in. left over and 17 ÷ 5 = 3, with 2 in. left over. Number of pieces = (7)(3) = 21. The waste is only (1)(2) = 2 sq.in.

14. Let x = cost of n pencils. Then, p/c = n/x. px = cn. Solving, x - cn/p

15. The increase in population is 1200 - 300 = 900. Then, 900/300 = 3 = 300%

———

TEST 7

DIRECTIONS:
    Each question or incomplete statement is followed by several suggested answers or completions. Select the one that *BEST* answers the question or completes the statement. *PRINT THE LETTER OF THE CORRECT ANSWER IN THE SPACE AT THE RIGHT.*

1. If a merchant makes a 20% profit based on the selling price of an article, *what* percent profit does he make on the cost?
    A. 15%   B. 25%   C. 75%   D. 300%   E. 400%

    1. ...

2. The dial of a meter is divided into equal divisions from 0 to 60. When the needle points to 48, the meter registers 80 amperes. *What* is the *MAXIMUM* number of amperes that the meter will register?
    A. 60   B. 92   C. 100   D. 102   E. 120

    2. ...

3. The scale of a certain map is 3/4 inch equals 12 miles. Find, in square miles, the actual area of a park represented on the map by a square whose side is 5/8 inch.
    A. 7½   B. 10   C. 40   D. 100   E. None of these

    3. ...

4. Two boys buy a radio for $15 contributing amounts in the ratio of 5:4. Find the *smaller* amount.
    A. 4   B. 5   C. 12   D. 6 2/3   E. 1 2/3

    4. ...

5. There are 25 equally placed poles in a row. If the distance from the first to the sixth is 30 feet, find the distance from the first to the twenty-fifth.
    A. 120   B. 125   C. 144   D. 150   E. 127½

    5. ...

6. A rectangular room 15' x 19' has a 10' x 10' rug in it. *What* percent of the room is covered?
    A. 25   B. 35   C. 45   D. 55   E. 65

    6. ...

7. .8% is the same as one out of
    A. 20   B. 40   C. 80   D. 100   E. 125

    7. ...

8. A painted wooden cube whose edge is 3 inches is cut into 27 one-inch cubes. *How many* of these have just two painted sides?
    A. 12   B. 18   C. 8   D. 9   E. None of these

    8. ...

9. Four tractors working together can plow a field in 12 hours. *How many* hours will it take 6 tractors to plow the field?
    A. 6   B. 9   C. 10   D. 18   E. None of these

    9. ...

10. A company offers a gas range for $63 cash or for $5 down and 10 months payments of $6.50 each. The installment price is, approximately, *what* percent *greater* than the cash price?
    A. 7%   B. 9%   C. 10%   D. 11%   E. None of these

    10. ...

11. A seesaw 12 feet long is balanced at the middle by a support 3 feet high. If one end of the seesaw is on the ground, *how many* feet above the ground is the other end?
    A. 3   B. 6   C. 9   D. 15   E. 18

    11. ...

12. A baseball team won W games and lost L games. *What* fractional part of its games did it win?
    A. $\dfrac{L}{W}$ B. $\dfrac{W}{L}$ C. $\dfrac{W-L}{W}$ D. $\dfrac{W+L}{W}$ E. $\dfrac{W}{W+L}$

    12. ...

13. A train left A for B, a distance of 290 miles, at 10:10   13. ...
    a.m. The train was scheduled to reach B at 3:45 p.m.
    If the average rate of the train was 50 m.p.h., it
    arrived in B
        A. 5 minutes *early*   B. *on time*
        C. 5 minutes *late*   D. 13 minutes *late*
        E. more than 15 minutes *late*

14. *How many* dollars would it cost to carpet a room r yards   14. ...
    long and w feet wide at x cents a square foot?

        A. wrx   B. .03wrx   C. $\dfrac{100\ wrx}{3}$

        D. $\dfrac{100\ wr}{3x}$ E. $\dfrac{3wr}{100x}$

15. Find the number of degrees between the hands of a clock   15. ...
    at 7:20.
        A. 90   B. 100   C. 97½   D. 108   E. 33 1/3

KEY (CORRECT ANSWERS)

1. B
2. C
3. D
4. D
5. C

6. B
7. E
8. A
9. E
10. D

11. B
12. E
13. D
14. B
15. B

SOLUTIONS TO PROBLEMS

1. Let x = selling price so that .20x = profit. Then, x - .20x = .80x = cost. Percent profit on cost is (.20x/.80x)(100) = 25%

2. Let x = maximum number of amperes. 48/80 = 60/x. Solving, x = 100

3. Let the actual length (or width) of the park = x. Then, $\frac{3}{4}/\frac{5}{8}$ = 12/x. Solving, x = 10. The actual area of the park is 10^2 = 100 square miles.

4. Let 5x and 4x represent the respective amounts. Then, 5x + 4x = 15, so x = $1\frac{2}{3}$. The smaller amount = $(4)(1\frac{2}{3})$ = $6\frac{2}{3}$ dollars.

5. From the 1st pole to the 25th pole represents 24 spaces, so the number of spaces from the 1st pole to the 6th pole is 5. 30 ft. ÷ 5 = 6 ft. = distance between successive poles. Thus, the distance from the 1st pole to the 25th pole is (6)(24) = 144 ft.

6. 10 × 10 = 100 and 15 × 19 = 285. Then, $\frac{100}{285}$ ≈ .351 ≈ 35%

7. .8% = .008 = $\frac{8}{1000}$ = $\frac{1}{125}$ = 1 out of 125

8. The 12 cubes occupying center positions would have only 2 painted sides.

9. The number of tractors is inversely proportional to the number of hours. Let x = required time. 4/6 = x/12, so x = 8 hours.

10. Paying on the installment plan, the cost is 5 + (10)(6.50) = $70. This represents (70 - 63)/63 × 100 = 11% more than the cash price.

11.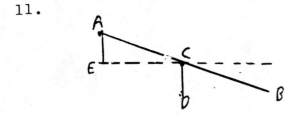
Let CD = 3' support. AC = CB = 6' Now, AE = 3', so point A must be 6' above the ground.

12. Games played = W + L. Fractional part of games won = $\frac{W}{W+L}$

13. Time of travel was $\frac{290}{50}$ = 5.8 hours = 5 hours 48 minutes. Since the train left point A at 10:10 AM, it arrived at point B at 3:58 PM. Thus, it was 13 minutes late.

14. x cents per square foot means 9x cents per square yard = 9x/100 dollars per square yard. The area of the room = (r yards) × ($\frac{w}{3}$ yards) = rw/3 square yards. Total cost to carpet the room = (9x/100)(rw/3) = $\frac{3}{100}$ xrw = .03 wrx dollars.

15. At 7:20, the minute hand is exactly on the numeral 4 and the hour hand lies $\frac{1}{3}$ of the way between the numerals 7 and 8. The distance of $7\frac{1}{3}$ - 4 = $3\frac{1}{3}$ numerals on the clock is equivalent to $(3\frac{1}{3}/12)(360°)$ = 100°.

———

TEST 8

1. If both the filling and emptying pipes of a pool are open, the pool fills in 10 hours. If just the filling pipes are open, the pool fills in 4 hours. *How many* hours does it take to empty the pool if only the emptying pipes are open?

    A. Less than 5   B. More than 5   C. Exactly 5
    D. More than 6   E. Exactly 6

1. ...

2. A cylindrical pail 14 inches in diameter and 7 inches high is full of water. The water is poured into a rectangular aquarium 22" long, 21" wide, and 14" high. To *what* depth in inches does the water rise in the aquarium?

    A. 2 1/3   B. 9 1/3   C. 5 2/3
    D. $7\frac{1}{4}$ E. None of these

2. ...

3. A poster is cut down by 10% of its height and 30% of its width. *What* percent of the original area remains?

    A. 3   B. 37   C. 70   D. 57   E. 63

3. ...

4.

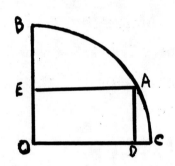

BOC is a quadrant of a circle.
AD = 3 and AE = 4.
Find the length of arc BC.

4. ...

    A. 5π B. $\frac{5\pi}{2}$ C. 10π D. 12
    E. Cannot be determined from the information given

5. A commuter runs from his house to the station, a distance of 132 feet. It takes him 9 seconds. *What* is his speed in miles per hour?

    A. 12   B. 9   C. 8   D. 11   E. 10

5. ...

6. A swimming pool is 4 yards deep, 6 yards wide, and 8 yards long. If it is filled to one foot from the top, *what* is the volume of water in cubic feet?

    A. 24 · 18 · 11   B. 24 · 18 . 12 ⁻ 1   C. 24 · 18 · 12
    D. 24 · 18 · 12 - 3   E. None of these

6. ...

7. A typist uses lengthwise a sheet of paper 9" x 12". She leaves a 1" margin on each side and a $1\frac{1}{2}$" margin on top and bottom. *What* fractional part of the page is used for typing?

    A. $\frac{63}{66}$ B. $\frac{7}{12}$ C. $\frac{5}{9}$ D. 3/4   E. None of these

7. ...

8. Eight blocks on one side of a scale balance two blocks   8. ...
and a one-pound weight on the other side. *What* is the
weight in pounds of *all* ten blocks?
    A. 1   B. 1½   C. 1 2/3   D. 2   E. None of these

9. How many numbers between 131 and 259 are divisible by 3?   9. ...
    A. 41   B. 42   C. 43   D. 44   E. None of these

10. The consecutive angles of a quadrilateral are 60, 120,   10. ...
60, and 120 degrees. If one side is 6 and another is
12, *what* is the perimeter?
    A. 18   B. 36   C. $24 + 6\sqrt{3}$
    D. $12 + 6\sqrt{3}$ E. Cannot be determined from the information given

11. Admission tickets for children are 1/3 the price for   11. ...
adults. The price for 3 children and 3 adults is $10.80.
How much is the price for one adult?
    A. $.90   B. $1.20   C. $1.80   D. $2.70   E. $3.00

12. A man walks 100 feet north, 150 feet west, and 100 feet   12. ...
north again. *How many* feet is the distance from where he
started to where he finished in a straight line?
    A. 350   B. 300   C. 250   D. 200   E. None of these

13. A ferris wheel has a diameter of 60 feet. It makes   13. ...
3 revolutions per minute. Find the distance in miles
that the occupant of one of the cars travels in 5 minutes.
($\pi = \frac{22}{7}$)
    A. $\frac{30}{28}$ B. $\frac{15}{28}$ C. $\frac{4}{7}$ D. $\frac{3}{5}$ E. $2\frac{1}{4}$

14. A box contains 2 red balls, 3 blue balls, and 4 white.   14. ...
What is the *LEAST* number of balls a blindfolded person
must draw to be sure of getting two of the same kind?
    A. 2   B. 3   C. 4   D. 5   E. 6

15. If an apple weighs 4/5 of its weight plus 4/5 of an   15. ...
ounce, *what* is its weight in ounces?
    A. 3½   B. 1 3/5   C. 4   D. 4 4/5   E. 5

KEY (CORRECT ANSWERS)

1. D
2. A
3. E
4. B
5. E

6. A
7. B
8. C
9. C
10. B

11. D
12. C
13. B
14. C
15. C

SOLUTIONS TO PROBLEMS

1. Let x = time required to empty the pool using only the emptying pipes. Then, $\frac{10}{4} - \frac{10}{x} = 1$. Simplifying, 10x - 40 = 4x. Solving, $x = 6\frac{2}{3}$ hours, which corresponds to *more than 6*.

2. Volume of pail = $(\pi)(7^2)(7) \approx 1078$ cu.in. Let x = height to which water will rise in aquarium. Then, 1078 = (22)(21)(x), so, $x = 2\frac{1}{3}$ in.

3. Let x = original height, y = original width, xy = original area. New height = .9x, new width = .7y, new area = .63xy, which is 63% of the original area.

4. Radius of circle = OA = $\sqrt{3^2 + 4^2} = 5$. Length of arc BC = $(\frac{1}{4})(2\pi)(5) = 5\pi/2$

5. 132 ft. in 9 sec. means $14\frac{2}{3}$ ft. per sec. Since 88 ft. per sec. is equivalent to 60 mph, the commuter's speed in mph = $(60)(14\frac{2}{3}/88) = 10$

6. 6 yds. = 18 ft., 8 yds. = 24 ft., 4 yds. - 1 ft. = 11 ft. The volume, in cubic feet, is 24·18·11.

7. The typing section has an area of (9 - 2)(12 - 3) = 63 sq.in. The entire sheet of paper has an area of (9)(12) = 108 sq.in. Finally, $63/108 = \frac{7}{12}$

8. Let x = weight of each block. Then, 8x = 2x + 1, so $x = \frac{1}{6}$ lbs. The weight of all ten blocks = $(10)(\frac{1}{6}) = 1\frac{2}{3}$ lbs.

9. The numbers divisible by 3 begin with 132 and end with 258. The total number of these numbers = (258 - 132)/3 + 1 = 43

10. Since opposite angles are equal, the given figure must be a parallelogram, wherein opposite sides are also equal. The perimeter = (2)(6) + (2)(12) = 36.

11. Let x = admission price per adult, $\frac{1}{3}x$ = admission price per child. $(3)(\frac{1}{3}x) + 3x = 10.80$. Solving, x = $2.70

12.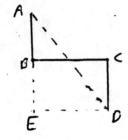

We are seeking the value of DA.
Now, ED = BC = 150 and AE = AB + CD = 200.
Since AED forms a right triangle,
DA = $\sqrt{150^2 + 200^2}$ = 250

13. In 1 min., each car of the ferris wheel travels $(\frac{22}{7})(60)(3)$ = 3960/7 ft. In 5 min., this distance = 19,800/7 ft.

Since 5280 ft. = 1 mi., the distance traveled in 5 min. becomes (19,800/7) ÷ 5280 = $\frac{15}{28}$ mi.

14. By drawing only 3 balls, the person might get exactly one of each color. However, by drawing 4 balls, at least 2 of them will be the same color.

15. Let x = weight in ounces. Then, x = $\frac{4}{5}$x + $\frac{4}{5}$.

Solving, x = 4.

DIRECTIONS:

Each question or incomplete statement is followed by several suggested answers or completions. Select the one that *BEST* answers the question or completes the statement. *PRINT THE LETTER OF THE CORRECT ANSWER IN THE SPACE AT THE RIGHT.*

1. If r + q = s and r + q + s = w, what does w equal in terms of r and q?   1. ...
   A. 2r + q   B. 2q + r   C. 2r + 2q
   D. r + q + s   E. 2s + 2r + q

2. In a circle a chord is cut off so that it equals the radius. How many degrees are there in the central angle formed by two radii and this chord?   2. ...
   A. 50   B. 52   C. 54   D. 57   E. 60

3. Find the shaded area formed by 4 overlapping squares, each having a 3" side and a 1" overlap.   3. ...
   A. 36
   B. 32
   C. 30
   D. 24
   E. 22

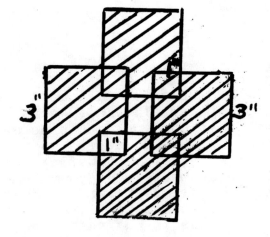

4. $(x+y)^2 - x^2 - y^2 = (?)$ 4. ...
   A. 2xy   B. xy   C. 0   D. $2x^2 + 2y^2$ E. y^2

5. If x-2 = x-2, what does x equal numerically?   5. ...
   A. Only 0   B. Any number   C. 7   D. 2   E. 5

6. What approximate percent of 72 is 43?   6. ...
   A. 56   B. 57   C. 58   D. 60   E. 61

7. What is the area of the shaded triangle?   7. ...
   A. $9\frac{1}{2}$
   B. 10
   C. $10\frac{1}{2}$
   D. 11
   E. 12

8. In a marine base 12% of the men are from California   8. ...
and 4% of these marines are from Anaheim. What percent of the men are from Anaheim?
    A. 48   B. 4.8   C. .48   D. .048   E. .0048

9. A book shelf is 4 feet long. How many books will fit   9. ...
on the shelf if each book is 3 1/3 inches thick?
    A. 11   B. 12   C. 13   D. 14   E. 15

10. The areas of the complete   10. ...
circles are x, y, and z.
The areas of the portions
of the circles are r, s,
t, u and w. What is the
area of x + y - z?
    A. r + t + w
    B. r + 2t + w
    C. s + t + u
    D. r + s + w
    E. s + u + w

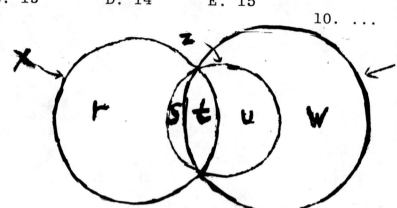

Questions 11-15.
DIRECTIONS: Each of the questions below is followed by two statements, labeled (1) and (2), in which certain data are given. In
these questions you do not actually have to compute an answer, but
rather you have to decide whether the data given in the statement
are *sufficient* for answering the question. Using the data given
in the statements *plus* your knowledge of mathematics and everyday
facts, you are to print in the space at the right the letter
    A if statement (1) *ALONE* is sufficient but statement (2)
       alone is not sufficient to answer the question asked;
    B if statement (2) *ALONE* is sufficient but statement (1)
       alone is not sufficient to answer the question asked;
    C if *BOTH* statements (1) and (2) *TOGETHER* are sufficient
       to answer the question asked, but *NEITHER* statement
       ALONE is sufficient;
    D if *EACH* statement is sufficient by itself to answer the
       question asked;
    E if statements (1) and (2) *TOGETHER* are *NOT* sufficient to
       answer the question asked and additional data specific
       to the problem are needed .

11. The distance to John's house is 40 miles from his   11. ...
college. John went to school Friday but then returned
home. *How long* did the entire trip take?
    (1) If John went 40 miles per hour faster it would have
       taken him half the time.
    (2) He traveled at a uniform rate, both going and coming,
       of 40 miles per hour.

12. $4x - 8y = 4$. $y = ?$ 12. ...
    (1) $x - 2y = 0$
    (2) $x = 5$

13. There are 75 people in the town that attend either   13. ...
meeting x or meeting y or both. How many attend each
meeting?
    (1) 30 people attend meeting x *only*
    (2) 45 people attend meeting y
14. In triangle RST, how many degrees is angle R if   14. ...
    (1) $\dfrac{RS}{ST} = 1$ (2) $\dfrac{RS}{TR} = 1$
angle R = 60 degrees
15. In triangle RST, angle S is 90 degrees and SR = ST.   15. ...
Find the area of triangle RST.
    (1) SR = 5
    (2) RT = $5\sqrt{2}$

KEY (CORRECT ANSWERS)

  1. C
  2. E
  3. B
  4. A
  5. B

  6. D
  7. E
  8. C
  9. D
10. A

11. D
12. B
13. E
14. C
15. D

TEST 2

DIRECTIONS:

Each question or incomplete statement is followed by several suggested answers or completions. Select the one that *BEST* answers the question or completes the statement. *PRINT THE LETTER OF THE CORRECT ANSWER IN THE SPACE AT THE RIGHT.*

1. A man runs 220 yards in 20.7 seconds. The first 90 yards he runs in 11.8 seconds. In approximately *how many* seconds does he run the first 100 yards if he runs the last 130 yards at a uniform rate?   1. ...
   A. 12.0   B. 12.2   C. 12.5   D. 12.7   E. 13.0

2. The symbol $\begin{vmatrix} a & b \\ c & d \end{vmatrix}$ is called the *determinant* of the quantities a, b, c, d. The value of the determinant is (ad-bc). Find the value of the determinant $\begin{vmatrix} 2 & 3 \\ 3 & 1 \end{vmatrix}$ 2. ...

   A. 3   B. -7   C. 5   D. 7   E. -5

3. In the figure, angle B is obtuse, AP = 8, BP = 5, and Q is any point on AB. *Which* of the following expresses possible values of the length of PQ?   3. ...
   A. 8 > PQ > 5
   B. 8 > 5 > PQ
   C. 5 > PQ > 8
   D. PQ > 8 > 5
   E. None of these

4. If a man buys several articles for n cents per dozen and sells them for $\frac{n}{9}$ cents per article, *what* is his profit, in cents, on each article?   4. ...
   A. $\frac{n}{36}$ B. $\frac{n}{12}$ C. $\frac{3n}{4}$ D. $\frac{4n}{3}$ E. $\frac{n}{18}$

5. Five billion dozen eggs are used in the United States each year. If every twelfth egg is made into powder, *how many* billion eggs per year are powdered?   5. ...
   A. 2   B. $2\frac{1}{2}$ C. 3   D. 4   E. 5

6. The symbols ° and * designate two different mathematical operations. If a °(b*c) = a°b*a°c, then the operation is said to be *distributive* with respect to the operation *. If ° represents the operation of multiplication (x), then * may represent *which* of the following operations: 6. ...
   I. +   II. -   III. ÷
The *CORRECT* answer is:
   A. I only   B. II only   C. I and II only
   D. I, II, and III   E. None of these

4

7. If the *additive inverse* of a number *a* is termed (-a) in the real number system, find the additive inverse of $-\frac{7}{2}$

    A. $\frac{2}{2}$ B. $-\frac{2}{7}$ C. -7   D. -2   E. $\frac{7}{2}$

7. ...

8. If $x = ay$, where *y* does not equal zero, express *a* in terms of *x* and *y*.

    A. $-\frac{y}{x}$ B. $\frac{x}{y}$ C. xy   D. x+y   E. x-y

8. ...

9. Which of the following has *no* finite value that can be determined?

    A. $\frac{0}{3}$ B. 3 x 0   C. 0 - 3   D. $\frac{3}{0}$

    E. None of these

9. ...

10. The coordinates of P_1 are (1,4).
What are the coordinates of P_2?
    A. (2,3)
    B. (1,2)
    C. (5,2)
    D. (2,2)
    E. (5,3)

10. ...

Questions 11-15.
DIRECTIONS: Each of the data sufficiency problems below consists of a question and two statements, labeled (1) and (2), in which certain data are given. You have to decide whether the data given in the statements are *sufficient* for answering the question. Using the data given in the statements *plus* your knowledge of mathematics and everyday facts, you are to print in the space at the right the letter
    A if statement (1) *ALONE* is sufficient, but statement (2) alone is not sufficient to answer the question asked;
    B if statement (2) *ALONE* is sufficient, but statement (1) alone is not sufficient to answer the question asked;
    C if *BOTH* statements (1) and (2) *TOGETHER* are sufficient to answer the question asked, but *NEITHER* statement *ALONE* is sufficient;
    D if *EACH* statement *ALONE* is sufficient to answer the question asked;
    E if statements (1) and (2) *TOGETHER* are *NOT* sufficient to answer the question asked, and additional data specific to the problem are needed.

11. Given triangle ABC. *How many* degrees in angle A?
    (1) AB = AC
    (2) Angle B = 40 degrees

11. ...

12. There are 24 pencils in a box. *How many* have both erasers and dull points?
    (1) 21 have erasers
    (2) 3 have dull points

12. ...

13. Given equilateral triangle
ABC and hexagon DEFGHI formed
as in the figure.
What is the ratio of the
area of the hexagon to the
area of triangle ABC?
(1) Triangles ADE, BFG
and CHI are all
equilateral
(2) AD = CH = BF

13. ...

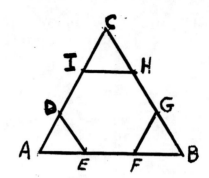

14. A and B go on a 300-mile trip by car. They take turns
driving, each driving for eight hours. Find the average
rate of each.
(1) A drove 48 miles more than B
(2) A averaged 6 miles an hour faster than B

14. ...

15. A table is 30 inches long and 9 inches wide. It is
covered by three overlapping napkins each 9 inches
wide. *How long* is each of the napkins?
(1) All three napkins are of equal length
(2) If the table were 1½ times as long as it is now,
the napkins would just cover the table without
overlapping.

15. ...

KEY (CORRECT ANSWERS)

1. C
2. B
3. A
4. A
5. E

6. C
7. E
8. B
9. D
10. D

11. C
12. E
13. E
14. D
15. C

6

TEST 3

DIRECTIONS:

Each question or incomplete statement is followed by several suggested answers or completions. Select the one that *BEST* answers the question or completes the statement. *PRINT THE LETTER OF THE CORRECT ANSWER IN THE SPACE AT THE RIGHT.*

Questions 1-10.
DIRECTIONS: In each of the problems below, *do not solve the problem,* but simply indicate one of the following choices:
  A if not enough information is given to solve the problem;
  B if just enough information is given to solve the problem;
  C if statement (1) is needed to solve the problem, but not statement (2);
  D if statement (2) is needed to solve the problem, but not statement (1);
  E if neither statement (1) nor (2) is needed to solve the problem.

1. The bases of an isosceles trapezoid are 6 and 10.   1. ...
Find the area of the trapezoid.
   (1) The diagonals of the trapezoid are 9.
   (2) The lower base angles are acute.

2. How far is A from C?   2. ...
   (1) A is 10 miles from B.
   (2) B is 15 miles from C.

3. A cylindrical glass 6 inches high is full of water.   3. ...
How many lbs. of water does the glass contain?
   (1) A cubic foot of water weighs 62.5 pounds.
   (2) The diameter of the glass is 4 inches.

4. Find the height of the flagpole.   4. ...
   (1) The shadow of a yardstick is 4 ft. long.
   (2) At the same time and place the shadow of a flagpole
      is 36 ft.

5. A man has 18 coins consisting of nickles and dimes.   5. ...
How many of each are there?
   (1) The total value is $1.20.
   (2) There are twice as many nickles as dimes.

6. Find each number.   6. ...
   (1) Three numbers are in the ratio 5:7:9.
   (2) The middle number is equal to half the sum of the
      first and third numbers.

7. How many pounds of each does he use?   7. ...
   (1) A dealer mixes coffee worth $1.80 a pound with
      coffee worth $2.10 a pound.
   (2) The mixture sells for $1.98 a pound.

8. The area of a square is 36 square inches. Find the   8. ...
side of the square.
   (1) A rectangle is formed equal in area to the square.
   (2) The length of the rectangle is 3 inches more than
      a side of the square.

7

9. Find the number of dollars invested at each rate.
    (1) A man invests a certain amount of money, part at 6% and the rest at 8%.
    (2) The total annual income from the two investments is $290.

                                                     9. ...

10. Find each integer.
    (1) The sum of three consecutive integers is 33.
    (2) The largest of the three integers is 2 more than the smallest.

                                                   10. ...

KEY (CORRECT ANSWERS)

1. C
2. A
3. B
4. B
5. D

6. A
7. A
8. E
9. A
10. C

TEST 4

DIRECTIONS:

Each question or incomplete statement is followed by several suggested answers or completions. Select the one that *BEST* answers the question or completes the statement. *PRINT THE LETTER OF THE CORRECT ANSWER IN THE SPACE AT THE RIGHT.*

Questions 1-5.

DIRECTIONS: Each of the data sufficiency problems below consists of a question and two statements, labeled (1) and (2), in which certain data are given. You have to decide whether the data given in the statements are *sufficient* for answering the question. Using the data given in the statements *plus* your knowledge of mathematics and everyday facts (such as the number of days in June or the meaning of *counterclockwise*), you are to print in the space at the right of the letter:

A if statement (1) *ALONE* is sufficient, but statement (2) alone is not sufficient to answer the question asked;

B if statement (2) *ALONE* is sufficient, but statement (1) alone is not sufficient to answer the question asked;

C if *BOTH* statements (1) and (2) *TOGETHER* are sufficient to answer the question asked, but *NEITHER* statement *ALONE* is sufficient;

D if *EACH* statement *ALONE* is sufficient to answer the question asked;

E if statements (1) and (2) *TOGETHER* are *NOT* sufficient to answer the question asked, and additional data specific to the problem are needed.

1. *Which* side of $\triangle$ RST is the longest?   1. ...
   (1) < S = 54 degrees, < T = 36 degrees
   (2) < R is a right angle

2. Is the sum of the three integers, x, y, and z, odd?   2. ...
   (1) xyz = 105
   (2) The sum and the difference of any two of the numbers are each even, and y is odd.

3. *What* is the two-digit number Q?   3. ...
   (1) The sum of its digits is 13 and the product of its digits is 36.
   (2) If it were multiplied by 2, the result would still be a two-digit number.

4. If x and y are integers, is x+y odd?   4. ...
   (1) xy = 6
   (2) x-y is odd.

5. x + y + z = (?)   5. ...
   (1) x + y = 3
   (2) x + z = 5

6. Two variables in a scientific experiment are such that   6. ...
   their product is always 1.
   If, for a certain time, one variable is greater than zero, less than 1, and decreasing, then *which* of the following describes the second variable?
   A. Greater than 1 and increasing

9

B. Greater than 1 and decreasing
C. Not changing
D. Less than 1 and increasing
E. Less than 1 and decreasing

7. If x, y, z, and w are all real numbers and none of them   7. ...
   is zero, *which* of the following expressions can equal zero?
   I. $x + y + z + w$
   II. $x^2 + y^2 + z^2 + w^2$
   III. $x^3 + y^3 + z^3 + w^3$
   IV. $x^4 + y^4 + z^4 + w^4$
   The *CORRECT* answer is:
   A. I *only*   B. III *only*   C. II and IV *only*
   D. I and III *only*   E. I, II, III, and IV

8. If $x(x - y) = 0$ and if y does not equal zero, *which* of   8. ...
   the following is true?
   A. $x = 0$ B. Either $x = 0$ or $x = y$ C. $x = y$
   D. $x^2 = y$ E. Both $x = 0$ and $x - y = 0$

9. If n is an integer and if the following are arranged   9. ...
   in order, *which* integer is in the middle?
   A. $n + 3$ B. $n - 9$ C. $n - 4$
   D. $n + 6$ E. $n - 1$

10. If ϕ is an operation on the positive numbers, for *which*   10. ...
    of the following definitions of ϕ is $x\phi y = y\phi x$?

    A. $x\phi y = \dfrac{x}{y}$ B. $x\phi y = x - y$

    C. $x\phi y = x(x + y)$ D. $x\phi y = \dfrac{xy}{x+y}$

    E. $x\phi y = x^2 + xy^2 + y^4$

11. In the figure to the right,   11. ...
    a card is covering part of
    the left number which is
    known to be in the hundred
    thousands.
    Which of the following is
    the *only* number that could
    possibly be the above product?
    A. 1, 107, 130, 464
    B. 1, 107, 130, 466
    C. 11, 076, 130, 444
    D. 11, 076, 130, 464
    E. 11, 076, 130, 466

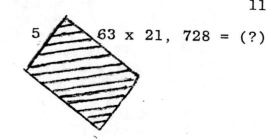

$5\diagdown 63 \times 21,\ 728 = (?)$

12. If $x^2 + 2xy + y^2 = k$, where x and y are positive   12. ...
    integers and x is odd and y is even, *which* of the
    following statements is true?
    A. k is odd and a perfect square
    B. k is even and a perfect square
    C. k is odd and not a perfect square
    D. k is even and not a perfect square
    E. None of these

13. If the average of 13 consecutive whole numbers is odd,   13. ...
    then the product of the first and last of these numbers
    must necessarily be
    A. odd   B. even
    C. a multiple of 7   D. a multiple of 13
    E. a multiple of the average of the 13 numbers

10

14. *How many* of the numbers between 100 and 300 begin or end with 2?

    A. 20   B. 40   C. 180   D. 100   E. 110

14. ...

15. A prime number is a number that can be divided only by itself and one. *Which* of the following is *NOT* a prime number?

    A. 101   B. 93   C. 53   D. 47   E. 17

15. ...

16. If $2x + 2 > 8$, x must be

    A. < 8 B. < 5 C. > 3 D. > 4 E. > 6

16. ...

17. *Which* one of the following must be excluded so that the remaining four are consistent?

    A. $a > b$ B. $a > d$ C. $b > c$ D. $c > a$ E. $d > c$

17. ...

18. The sides of a triangle are 9, 12, and x. *What* are all the values of x for which the triangle will be acute?

    A. $x < 21$ B. $x > 3$ C. $3 < x < 21$
    D. $x < 15$ E. $3 \sqrt{7} < x < 15$

18. ...

19. The fraction $\frac{a}{b}$ (a and b positive) will have a value greater than 2 *if*

    A. $2a = 2b$ B. $a > b$ C. $a > 2$
    D. $a > 2b$ E. $2b > a$

19. ...

20. If Tom knows that x is an integer > 3 but < 8 and Charley knows that x is an integer > 6 but < 11, then Tom and Charley can *correctly* conclude that

    A. x can be exactly determined
    B. x may be either of 2 values
    C. x may be any of 3 values
    D. x may be any of 4 values
    E. there is no value of x satisfying these conditions

20. ...

KEY (CORRECT ANSWERS)

1. D	11. D
2. D	12. A
3. C	13. A
4. D	14. E
5. E	15. B
6. A	16. C
7. D	17. D
8. B	18. E
9. E	19. D
10. D	20. A

SOLUTIONS TO PROBLEMS
TEST 1

1. Since $r + q = s$ and $r + q + s = w$, we get $r + q + r + q = w$. Simplified, $w = 2r + 2q$

2. In a circle with center O, if chord $\overline{AB}$ equals the radius, that $\triangle AOB$ is equilateral. Then, the central angle = 60°.

3. By adding up the areas of the 4 large squares, each little square has been added twice. The shaded area will be $(4)(3^2) - 4(1^2) = 32$ sq.in.

4. $(x+y)^2 - x^2 - y^2 = x^2 + 2xy + y^2 - x^2 - y^2 = 2xy$

5. Since $x - 2 = x - 2$ is an identity, x can equal any number.

6. $43/72 \approx .597 \approx 60\%$

7. Area $= (\frac{1}{2})(\text{base})(\text{height}) = (\frac{1}{2})(4)(6) = 12$

8. The percent of men from Anaheim is $(.04)(.12) = .0048 = .48\%$

9. 4 ft. = 48 in. Then, $48 \div 3\frac{1}{3} = 14.4$. So, 14 books will fit on the shelf.

10. $x + y - z = (r+s+t) + (t+u+w) - (s+t+u) = r + t + w$

11. Let x = rate. Statement 1 alone is sufficient, since we could solve $40/(x + 40) = \frac{1}{2}(40/x)$, yielding $x = 40$. Thus, time = 1 hour. Statement 2 alone is also sufficient since letting x = time we get $x = \frac{40}{40} = 1$ hour.

12. Statement 1 alone will not be sufficient to solve for y, since substituting $x = 2y$ into the given equation yields $4(2y) - 8y = 4$ which has no solution. Statement 2 alone would be sufficient. If $x = 5$, $(4)(5) - 8y = 4$, so $y = 2$.

13. Statement 1 alone would not be sufficient because we don't know how many people attended meeting y only and how many attended both x and y. Statement 2 alone is not sufficient because we don't know how many of the 45 attended both x and y, versus how many attended only y. Finally, the two statements together are still insufficient.

14. Each of statements 1 and 2 separately is not sufficient to find $\angle R$, but together they imply that $RS = ST = TR$. So, $\angle R = 60°$.

15. Statement 1 alone is sufficient because $ST = SR = 5$. Then, the area of the triangle is $(\frac{1}{2})(5)(5) = 12.5$. Statement 2 alone is also sufficient because given $RT = 5\sqrt{2}$ and $SR = ST$, we let $SR = x$. Then, $x^2 + x^2 = (5\sqrt{2})^2$. Solving, $x = 5$. Area of triangle $= (\frac{1}{2})(5)(5) = 12.5$.

———

TEST 2

1. $(220 - 90) \div (20.7 - 11.8) \approx 14.6$ yds. per second for the last 130 yards. The time needed to run the 10 yards from the 90-yard marker to the 100-yard marker $= 10 \div 14.6 \approx .7$ sec. Since he ran the first 90 yards in 11.8 seconds, his time, in seconds, for the first 100 yards $= 11.8 + .7 = 12.5$.

2. $\begin{vmatrix} 2 & 3 \\ 3 & 1 \end{vmatrix} = (2)(1) - (3)(3) = -7$

3. In $\triangle PQB$, $\overline{PQ}$ must be the longest side since $\angle B$ is obtuse. Then, $PQ > 5$. In $\triangle APQ$, $\angle Q$ is obtuse, so $AP = 8$ must be the longest side. This implies $PQ < 8$. Finally, $8 > PQ > 5$.

4. n cents per dozen articles means $\frac{n}{12}$ cents per article. His profit in cents on each article $= \frac{n}{9} - \frac{n}{12} = \frac{n}{36}$.

5. Five billion dozen $\div$ 1 dozen = 5 billion.

6. Only statements I and II are correct since $a \cdot (b+c) = a \cdot b + a \cdot c$ and $a \cdot (b-c) = a \cdot b - a \cdot c$.

7. The additive inverse of $-\frac{7}{2} = -(-\frac{7}{2}) = +\frac{7}{2}$

8. If $x = ay$, dividing by y yields $a = \frac{x}{y}$

9. $\frac{3}{0}$ has no finite value since division by zero has no meaning.

10. Since P_2 lies 1 unit to the right and 2 units below P_1, the coordinates of P_2 are (2,2).

11. If $AB = AC$, then $\angle B = \angle C$, but we cannot determine the measurement of $\angle A$. If $\angle B$ is known to be 40°, $\angle A + \angle C$ must equal 180°, but we could not determine $\angle A$. These two statements together would be sufficient to determine $\angle A$. Since $\angle B = 40°$, $\angle C = 40°$. Then, $\angle A = 180° - 40° - 40° = 100°$.

12. The two statements together are insufficient. For example, we might have 21 pencils with erasers and no dull points along with 3 pencils with dull points but no erasers. Another possibility is 20 pencils with erasers and no dull points, 3 pencils with dull points and no erasers, 1 pencil with both an eraser and a dull point, and 1 pencil with no eraser and no dull point.

13. Statement 1 alone is not sufficient to determine the sides of
    the hexagon. Statement 2 alone is not sufficient since we
    do not know if $\triangle ADE$, $\triangle BFG$, $\triangle CIH$ are equilateral. So the sides
    of the hexagon are still unknown. Together, statements 1 and 2
    are still not sufficient. (The required information would be:
    $\triangle ADE$, $\triangle BFG$, $\triangle CHI$ are equilateral and $AD = DI = IC$.)

14. Statement 1 alone is sufficient. Let x = distance driven by B
    and $x + 48$ = distance driven by A. Then, $x + x + 48 = 300$,
    so $x = 126$, $x + 48 = 174$. The average rates of A and B are
    $174/8 = 21.75$ and $126/8 = 15.75$. Using statement 2 alone, let
    x = average rate for B and $x + 6$ = average rate for A. Then,
    $(x+6)(8) + 8x = 300$. Thus, $x = 15.75$, $x + 6 = 21.75$.

15. Each statement alone is not sufficient, but taken together
    let x = each napkin's length. Then, $3x = (30)(1\frac{1}{2}) = 45$.
    Thus, $x = 15$.

———

TEST 3

1. 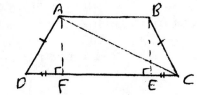 Let AB = 6, DC = 10. Using statement 1, in right triangle AFC, FC = 6 + 2 = 8, AC = 9, so AF = $\sqrt{9^2 - 8^2} = \sqrt{17}$. The area of the trapezoid = $\frac{1}{2}(\sqrt{17})(6 + 10)$ or $8\sqrt{17}$. This means statement 2 will not be needed.

2. There is insufficient information to find the distance from A to C. (Note that AC = 25 ONLY if points A, B, C are collinear.)

3. Using both statements together, the volume of the glass is $(\pi)(4^2)(6) = 96\pi$ cu.in. = $\frac{2}{3}\pi$ cu.ft. Since a cubic foot of water weighs 62.5 pounds, the weight of water in the glass = $(62.5)(\frac{2}{3}\pi)$ = $41\frac{2}{3}\pi$ pounds.

4. Using both statements together, let x = height of the flagpole. Then, x/36 = 3/4. Thus, x = 27 ft.

5. Statement 1 is not needed. With statement 2 alone, let x = number of dimes, 2x = number of nickels. Then, x + 2x = 18, so x = 6. There are 6 dimes and 12 nickels.

6. Let the three numbers be represented as 5x, 7x, 9x. Since 7x = $\frac{1}{2}$(5x + 9x) anyway, statement 2 is not needed. We now conclude that there is insufficient information to find each number.

7. There is insufficient information to find the number of pounds of each type of coffee. The only conclusion we can reach is that UNEQUAL number of pounds of each type is used since 1.98 ≠ (1.80 + 2.10)/2.

8. From the given information, each side of the square = $\sqrt{36}$ = 6. Neither of statements 1 nor 2 is needed.

9. Let x = amount invested at 6%, y = amount invested at 8%. Then, .06x + .08y = 290, if we use both statements. This is still insufficient to find x or y.

10. From statement 1, x, x + 1, x + 2 could represent the integers. Then, x + x + 1 + x + 2 = 33. Solving, the numbers are 10, 11, and 12. This means statement 2 will not be needed.

15

TEST 4

1. From statement 1, $\angle S = 54°$, $\angle T = 36°$, so $\angle R = 90°$. Then the hypotenuse $\overline{ST}$ of this right triangle must be the longest. From statement 2, $\overline{ST}$ must be the hypotenuse, and so must be the longest side. Each of statements 1 and 2 is sufficient to find the longest side of $\triangle RST$.

2. From statement 1, if $xyz = 105$, then all three numbers must be odd. This implies $x + y + z$ is odd. From statement 2, y is odd and since $|x-y|$, $|x-z|$, $|z-y|$ must each be even, we know that x and z must also be odd. Thus, $x + y + z$ must be odd. Each of statements 1 and 2 is sufficient.

3. Let $10x + y$ represent Q. From statement 1 alone, $x + y = 13$ and $xy = 36$. Solving this system of equations, $x = 9$ and $y = 4$ or $x = 4$ and $y = 9$. $Q = 49$ or 94. Now using statement 2, we have $2(10x + y) < 100$. With both statements 1 and 2, Q must be 49 since $2(94)$ exceeds 100.

4. From statement 1, if $xy = 6$, one of x,y is odd and the other is even. So, $x + y$ must be odd. From statement 2, $x - y$ is odd would mean that one of x, y is odd and the other is even. Again, $x + y$ must be odd. Each of statements 1 and 2 is sufficient.

5. Using both statements together, we could determine only that $z - y = 2$. This would still be insufficient to determine the value of $x + y + z$.

6. If $0 < x < 1$, $xy = 1$, and x is decreasing, then y must be increasing and $y > 1$. For example, if $x = .5$ and $y = 2$, when x decreases to $.25$, $y = 4$.

7. $x + y + z + w$ could be zero. (For example, $x = 1$, $y = -1$, $z = 2$, $w = 2$.) Those same values would also make $x^3 + y^3 + z^3 + w^3 = 0$. But $x^2 + y^2 + z^2 + w^2 > 0$ and $x^4 + y^4 + z^4 + w^4 > 0$. Only statements I and III could be zero.

8. Given $x(x-y) = 0$ and $y \neq 0$, then $x = 0$ or $x-y = 0$. This means $x = 0$ or $x = y$.

9. The 5 selections arranged in ascending order are: $n-9$, $n-4$, $n-1$, $n+3$, $n+6$. Thus, $n-1$ is the middle integer.

10. If $x \emptyset y = \dfrac{xy}{x+y}$, then $y \emptyset x = \dfrac{yx}{y+x}$, which is equivalent to $\dfrac{xy}{x+y}$. Thus, $x \emptyset y = y \emptyset x$.

16

11. Since $500,000 \times 21,728 > 11,000,000,000$, only choices C, D, E are possible. Since the last digits of each factor are 3 and 8, respectively, the product must end in 4. We now eliminate choice E. Consider the first line of the multiplication. $8 \times 3 = 4$ with a carry of 2 and $8 \times 6 + 2 = 0$ digit in the ten's column. Another contribution to the ten's column will be the result of multiplying 3 (from the unknown number) by 2 (from 21,728) to get a 6 digit. The answer must now have a digit of $0 + 6 = 6$ in the ten's column. Only choice D is possible. Note: $11,076,130,464 \div 21,728 = 509,763$.

12. $x^2 + 2xy + y^2 = (x+y)^2 = k$. Since x is odd and y is even, $x + y$ is odd and so is $(x+y)^2$ an odd number. This means that k is odd and a perfect square.

13. The average of 13 consecutive whole numbers must be the 7th number. If this 7th number is odd, then both the first and last numbers must also be odd. Consequently, their product must be odd.

14. There are 10 numbers between 100 and 200 (non-inclusive) which end with a 2, namely 102, 112, 122,..., 182, 192. Between 200 and 300 (inclusive), there are 100 numbers beginning with a 2 (and some ending with a 2 as well), namely, 200, 201, 202,..., 298, 299. The total of numbers satisfying the given requirements $= 100 + 10 = 110$.

15. 93 is not a prime number since it has factors other than 1 and 93, namely 3 and 31.

16. If $2x + 2 > 8$, then $2x > 6$, so $x > 3$.

17. By excluding choice D, there is consistency among the others, so that a > b or d and b or d > c.

18. If x is the largest side, then $x^2 = 9^2 + 12^2$ will result in a right triangle. Solving, $x = 15$. This would mean if $x \geq 15$, this will not be an acute triangle. (If $x > 15$, this will be an obtuse triangle.) Now suppose x is the smallest side. The largest angle will lie opposite the side which is 12. We know that $12^2 = 9^2 + x^2 - (2)(9)(x) \cdot \cos$ (angle opposite 12). To maintain an acute triangle, cos (any angle) must be positive. To insure this, $12^2 - 9^2 - x^2$ must be negative. This leads to $x^2 > 144 - 81 = 63$, so $x > \sqrt{63} = 3\sqrt{7}$. Finally, the restrictions on x are $3\sqrt{7} < x < 15$.

19. If $a/b > 2$, then $a > 2b$. (Both $a, b > 0$.)

20. If x fulfills both $3 < x < 8$ and $6 < x < 11$, then $x = 7$ (if x must be an integer).

QUANTITATIVE COMPARISON

COMMENTARY

The item-type designated as *QUANTITATIVE COMPARISON* is a novel form of mathematics problem stressing the finest and highest types of conceptualizing, reasoning, and evaluating.

The examinee is directed to compare two quantities and to decide, on the basis of the information given, which, if either, is greater.

For example, if you were requested to compare 5/8 X 1/4 X 1/5 X 1/6 with 3/7 X 1/4 X 1/5 X 1/6, it would NOT be necessary to compute *each* product. It would suffice, *preferably*, to see at once that 1/4 X 1/5 X 1/6 is common to both items and, immediately, to appreciate that 5/8 > 3/7. Therefore, 5/8 X 1/4 X 1/5 X 1/6 must be, of course, the greater quantity.

Fundamental to the quantitative-comparison question are the concepts *greater than*, *less than*, and *equal to*, and the meaning and use of the symbols, > ("greater than"), and < ("less than"), which should be overlearned since these symbols appear or are implied in practically every question.

It would be wise to review the basic principles and concepts of algebra and geometry as a necessary preparation for this question-type. However, the candidate is advised that advanced mathematics is *not* required in the solution or interpretation of any of these problems.

Following are the directions in detail for the quantitative-comparison question:

DIRECTIONS: Each question in this section consists of two quantities, one in Column A and one in Column B. You are to compare the two quantities and, on the answer sheet, blacken space

    (A) if the quantity in Column A is the greater;
    (B) if the quantity in Column B is the greater;
    (C) if the two quantities are equal;
    (D) if the relationship cannot be determined from the information given.

DIAGRAMS

Position of points, angles, regions, etc., can be assumed to be in the order shown.

Figures are NOT NECESSARILY drawn to scale and may NOT agree to measure shown unless a note states that the figure is drawn to scale.

Lines shown as straight can be assumed to be straight.

Figures are assumed to lie in the plane unless otherwise indicated.

Note: All numbers used are real numbers. In a question, information concerning one or both of the quantities to be compared is centered above the two columns. A symbol that appears in both columns represents the same thing in Column A as it does in Column B.

Definitions of symbols:

<   is less than $\leq$ is less than or equal to
>   is greater than $\geq$ is greater than or equal to
$\perp$ is perpendicular to $\parallel$ is parallel to
                            $\neq$ is not equal to

SAMPLE QUESTIONS

DIRECTIONS FOR THIS SECTION: See page 1.

1.
    Column A   Column B
    2 X 6   2 + 6
                                     1. ...

The correct answer is A, since, obviously, 2 *times* a number is patently greater than 2 *more than* that same number.

Questions 2-4.

DIRECTIONS: Questions 2 - 4 refer to $\triangle$PQR.

2.
        Column A   Column B
          PN   NQ   2. ...

The correct answer is D, since nothing can be assumed about measures from the figure.

3.
        Column A   Column B
           y   x   3. ...

The correct answer is B, since N is between P and Q.

4.
        Column A   Column B
        w + z   180   4. ...

The correct answer is C, since $\overline{PQ}$ is a straight line.

EXAMINATION SECTION

TEST 1

1.   Column A   Column B   1. ...

$BA \mid AD$
$x° = y°$
$AE \perp BD$

        BE   ED

2.   Column A   Column B   2. ...

$BA \perp BC$
$BA = BC$
$AC \perp BD$

       W°   X°

3.   Column A   Column B   3. ...

$e \perp d$
$e \perp b$
$a \parallel c$

       a   c

2

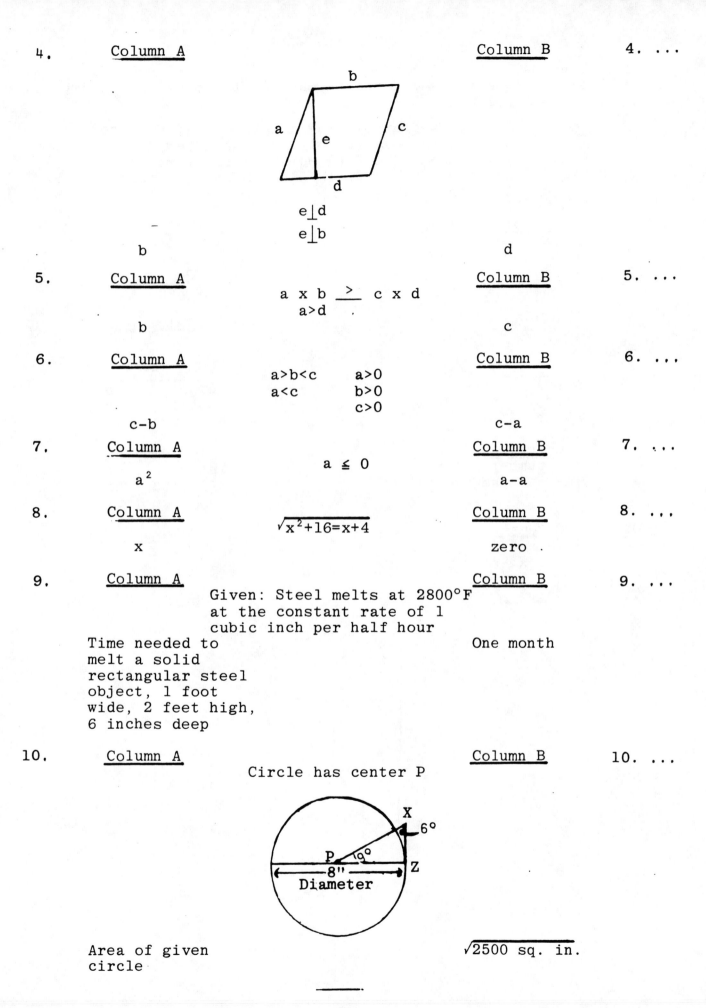

4.   Column A   Column B   4. ...

b

e⊥d
e⊥b

b   d

5.   Column A   Column B   5. ...

a x b ≥ c x d
a>d

b   c

6.   Column A   Column B   6. ...

a>b<c   a>0
a<c   b>0
          c>0

c-b   c-a

7.   Column A   Column B   7. ...

a ≤ 0

a^2 a-a

8.   Column A   Column B   8. ...

$\sqrt{x^2+16}=x+4$

x   zero

9.   Column A   Column B   9. ...

Given: Steel melts at 2800°F
at the constant rate of 1
cubic inch per half hour

Time needed to   One month
melt a solid
rectangular steel
object, 1 foot
wide, 2 feet high,
6 inches deep

10.   Column A   Column B   10. ...

Circle has center P

Area of given $\sqrt{2500}$ sq. in.
circle

3

TEST 2

Questions 1-2.
DIRECTIONS: Questions 1-2 are based upon the description given
below.

A line is drawn from P (center of given circle)
to X (point outside circle). Another line is
drawn from P to Z (a point on the circle).
Another line connects X and Z and is tangent to
the circle at A.

1.   <u>Column A</u>   <u>Column B</u>   1. ...
        Line PZ   Line PX

2.   <u>Column A</u>   <u>Column B</u>   2. ...
        Angle a°   Angle b°

3.   <u>Column A</u>   <u>Column B</u>   3. ...
        7/2   √10

4.   <u>Column A</u>   <u>Column B</u>   4. ...
        Number of one-inch   Number of one-
        links in a 12-foot   foot links in a
        chain   45-yard chain

5.   <u>Column A</u>   <u>Column B</u>   5. ...
        The number of sides   The cube root of
        in a pentagon   343 minus the
                                                cube root of 27

6.   <u>Column A</u>   <u>Column B</u>   6. ...
        9/16 x 4/3 x 3 x   8/16 x 3/4 x 11 x
        1/2 x 8   4 x 5/8

7.   <u>Column A</u>   <u>Column B</u>   7. ...

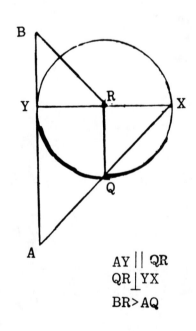

AY ∥ QR
QR ⊥ YX
BR > AQ

        AX   AB

4

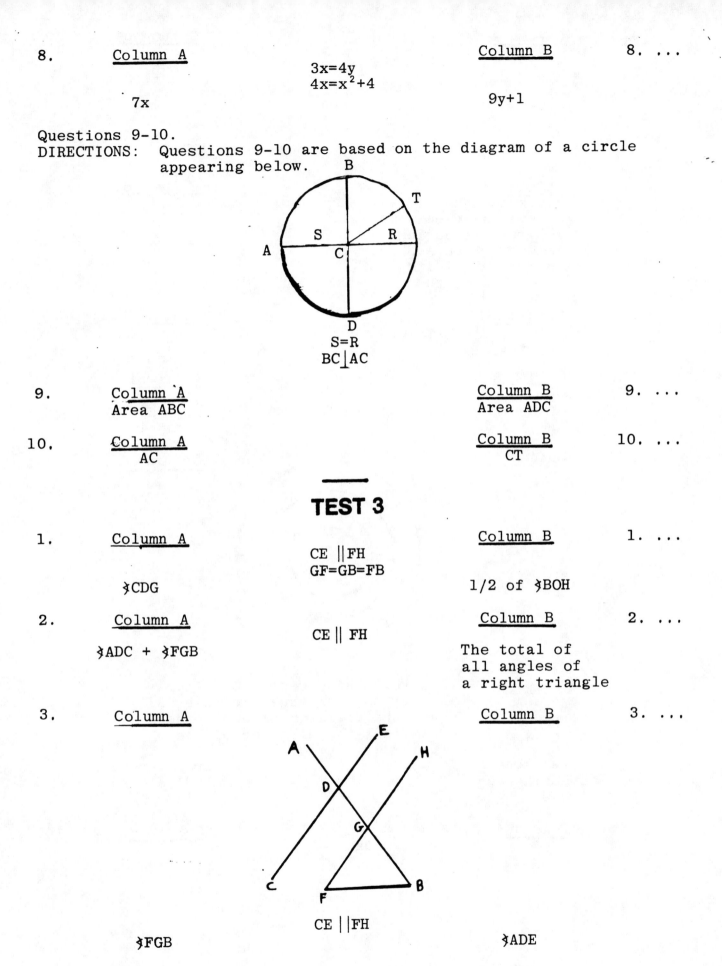

8.   <u>Column A</u>   <u>Column B</u>   8. ...

$$3x=4y$$
$$4x=x^2+4$$

        7x   9y+1

Questions 9-10.
DIRECTIONS: Questions 9-10 are based on the diagram of a circle
appearing below.

S=R
BC⊥AC

9.   <u>Column A</u>   <u>Column B</u>   9. ...
      Area ABC   Area ADC

10.   <u>Column A</u>   <u>Column B</u>   10. ...
        AC   CT

TEST 3

1.   <u>Column A</u>   <u>Column B</u>   1. ...

CE ‖ FH
GF=GB=FB

      ∢CDG   1/2 of ∢BOH

2.   <u>Column A</u>   <u>Column B</u>   2. ...

CE ‖ FH

  ∢ADC + ∢FGB   The total of
                                        all angles of
                                        a right triangle

3.   <u>Column A</u>   <u>Column B</u>   3. ...

CE ‖FH

      ∢FGB   ∢ADE

4.   Column A   Column B   4. ...

$$a \leq 0$$
$$b \geq 0$$
$$a \neq b$$

          b-a   b+a

5.   Column A   Column B   5. ...
          9 X 8 X 283   283 X 6 X 12

6.   Column A   Column B   6. ...
          The average number   10
          of leaves shed per
          day by tree X during
          November if tree X
          shed all 300 of its
          leaves that month

7.   Column A   Column B   7. ...
                                     $$0 > a$$
              $a^3 + 1$ 0

8.   Column A   Column B   8. ...
                                     $$a < 0$$
                                     $$b < 0$$
              a - b   a + b

9.   Column A   Column B   9. ...

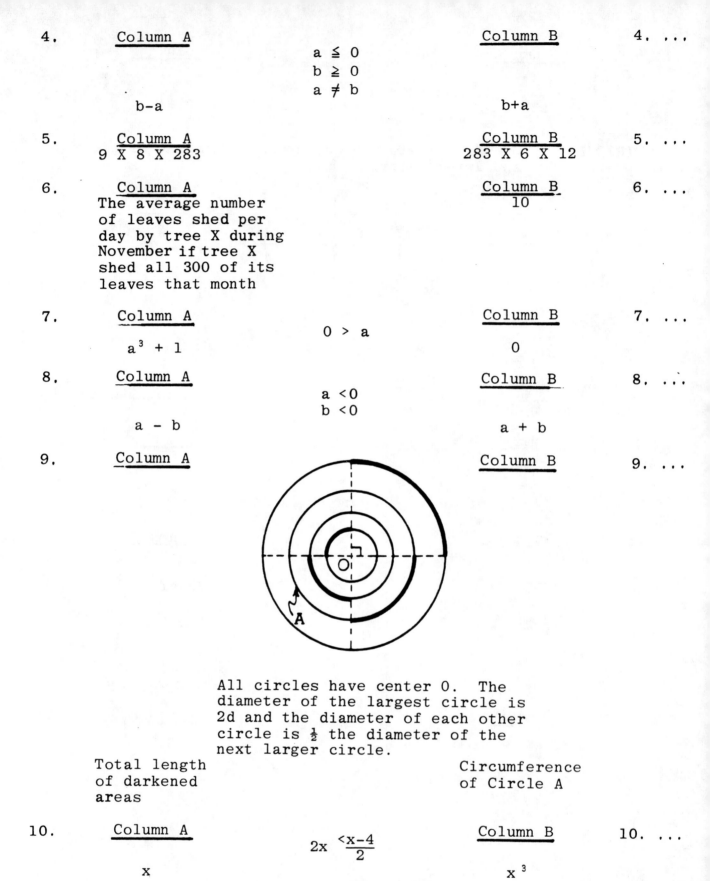

All circles have center O. The
diameter of the largest circle is
2d and the diameter of each other
circle is ½ the diameter of the
next larger circle.

Total length   Circumference
of darkened   of Circle A
areas

10.   Column A   Column B   10. ...
                              $2x \quad \dfrac{<x-4}{2}$
              x x^3

6

TEST 4

Questions 1-3.
DIRECTIONS: Questions 1-3 refer to the diagram below.

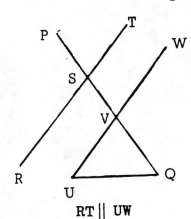

RT ∥ UW

1.   <u>Column A</u>   <u>Column B</u>   1. ...

∢ UVQ   ∢ PST

2.   <u>Column A</u>   <u>Column B</u>   2. ...

RT ∥ UW

∢FSR + ∢UVQ   180°

3.   <u>Column A</u>   <u>Column B</u>   3. ...

RT ∥ UW

UV = VQ = UQ

∢RSV   ½ of ∢WVQ

4.   <u>Column A</u>   <u>Column B</u>   4. ...
      5/2
      5/2 $\sqrt{6}$

Questions 5-7.
DIRECTIONS: Questions 5-7 refer to the diagram below:

Circle has center O

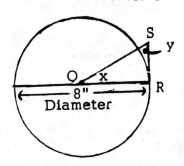

5.   <u>Column A</u>   <u>Column B</u>   5. ...

Area of circle   500 sq. in.

7

6.   <u>Column A</u>   <u>Column B</u>   6. ..

        OR   OS

7.   <u>Column A</u>   <u>Column B</u>   7. ..

        ʒX   ʒY

8.   <u>Column A</u> $2a < \dfrac{a}{2} - 2$ <u>Column B</u>   8. ..

        a a^3

Questions 9-10.
DIRECTIONS: Questions 9 and 10 refer to the diagram below:

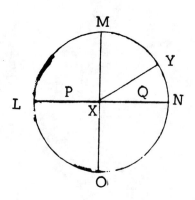

Point X bisects line LN
MO ⊥ LN

9.   <u>Column A</u>   <u>Column B</u>   9. ...

     Area LMX   Area LXO

10. <u>Column A</u>   <u>Column B</u>   10. ...

        LX   XY

———

KEYS (CORRECT ANSWERS)

<u>TEST 1</u>				<u>TEST 2</u>				<u>TEST 3</u>				<u>TEST 4</u>			
1.	C	6.	A	1.	B	6.	B	1.	C	6.	B	1.	C	6.	B
2.	D	7.	D	2.	B	7.	D	2.	C	7.	D	2.	C	7.	D
3.	C	8.	C	3.	A	8.	B	3.	C	8.	B	3.	C	8.	A
4.	D	9.	A	4.	A	9.	D	4.	D	9.	B	4.	A	9.	D
5.	D	10.	A	5.	A	10.	D	5.	C	10.	A	5.	A	10.	D

———

QUANTITATIVE COMPARISONS

TEST 1

DIRECTIONS: Each of the following questions has two parts. One is
in Column A. The other part is in Column B. You must
find out if one part is greater than the other, or if
the parts are equal.
Mark the answer:
   A if the part in Column A is greater,
   B if the part in Column B is greater,
   C if the two parts are equal.
*PRINT THE LETTER OF THE CORRECT ANSWER IN THE SPACE AT
THE RIGHT.*

COLUMN A	COLUMN B	
1. 2 + 3	4 + 1	1.___
2. 1 dozen	10	2.___

3.

    ● ● ● ● ●   ● ● ● ●
    ● ● ● ● ●   ● ● ● ●
    ● ● ● ● ●   ● ● ● ●

Number of dots   Number of dots

3.___

4.

Area of the shaded region   One-half the area of the circle

4.___

5. Time: 60 minutes   Time: 60 seconds   5.___

6.

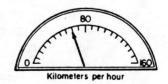

Speed as shown above   Speed as shown above

6.___

COLUMN A	COLUMN B	

7.
$$\begin{array}{r} 27 \\ \times 3 \\ \hline \end{array}$$

$$\begin{array}{r} 27 \\ 27 \\ 27 \\ +27 \\ \hline \end{array}$$
          7.____

8. This morning   This afternoon   8.____

Minutes <u>before</u> noon today on this <u>clock</u>   Minutes <u>after</u> noon today on this <u>clock</u>

9. One-tenth $\frac{1}{10}$ 9.____

10.   10.____

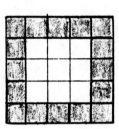

Number of white squares   Number of dark squares

11. $0.90   3 × $0.03   11.____

Questions 12-13.

DIRECTIONS: Questions 12 through 13 are to be answered on the basis of the following table.

DAVID'S SPELLING SCORES

12. David's score on Monday   His score on Friday   12.____

2

COLUMN A	COLUMN B	
13. His average score for Thursday and Friday	His average score for Tuesday and Wednesday	13.____
14. (5 × 60) – (4 × 60)	(7 × 60) – (5 × 60)	14.____

15. 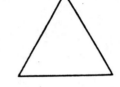

15.____

The number of <u>even</u> numbers that are not named on this segment of the number line.   The number of <u>odd</u> numbers that are not named on this segment of the number line.

16.

16.____

Distance around the square if each side has length 3   Distance around the triangle if each side has length 4

17. $\frac{1}{3} + \frac{1}{4}$	$\frac{1}{12}$	17.____
18. 378 + 381	379 + 380	18.____
19. Number of eighths equal to $\frac{1}{4}$	Number of sixths equal to $\frac{1}{3}$	19.____
20. Number of days in 6 weeks, not counting Sundays	Number of days in 7 weeks, not counting Saturdays and Sundays	20.____

21.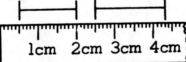

21.____

Length of AB   Length of CD

22.   100 centimeters = 1 meter

22.____

Length of 0.2 meter   Length of 20 centimeters

COLUMN A   COLUMN B

23. $300 + \square + 6 = 346$ $\triangle + 40 + 6 = 346$ 23.___

The number that goes in   The number that goes in $\triangle$

$\square$

24. Speed at 1 kilometer per   Speed at 60 kilometers per   24.___
minutes   hour

25. $\dfrac{1 + 1 + 1}{3}$ $\dfrac{1 + 1 + 1 + 1}{4}$ 25.___

___

TEST 2

DIRECTIONS: Each of the following questions has two parts. One is
in Column A. The other part is in Column B. You must
find out if one part is greater than the other, or if
the parts are equal.
Mark the answer:
   A if the part in Column A is greater,
   B if the part in Column B is greater,
   C if the two parts are equal.
*PRINT THE LETTER OF THE CORRECT ANSWER IN THE SPACE AT
THE RIGHT.*

COLUMN A   COLUMN B

1. The sum: The sum: 1.___
3 + 5 plus any whole   3 + 5 + 1
number greater than 1

2. The next <u>whole</u> number   The next <u>even</u> number after 6   2.___
after 6

3.   3.___

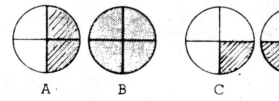

A   B   C   D

Each of the four equal circles is divided into four equal
parts.

Sum of shaded parts in   Sum of shaded parts in C
A and B   and D

4

	COLUMN A	COLUMN B	
4.	3)63̄	2)42̄	4._____

5.

The number □ on this number line

The number Δ on this number line

5._____

6. 400 minus 110   400 minus 120   6._____

7. $\frac{1}{2} + \frac{1}{2}$ $\frac{1}{3} + \frac{2}{3}$ 7._____

8. Some number between 2 and 6   Some number between 7 and 11   8._____

9. The number of tens in 38   The number of hundreds in 438   9._____

10. Amount of milk in 1,000 liters of milk   Amount of milk in 1 kiloliter of milk   10._____

11. $1.11   Value of 11 dimes   11._____

12. 9,634 ×6,825   6,825 ×9,634   12._____

13. 3 × (1+1+1+1+1)   5 × (1+1+1)   13._____

14. Number of years since you were 2 years old   Number of years since you were 4 years old   14._____

15. 3 × 9 × 2   3 × 3 × 5   15._____

16. 100 centigrams = 1 gram   16._____

Weight of 100 grams   Weight of 1 centigram

17. $\frac{1}{5}$ $\frac{1}{4}$ 17._____

18. $4.00   Cost of 4 boxes of candy at $0.99 per box   18._____

19. The number □ if   The number Δ if   19._____

    □ + 3 = 5   Δ − 2 = 2

20. 64 ÷ 8   63 ÷ 9   20._____

COLUMN A	COLUMN B	
21. Number of dimes equal to $0.50	Number of nickels equal to $0.25	21.___
22. 8 + 8	~~||||~~ ||| + ~~||||~~ |||	22.___
23. Total number of apples in 3 baskets of 9 apples each	Total number of apples in 4 baskets of 7 apples each	23.___
24. 0	0 × 2	24.___
25. 10,000	100 × 100	25.___

TEST 3

DIRECTIONS: Each of the following questions has two parts. One part is in Column A. The other part is in Column B. You must find out if one part is greater than the other, or if the parts are equal, or if not enough information is given for you to decide.
Mark the answer:
   A if the part in Column A is greater,
   B if the part in Column B is greater,
   C if the two parts are equal,
   D if not enough information is given for you to decide.
Note: Letters such as x, n, and k stand for real numbers. If the same letter appears in both columns of a question, it stands for the same number.
PRINT THE LETTER OF THE CORRECT ANSWER IN THE SPACE AT THE RIGHT.

COLUMN A	COLUMN B	
1. 2 + 8	13 - 2	1.___
2. 10	Number of centimeters in 1 meter	2.___
3. 2.5	5.2	3.___
4. The amount of money Jim has if he has 4 coins	The amount of money Bill has if he has 7 coins	4.___

6

COLUMN A	COLUMN B	
5. Amount of money in one quarter, one dime, and one nickel	$0.35	5.____
6. (350×860) + (350×1)	(350×861)	6.____

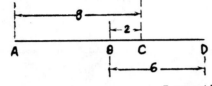

7.____

Length of AB	Length of CD	
8. (2 × 6) + 3	(15 × 2) – 15	8.____
9. 50%	$\dfrac{49}{100}$	9.____
10. 467	4 + (6×10) + (7×100)	10.____

11.____

11.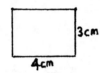

Area of this rectangle	Area of this rectangle	
12. 13 + 15 + 16 + 18	14 + 15 + 16 + 17	12.____
13. Distance traveled in $\frac{1}{2}$ hour at 70 kilometers per hour	Distance traveled in $\frac{1}{3}$ hour at 105 kilometers per hour	13.____
14. Mrs. Stein's weight, if she weighs twice as much as her daughter	Mrs. Barnum's weight if she weighs three times as much as her daughter	14.____
15. (6 × 8) + (3 × 8)	72	15.____
16. $\dfrac{2 \times 3 \times 5 \times 7}{10}$	$\dfrac{2 \times 3 \times 5 \times 7}{14}$	16.____

	COLUMN A	COLUMN B	

17. The number of <u>even</u> numbers greater than 2 but less than 9

The number of <u>odd</u> numbers greater than 2 but less than 9

17.____

18. z if $(2 \times z) - 6 = 0$

y if $(3 \times y) - 9 = 0$

18.____

19. 0.472

$\dfrac{400}{1,000} + \dfrac{70}{1,000} + \dfrac{2}{1,000}$

19.____

20. The number of days in a year

356 days

20.____

21. x if $9 + x = 21$

y if $9 + y = 11$

21.____

22. Number of integers between -10 and $+10$

Number of integers between -20 and $+20$

22.____

23. 3×25

$\dfrac{3 \times 100}{4}$

23.____

24.

1 rallod = 10 paldas
1 palda = 5 kanigs

24.____

The value in rallods of 30 paldas and 10 kanigs

The value in rallods of 50 paldas and 5 kanigs

25.

25.____

25% of the liquid in the container

50% of the liquid in this container

8

TEST 4

DIRECTIONS: Each of the following questions has two parts. One part is in Column A. The other part is in Column B. You must find out if one part is greater than the other, or if the parts are equal, or if not enough information is given for you to decide.
Mark the answer:
    A if the part in Column A is greater,
    B if the part in Column B is greater,
    C if the two parts are equal,
    D if not enough information is given for you to decide.
Note: Letters such as x, n, and k stand for real numbers. If the same letter appears in both columns of a question, it stands for the same number.
PRINT THE LETTER OF THE CORRECT ANSWER IN THE SPACE AT THE RIGHT.

COLUMN A	COLUMN B	
1. $\dfrac{473}{31}$	$\dfrac{473}{3.1}$	1.___

2.

Sum of the missing whole numbers on the part of the number line above	The missing whole number on the part of the number line above	2.___

| 3. $\dfrac{6}{7} \times \dfrac{7}{6}$ | $\dfrac{3}{5} \times \dfrac{5}{3}$ | 3.___ |

4.   x is a whole number   4.___

$$\begin{array}{r} 2 \\ 9 \\ +3 \\ \hline \end{array} \qquad \begin{array}{r} 4 \\ 7 \\ +x \\ \hline \end{array}$$

| 5. $\dfrac{9}{30}$ | $33\dfrac{1}{3}\,\%$ | 5.___ |

| 6. $\dfrac{1}{3} + \dfrac{1}{3} + \dfrac{1}{3}$ | $\dfrac{1}{4} + \dfrac{1}{4} + \dfrac{1}{4} + \dfrac{1}{4}$ | 6.___ |

COLUMN A	COLUMN B	
7. 1.00073	1.0063	7.___

8.    8.___

Circle with center C

Length of segment XY	Length of segment AB	
9. A whole number that is greater than 3	A whole number that is less than 8	9.___

Questions 10-13.

DIRECTIONS: Questions 10 through 13 are to be answered on the basis of the circle graph below which gives information about the distribution of the world population.

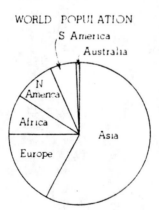

WORLD POPULATION

10. Population of South America	Population of Australia	10.___
11. Population of Asia	Population of the world, not counting Asia	11.___
12. 50% of the world population	Population of Asia	12.___

10

	COLUMN A	COLUMN B	
13.	Population of Australia	Population of Pakistan	13.___
14.	32 ×20	20 ×30	14.___
15.	$\frac{9}{8} \div \frac{3}{8}$	3	15.___
16.	One million	$1{,}000 \times 100$	16.___
17.	The average of 15 and 45	The average of 15, 30, and 45	17.___
18.	An area of 1 square meter	Area of rectangle 150 centimeters long and 50 centimeters wide	18.___
19.	Distance represented by 0.5 centimeter on a map with scale: 1 centimeter represents 8 kilometers	Distance represented by 2 centimeters on a map with scale: 1 centimeter represents 4 kilometers	19.___

20.   x is greater than zero   20.___

        $\frac{3}{x}$ 3x

21.   r, s, and t are consecutive whole numbers listed in   21.___
increasing order

     r + 3   t + 1

22.	$\frac{1 + 0}{1 + 1 - 0}$	$\frac{0 + 1}{1 + 1 - 1}$	22.___
23.	3% of the cost of 5 books	5% of the cost of 3 books	23.___
24.	The number obtained by rounding 7,372 to the nearest 1,000	7,000	24.___

COLUMN A   COLUMN B

25.

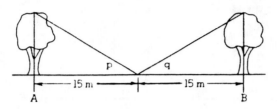

25.___

Angle p is greater than angle q.

Height of tree A   ___   Height of tree B

TEST 5

DIRECTIONS: Each of the following questions has two parts. One
part is in Column A. The other part is in Column B.
You must find out if one part is greater than the
other, or if the parts are equal, or if not enough
information is given for you to decide.
Mark your answer:
    A if the part in Column A is greater,
    B if the part in Column B is greater,
    C if the two parts are equal,
    D if not enough information is given for you to decide.
Note: Letters such as x, n, and k stand for real numbers.
If the same letter appears in both columns of a question,
it stands for the same number.
*PRINT THE LETTER OF THE CORRECT ANSWER IN THE SPACE AT
THE RIGHT.*

COLUMN A   COLUMN B

1. 100% $\frac{16}{17}$ 1.___

2. 6 × 6 × 2   12 × 12   2.___

3.   3.___

A   B   C   D

Segments AC and BD have equal lengths.

Length of AB   Length of CD

12

COLUMN A   COLUMN B

4.   Z is a number greater than zero.   4.___

   Z × Z   2 × Z × Z

5. 0.600 + 0.080 + 0.003   0.600 + 0.030 + 0.008   5.___

6.   Two circles with center O   6.___

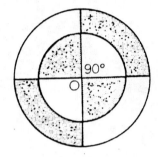

Area of shaded portion of   Area of unshaded portion
figure   of figure

7. $\frac{2}{3} = \frac{4}{x}$ 7.___

   x   5

8. Number of days in   Number of days in   8.___
    month X   4 weeks

9. x if 0.2x = 5   y if 0.2y = 6   9.___

10. $\frac{4 + 6 + 8}{3}$ $\frac{2 + 4 + 6 + 8 + 10}{5}$ 10.___

11. 1 ÷ 2   2 ÷ 1   11.___

12. 100,000 ÷ 1,000   100,000 ÷ 100   12.___

13

	COLUMN A	COLUMN B	

13. $\frac{1}{3}$, $\frac{1}{8}$, $\frac{1}{4}$ $\frac{1}{7}$, $\frac{1}{5}$, $\frac{1}{2}$ 13.___

     The greatest fraction above   The greatest fraction above

14. x, y, and z are consecutive whole numbers in increasing   14.___
order

     $\frac{x + z}{2}$ y

15.   x and y are positive numbers   15.___
$$x - y = 3$$

     x   3

16. Three times the diameter of circle A   Circumference of circle A   16.___

17. $\frac{60}{80} = \frac{x}{100}$ $\frac{3}{4} = y\%$ 17.___

     x   y

18. $\frac{5}{0.1}$ 5   18.___

19.   19.___

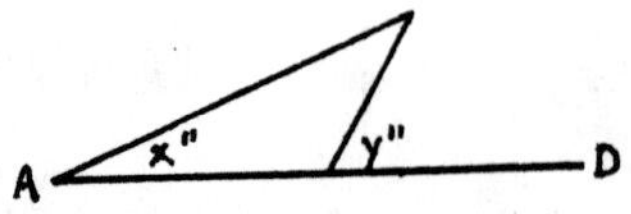

AD is a straight line.

     x   y

20. $(30 \times 575) - (29 \times 575)$ $(40 \times 575) - (39 \times 575)$ 20.___

21. $x + 2$ $2x$ 21.___

COLUMN A   COLUMN B

Questions 22-25.

DIRECTIONS: Questions 22 through 25 are to be answered on the basis
              of the following graph.

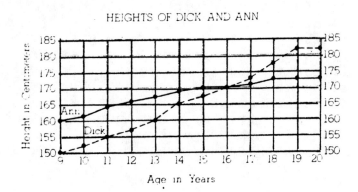

HEIGHTS OF DICK AND ANN

22.   The height of Dick at   The height of Ann at   22.____
      18 years of age   18 years of age

23.   The height of Ann at   The height of Dick at   23.____
      16 years of age   16 years of age

24.   Ann's age when she was   Dick's age when he was   24.____
      taller than Dick   taller than Ann

25.   Difference between Ann's   Difference between Ann's   25.____
      and Dick's ages when   and Dick's ages in 1956
      Dick was 16 years of age

_____

TEST 6

DIRECTIONS: Each of the following questions has two parts. One part is in Column A. The other part is in Column B. You must find out if one part is greater than the other, or if the parts are equal, or if not enough information is given for you to decide.
Mark your answer:
    A if the part in Column A is greater,
    B if the part in Column B is greater,
    C if the two parts are equal,
    D if not enough information is given for you to decide.
Note: Letters such as x, n, and k stand for real numbers. If the same letter appears in both columns of a question, it stands for the same number.
PRINT THE LETTER OF THE CORRECT ANSWER IN THE SPACE AT THE RIGHT.

COLUMN A	COLUMN B	
1. $\frac{1}{8}$ of 8	$\frac{1}{9}$ of 9	1.____

2.

$$\boxed{\text{area } 64} \; W$$
$$L$$

$$L + W = 16$$

Length L	Length W	2.____
3. 3^3	3×3	3.____

4.
$$x = 1$$
$$y = 2$$

2x + y	2y + x	4.____

5.
$$N > 6$$

N	8	5.____
6. $\frac{2}{3} + \frac{3}{4}$	$\frac{5}{12}$	6.____

COLUMN A   COLUMN B

7.

x   y

8.   x + y = 6

x   y   8.___

9.   4,564   2,096   9.___
    – __y__   + __z__
     2,096   4,564

y   z

10. 243,000   2.43 × 100,000   10.___

11.   11.___

Each region is rectangular

The area of shaded   The area of shaded
region A   region B

12. $10,428 ÷ 2 $521.40   12.___

13. An odd number less than 5   An even number less than 10   13.___

14.   14.___

Area of this triangle   Area of this triangle

17

	COLUMN A	COLUMN B	

15. $\frac{9}{8} \div \frac{3}{8}$ $\frac{9}{8} \times \frac{8}{3}$ 15.___

16.

Car A circles Track A in 10 seconds.
Car B circles Track B in 10 seconds.

Car A's average speed in kilometers per hour   Car B's average speed in kilometers per hour   16.___

17. $3.00   The simple interest earned on $100 for 6 months if the rate is 6% per year   17.___

18. The number of whole numbers between 4 and 10   The number of fractions between 1 and 2   18.___

19.

☆ ☆ ○

The ratio of stars to circles after 400 stars and 200 circles are added to those above   The ratio of stars to circles after 50 stars and 25 circles are added to those above   19.___

20. $\frac{x}{3} + \frac{x}{3} + \frac{x}{3} = 3$ $\frac{y}{4} + \frac{y}{4} + \frac{y}{4} + \frac{y}{4} = 4$ 20.___

x   y

21.   The last digit of M is 2.
The last digit of N is 3.   21.___

The remainder when M is divided by 5   The remainder when N is divided by 5

18

COLUMN A	COLUMN B	
22. The average of 10, 20, and 30	The average of 5, 10, and x, if x is a number greater than 30	22.___

23.

The area of regular hexagon P

The area of square Q

23.___

24. An area of 100 square centimeters

An area of 1 square meter

24.___

25.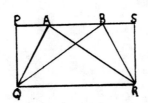

Rectangle PQRS

Perimeter △AQR   Perimeter △BQR

25.___

_____

KEY (CORRECT ANSWERS)

TEST 1	TEST 2	TEST 3	TEST 4	TEST 5	TEST 6
1. C	1. A	1. B	1. B	1. A	1. C
2. A	2. B	2. B	2. A	2. B	2. C
3. B	3. A	3. B	3. C	3. C	3. A
4. B	4. C	4. D	4. D	4. B	4. B
5. A	5. C	5. A	5. B	5. A	5. D
6. A	6. A	6. C	6. C	6. D	6. A
7. B	7. C	7. A	7. B	7. A	7. A
8. B	8. B	8. C	8. A	8. D	8. D
9. C	9. B	9. A	9. D	9. B	9. C
10. B	10. C	10. B	10. A	10. C	10. C
11. A	11. A	11. C	11. A	11. B	11. B
12. B	12. C	12. C	12. B	12. B	12. A
13. A	13. C	13. C	13. D	13. B	13. D
14. B	14. A	14. D	14. A	14. C	14. C
15. C	15. A	15. C	15. C	15. A	15. C
16. C	16. A	16. A	16. A	16. B	16. A
17. A	17. B	17. C	17. C	17. C	17. C
18. C	18. A	18. C	18. A	18. A	18. B
19. C	19. B	19. C	19. B	19. B	19. C
20. A	20. A	20. A	20. D	20. C	20. B
21. B	21. C	21. A	21. C	21. D	21. B
22. C	22. C	22. B	22. B	22. A	22. D
23. B	23. B	23. C	23. D	23. C	23. A
24. C	24. C	24. B	24. C	24. B	24. B
25. C	25. C	25. D	25. A	25. D	25. D

———

ANSWER SHEET

ST NO. _____ PART _____ TITLE OF POSITION _____

(AS GIVEN IN EXAMINATION ANNOUNCEMENT - INCLUDE OPTION, IF ANY)

ACE OF EXAMINATION _____ DATE_____

(CITY OR TOWN) (STATE)

RATING

USE THE SPECIAL PENCIL.   MAKE GLOSSY BLACK MARKS.

	A B C D E		A B C D E		A B C D E		A B C D E		A B C D E
1	:: :: :: :: ::	26	:: :: :: :: ::	51	:: :: :: :: ::	76	:: :: :: :: ::	101	:: :: :: :: ::
2	:: :: :: :: ::	27	:: :: :: :: ::	52	:: :: :: :: ::	77	:: :: :: :: ::	102	:: :: :: :: ::
3	:: :: :: :: ::	28	:: :: :: :: ::	53	:: :: :: :: ::	78	:: :: :: :: ::	103	:: :: :: :: ::
4	:: :: :: :: ::	29	:: :: :: :: ::	54	:: :: :: :: ::	79	:: :: :: :: ::	104	:: :: :: :: ::
5	:: :: :: :: ::	30	:: :: :: :: ::	55	:: :: :: :: ::	80	:: :: :: :: ::	105	:: :: :: :: ::
6	:: :: :: :: ::	31	:: :: :: :: ::	56	:: :: :: :: ::	81	:: :: :: :: ::	106	:: :: :: :: ::
7	:: :: :: :: ::	32	:: :: :: :: ::	57	:: :: :: :: ::	82	:: :: :: :: ::	107	:: :: :: :: ::
8	:: :: :: :: ::	33	:: :: :: :: ::	58	:: :: :: :: ::	83	:: :: :: :: ::	108	:: :: :: :: ::
9	:: :: :: :: ::	34	:: :: :: :: ::	59	:: :: :: :: ::	84	:: :: :: :: ::	109	:: :: :: :: ::
10	:: :: :: :: ::	35	:: :: :: :: ::	60	:: :: :: :: ::	85	:: :: :: :: ::	110	:: :: :: :: ::

Make only ONE mark for each answer.   Additional and stray marks may be
counted as mistakes.   In making corrections, erase errors COMPLETELY.

	A B C D E		A B C D E		A B C D E		A B C D E		A B C D E
11	:: :: :: :: ::	36	:: :: :: :: ::	61	:: :: :: :: ::	86	:: :: :: :: ::	111	:: :: :: :: ::
12	:: :: :: :: ::	37	:: :: :: :: ::	62	:: :: :: :: ::	87	:: :: :: :: ::	112	:: :: :: :: ::
13	:: :: :: :: ::	38	:: :: :: :: ::	63	:: :: :: :: ::	88	:: :: :: :: ::	113	:: :: :: :: ::
14	:: :: :: :: ::	39	:: :: :: :: ::	64	:: :: :: :: ::	89	:: :: :: :: ::	114	:: :: :: :: ::
15	:: :: :: :: ::	40	:: :: :: :: ::	65	:: :: :: :: ::	90	:: :: :: :: ::	115	:: :: :: :: ::
16	:: :: :: :: ::	41	:: :: :: :: ::	66	:: :: :: :: ::	91	:: :: :: :: ::	116	:: :: :: :: ::
17	:: :: :: :: ::	42	:: :: :: :: ::	67	:: :: :: :: ::	92	:: :: :: :: ::	117	:: :: :: :: ::
18	:: :: :: :: ::	43	:: :: :: :: ::	68	:: :: :: :: ::	93	:: :: :: :: ::	118	:: :: :: :: ::
19	:: :: :: :: ::	44	:: :: :: :: ::	69	:: :: :: :: ::	94	:: :: :: :: ::	119	:: :: :: :: ::
20	:: :: :: :: ::	45	:: :: :: :: ::	70	:: :: :: :: ::	95	:: :: :: :: ::	120	:: :: :: :: ::
21	:: :: :: :: ::	46	:: :: :: :: ::	71	:: :: :: :: ::	96	:: :: :: :: ::	121	:: :: :: :: ::
22	:: :: :: :: ::	47	:: :: :: :: ::	72	:: :: :: :: ::	97	:: :: :: :: ::	122	:: :: :: :: ::
23	:: :: :: :: ::	48	:: :: :: :: ::	73	:: :: :: :: ::	98	:: :: :: :: ::	123	:: :: :: :: ::
24	:: :: :: :: ::	49	:: :: :: :: ::	74	:: :: :: :: ::	99	:: :: :: :: ::	124	:: :: :: :: ::
25	:: :: :: :: ::	50	:: :: :: :: ::	75	:: :: :: :: ::	100	:: :: :: :: ::	125	:: :: :: :: ::

ANSWER SHEET

TEST NO. _____ PART _____ TITLE OF POSITION _____
(AS GIVEN IN EXAMINATION ANNOUNCEMENT - INCLUDE OPTION, IF ANY)

PLACE OF EXAMINATION _____ DATE _____
(CITY OR TOWN)   (STATE)

RATING

USE THE SPECIAL PENCIL.   MAKE GLOSSY BLACK MARKS.

	A B C D E		A B C D E		A B C D E		A B C D E		A B C D E
1	:: :: :: :: ::	26	:: :: :: :: ::	51	:: :: :: :: ::	76	:: :: :: :: ::	101	:: :: :: :: ::
2	:: :: :: :: ::	27	:: :: :: :: ::	52	:: :: :: :: ::	77	:: :: :: :: ::	102	:: :: :: :: ::
3	:: :: :: :: ::	28	:: :: :: :: ::	53	:: :: :: :: ::	78	:: :: :: :: ::	103	:: :: :: :: ::
4	:: :: :: :: ::	29	:: :: :: :: ::	54	:: :: :: :: ::	79	:: :: :: :: ::	104	:: :: :: :: ::
5	:: :: :: :: ::	30	:: :: :: :: ::	55	:: :: :: :: ::	80	:: :: :: :: ::	105	:: :: :: :: ::
6	:: :: :: :: ::	31	:: :: :: :: ::	56	:: :: :: :: ::	81	:: :: :: :: ::	106	:: :: :: :: ::
7	:: :: :: :: ::	32	:: :: :: :: ::	57	:: :: :: :: ::	82	:: :: :: :: ::	107	:: :: :: :: ::
8	:: :: :: :: ::	33	:: :: :: :: ::	58	:: :: :: :: ::	83	:: :: :: :: ::	108	:: :: :: :: ::
9	:: :: :: :: ::	34	:: :: :: :: ::	59	:: :: :: :: ::	84	:: :: :: :: ::	109	:: :: :: :: ::
10	:: :: :: :: ::	35	:: :: :: :: ::	60	:: :: :: :: ::	85	:: :: :: :: ::	110	:: :: :: :: ::

Make only ONE mark for each answer.   Additional and stray marks may be
counted as mistakes.   In making corrections, erase errors COMPLETELY.

	A B C D E		A B C D E		A B C D E		A B C D E		A B C D E
11	:: :: :: :: ::	36	:: :: :: :: ::	61	:: :: :: :: ::	86	:: :: :: :: ::	111	:: :: :: :: ::
12	:: :: :: :: ::	37	:: :: :: :: ::	62	:: :: :: :: ::	87	:: :: :: :: ::	112	:: :: :: :: ::
13	:: :: :: :: ::	38	:: :: :: :: ::	63	:: :: :: :: ::	88	:: :: :: :: ::	113	:: :: :: :: ::
14	:: :: :: :: ::	39	:: :: :: :: ::	64	:: :: :: :: ::	89	:: :: :: :: ::	114	:: :: :: :: ::
15	:: :: :: :: ::	40	:: :: :: :: ::	65	:: :: :: :: ::	90	:: :: :: :: ::	115	:: :: :: :: ::
16	:: :: :: :: ::	41	:: :: :: :: ::	66	:: :: :: :: ::	91	:: :: :: :: ::	116	:: :: :: :: ::
17	:: :: :: :: ::	42	:: :: :: :: ::	67	:: :: :: :: ::	92	:: :: :: :: ::	117	:: :: :: :: ::
18	:: :: :: :: ::	43	:: :: :: :: ::	68	:: :: :: :: ::	93	:: :: :: :: ::	118	:: :: :: :: ::
19	:: :: :: :: ::	44	:: :: :: :: ::	69	:: :: :: :: ::	94	:: :: :: :: ::	119	:: :: :: :: ::
20	:: :: :: :: ::	45	:: :: :: :: ::	70	:: :: :: :: ::	95	:: :: :: :: ::	120	:: :: :: :: ::
21	:: :: :: :: ::	46	:: :: :: :: ::	71	:: :: :: :: ::	96	:: :: :: :: ::	121	:: :: :: :: ::
22	:: :: :: :: ::	47	:: :: :: :: ::	72	:: :: :: :: ::	97	:: :: :: :: ::	122	:: :: :: :: ::
23	:: :: :: :: ::	48	:: :: :: :: ::	73	:: :: :: :: ::	98	:: :: :: :: ::	123	:: :: :: :: ::
24	:: :: :: :: ::	49	:: :: :: :: ::	74	:: :: :: :: ::	99	:: :: :: :: ::	124	:: :: :: :: ::
25	:: :: :: :: ::	50	:: :: :: :: ::	75	:: :: :: :: ::	100	:: :: :: :: ::	125	:: :: :: :: ::